OCR GENERAL STUDIES
for A level

OCR RECOGNISING ACHIEVEMENT / HODDER EDUCATION

Official Publisher Partnership

OCR GENERAL STUDIES
for A level

John Chiverrell
Paul Fletcher
John Pearce
Jan Robinson

HODDER EDUCATION

PART OF HACHETTE LIVRE UK

032
CH1

Although every effort has been made to ensure that website addresses are correct at time of going to press, Hodder Education cannot be held responsible for the content of any website mentioned in this book. It is sometimes possible to find a relocated web page by typing in the address of the home page for a website in the URL window of your browser.

Hachette Livre UK's policy is to use papers that are natural, renewable and recyclable products and made from wood grown in sustainable forests. The logging and manufacturing processes are expected to conform to the environmental regulations of the country of origin.

Orders: please contact Bookpoint Ltd, 130 Milton Park, Abingdon, Oxon OX14 4SB. Telephone: +44 (0)1235 827720. Fax: +44 (0)1235 400454. Lines are open 9.00–5.00, Monday to Saturday, with a 24-hour message answering service. Visit our website at www.hoddereducation.co.uk.

First published in 2008 by
Hodder Education, part of Hachette Livre UK
338 Euston Road
London NW1 3BH

Impression number   5 4 3 2
Year   2012 2011 2010 2009 2008

Illustrations by Oxford Designers and Illustrators and Tony Jones
Layouts by Stephen Rowling/Springworks
Typeset in 11.5/14pt Goudy
Printed in Italy

A catalogue record for this title is available from the British Library

ISBN 978 0340 96521 4

Contents

Joined-up thinking for General Studies

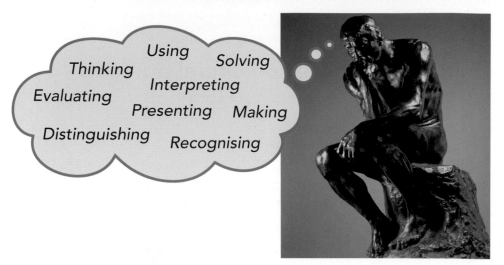

Thinking · Using · Solving · Evaluating · Interpreting · Presenting · Making · Distinguishing · Recognising

> 66 *Intelligence is something we are born with. Thinking is a skill that must be learned.* 99

Edward de Bono

Getting started

Welcome to General Studies! This book has been designed to help you get the most out of the OCR General Studies AS and A2 courses. Because it works a little differently from textbooks for other AS and A2 courses that you might be studying, and because General Studies is a different sort of course, it may be helpful to explain a few features of the course and this book.

To begin with, this textbook is written to support a new specification for General Studies from the OCR exam board. The aim of this specification is to help you explore the world you live in and some of the most important issues we all face in the 21st century. For example, at AS you will be studying the cultural, social and scientific domains. This means that you will be exploring political systems, social and economic trends, human behaviour, beliefs, values, media, communication, creativity and innovation, scientific methods and principles, mathematical reasoning and its application, and other subjects – a range of fascinating topics that link into and across many subjects and areas of interest. At A2, there is the opportunity to investigate the relationships and links between these domains and make connections that will provide you with invaluable study skills and a real perspective on the world around you.

Exploring and connecting is at the heart of General Studies. To do this successfully is as much about the skills of General Studies as it is about knowing information, facts and examples – what we call the content of General Studies. You need to know how to *apply* what you know to the questions you will be asked in your General Studies exams. This book is designed to help you develop these skills. This is not a 'knowledge' textbook. The internet has all the information anyone could ever need, and it can be much more up to date than any textbook – but it's important that you know how to use this information in the best way for success. This book is about how to develop skills and approaches for General Studies, to encourage you and your group to investigate and explore topics and issues for yourself, and to promote discussion.

The OCR specification is divided into three domains

- the social domain
- culture, arts and humanities
- science, mathematics and technology.

In this book, the three domains are covered in Units 1 and 2.

How the exam works, however, means that you will be assessed in different ways at AS and at A2 on what you know about these domains.

- At AS you have two exams, one on the cultural and social domains and one on the scientific domain. For both exams, you will have a series of short questions to work through, and then an extended answer: an essay.
- A2 is all about drawing together what you know and making connections. There are two exams. One is based on assessing your thinking skills (see below) in questions covering all three domains. This area is covered in Unit 3 of this book. The other exam is about the connections you make between the domains as you tackle two questions. The skills of making connections are explored later in this introduction, and some examples are given in Unit 4 of this book.

This book has been designed around a series of topic blocks. You will see that whatever unit you are in, the blocks work in broadly similar ways. They start off with an overview of the block of topics and what the specification says needs to be covered. The topic block is introduced and you will see some questions listed that cover the whole area of the block. Some starting points are given in the text to get you thinking about the issues, and these are then explored some more in tasks and then exam practice sections at the end of the block, which give you an idea of the way exam questions work at AS (units 1 and 2) and A2 (units 3 and 4) in General Studies. Most important, perhaps, are the 'What next?' sections. They give you suggestions on ways to take your exploration of these topic areas further.

Thinking and analysing skills

Throughout your General Studies course, the skills you develop are as important as the information you gather. As we said above, there is more information and knowledge on the internet, accessible to anyone with an internet connection, than anyone could ever need. The trick is knowing what to look for and what to do with it when you've found it. These skills are deeply embedded into General Studies and this section explains the skills that you will need to develop for General Studies success – but which will also serve you well throughout your life. You will use them throughout this book and, while they are given in outline form here, you will find examples and case studies, together with exam practice opportunities, that use all these thinking and analysing skills in Unit 3 of this textbook.

We need to think in different ways according to what we are thinking about. Opinion, whether informed or not, cuts little ice in the deductive world of mathematics: logic is not the best tool to apply to the critical appreciation of poetry.

General Studies requires thinking in many styles, and uses a variety of skills. These thinking styles and analytical/practical skills overlap. In working through a topic you will use different skills at different phases.

Joined-up thinking, like joined-up handwriting, connects things together in order to make their significance clearer. It is essential to success in General Studies. This is particularly true in the examination, where good answers must explore all aspects of a question. There is no such thing as an easy General Studies question: a question that seems simple is merely concealing its difficulty.

TA 1 Thinking critically and logically

Critical thinking is a process which explores issues and ideas at the same time as testing the accuracy of the information cited, as well as the authenticity of the logic applied to a process of reasoning. Critical and logical thinking starts with observation, and proceeds, via interpretation, analysis and evaluation, to a conclusion. It is a process in which feeling and opinion, ideally, play no part at all.

In reality, this kind of thinking does not come naturally. In discussion and argument we put the cart before the horse. We express an opinion – in effect our conclusion – and then support it by selecting only evidence in its favour.

You may already have strong views about some of the topics in this book. A key learning experience of this course is the opportunity to apply critical and logical thinking skills to them. This may not be a comfortable experience necessarily, but it will always be worthwhile.

Computer circuitry is logical, relying on processes which are essentially binary – *either/or, yes/no, on/off*. It is almost impossible for a human mind to work in this way, but critical and logical thinking attempts to use a similar kind of objectivity.

TA 2 Evaluating information against available observations and data

The internet provides information in massive and bewildering quantities. For the non-expert reader this is as much of a minefield as a treasure-trove. How can we tell what is useful, what is bogus and what is propaganda?

When we evaluate information we weigh its value and test the extent to which it supports, modifies or contradicts what we think we know already. The process of evaluating information often consists of asking simple questions such as these.

- Where does this information come from?
- Is the source apparently authoritative and, if so, by what criteria?
- Is it published by a reputable body such as a university?
- Has this information been peer-reviewed – i.e. subjected to scrutiny and appraisal by recognised experts in the field?
- Is a point of view or bias discernible in this information?
- Who has funded the research and on what terms?

There is particular need for caution when collecting and collating information in fast-moving areas such as medicine and technology. Although the internet provides us with mountains of facts, it has yet to provide us with a quick means of evaluating their authenticity.

TA 3 Solving quantitative and qualitative problems

A **quantitative problem** can be solved by a mathematical process of reasoning. These days such problems often form part of job-selection processes. In solving such problems a major factor is deciding what kind of knowledge can be taken as axiomatic (self evident). For example, in the task in the margin you need to assume that the hands on the clock move at a constant speed, and also to know that there are 60 minutes in an hour.

A **qualitative problem** is non-mathematical, and may have several possible answers. Of these, the best – or least worst – will be chosen. Solving such a problem can often begin by carrying out a SWOT analysis, in which the Strengths, Weakness, Opportunities and Threats offered or posed by various solutions may be assessed. An example is in the margin.

TA 4 Making predictions and proposing hypotheses

A credible prediction must satisfy three criteria. It should be based on repeated past experience, have a factual basis, and connections must not be assumed between unrelated facts. A good example is a weather forecast.

Historically, areas of high pressure are associated with light winds, clear skies and, in summer, warm days and cooler nights. Rising air pressures credibly forecast good summer weather.

The factual basis of the forecast relies on atmospheric subsidence causing the evaporation of water droplets (clear skies). There are no clouds to reflect daytime solar radiation (warm days) or to reflect back heat radiated from the Earth at night (cooler nights).

That two things happen consecutively does not mean that one causes the other. Weather forecasting rhymes often imply this, for example, *if*

TASK

Many people use the website Wikipedia to check facts. Visit http://en.wikipedia.org and find out how it is put together. Give one reason to explain why you could trust Wikipedia as a reliable source of information and one reason why you could not.

TASK

In a 12-hour period the hands on an analogue clock will overlap each other 12 times. Starting at 12 o'clock, how would you work out the exact times when this would occur?

TASK

It is proposed to solve a serious truancy problem in your school or college by expelling all students who truant more than six times in a term. What light might a SWOT analysis of this problem and the proposed solution shed on the situation?

TASK

Based on your experience of life as an A level student so far, make a prediction about your next day at school or college that satisfies the three criteria of a credible prediction. Did it turn out to be right or not?

there is dew upon the ground, no rain that day will be found. This particular example, incidentally, hedges its own prediction in the second line – *unless it rained the night before, then you had better keep the score.*

A hypothesis is also a prediction, suggesting ways in which two phenomena interrelate. Based on observation and reinforced by experiment, a hypothesis is a stage in the development of a scientific theory.

TA 5 Presenting reasoned explanations for phenomena, patterns and relationships

The important word in this phrase is *reasoned*. Observations can provide narratives suggesting explanations – but this does not mean that those explanations should not be questioned. Alternative explanations for phenomena, patterns and relationships need to be sought and tested.

The appearance of maggots in rotting meat, for example, led to the theory of the spontaneous generation of life, which also held that frogs and worms were incubated in mud, and that mice could be bred by leaving cut wheat where it fell in the field.

Such explanations were in their way empirical – i.e. derived from observation – but, once tested scientifically, fell apart. If meat is covered so that flies cannot lay eggs on it, no maggots will appear.

The simplest explanation for phenomena, patterns and relationships is often the best – this basic principle is called Occam's Razor. However, simplicity can be the enemy of reason, especially in scientific matters.

Equally, we sometimes explain simple phenomena with ideas more complex than they deserve. People complain of things they have mislaid that *it's always in the last place you look*, as if this were a law of nature, or the purse or bunch of keys had hidden itself. Once you have found something, where else would it be?

TA 6 Interpreting and evaluating opinions

Everyone is entitled to their own opinion – but not every opinion is of equal value, and worth equal consideration. Opinions supported only by ignorance have little value. Expert witnesses in court proceedings offer opinions based on sound knowledge and extensive experience, which is why we trust them. Genuinely objective scientific witnesses will also acknowledge that, however well informed their opinions may be, they can be invalidated by someone with greater understanding and information.

Opinion can be evaluated according to the credentials of its holder, but where ideas rather than facts are concerned, interpretation is equally important. Opinions are formed at least partially in the light of the beliefs we absorb from our social, religious, racial and ethical backgrounds, as well as by what we know.

TASK

What factors help you to decide what you think? When you meet someone new, how do you form an opinion about them? List the things that influence you.

If we know *why* someone thinks what they think, we have a better chance of interpreting that opinion realistically. Someone's views on foxhunting, say, may not be invalidated by their vegetarianism, but to the extent that it could inform their thinking, it needs to be considered. Equally, when interpreting opinions, we need to consider the extent of our own knowledge, as well as allowing for the effect of our own beliefs on the process.

TA 7 Distinguishing between fact, truth and belief

The fact that we believe something to be true does not make it factual, true or believable. The relationship between fact, truth and belief is complex.

A **fact** can be a scientific truth for which there is empirical evidence. It can be something accepted as fact by many people. A **truth** can sometimes be objectively tested and proved. It may be an idea that is central to someone's life, helping to make sense of it. (Those unable to credit such truth might write it off as a delusion.)

Only in the area of **belief** can we find some certainty as to meaning: belief, like faith, is concerned with things we cannot prove.

In distinguishing between fact, truth and belief we need to be aware of the overlap between the concepts. Here is an example.

Even a small amount – 2 units – of alcohol has a depressant effect on the central nervous system.

After a couple of drinks people feel so much more relaxed, in control and ready to enjoy themselves.

Drink causes emotional sensitivity as well as sexual inadequacy, and to that extent is a major cause of difficulty in personal relationships.

What elements of fact, truth and belief play a part in these statements?

TA 8 Recognising common fallacies

There are many types of logical **fallacy**. This list selects some common ones.

An **ad hominem** (Latin, *to the man*) argument plays the man and not the ball, attacking the person rather than addressing their argument.

The argument of **omniscience** says that *every school student knows that* – how can anyone know what everyone else knows? Compare **the bandwagon effect**: when people support a view because everyone else seems to agree with it.

The **appeal to faith** says that if you believe something then it is correct. That it is correct for you does not mean that it must be for anyone else.

The argument from **authority** says that if an eminent person believes something, then it will be true. This may apply to their specialism, but guarantees nothing in other areas.

> **KEY TERMS**
>
> A fallacy is a weakness or a flaw in an argument.

TASK

What sort of logical fallacies are being used in these three examples?

- Everyone always says that you should never generalise.
- Your baby just smiled! He likes me!
- Your football knowledge stinks as badly as your feet do.

Begging the question and **assuming the answer** are similar fallacies. *We must reintroduce corporal punishment to deter violent behaviour among young people.* Did corporal punishment deter violent behaviour?

Circular reasoning contains in its proposition that which it seeks to prove. *God exists because the Bible says that he does, and the Bible is the word of God.*

Post hoc, propter hoc reasoning says that what happens after an event is caused by it. *He's gone quite bald since his wife left him.*

TA 9 Using deductive and inductive arguments

A **deductive argument** is one in which conclusions follow from premises stated at its outset. It is also known as reasoning from the general to the specific, because a specific conclusion can be drawn from general principles.

A principal tool of deductive reasoning is the **syllogism**. This consists of a major premise, a minor premise and a conclusion. Here is an example.

All human beings are mortal	*(major premise, a general statement)*
I am a human being	*(minor premise, moving from the general towards the particular)*
therefore, I am mortal	*(a specific conclusion)*

Inductive arguments work in the opposite direction, from the particular to the general. The classic example of inductive reasoning is *all the crows I have ever seen were black, therefore all crows are black.* This line of reasoning raises practical questions: are there no such things as green crows? How would we know if there were if we have not seen all the crows? How would we know if we had seen all the crows anyway?

Inductive arguments can be as powerful as deductive ones to the extent that they are based on empirical evidence, so that the premises of a conclusion support it strongly without proving it. Despite the inductive gap between what can be proved by deduction, and what must be supposed from observation and common sense, inductive reasoning works.

Synoptic skills

General Studies requires a wide variety of synoptic skills. Because you will be developing and practising them in your other subjects there is need only for a brief survey of them here.

Synoptic skills fall into two groups. **Skills S1–S5** are vital to writing a successful essay in any subject. **Skills S6–S10** are more relevant to lengthier projects, or to group activities in which you may participate.

S1 Locating and selecting relevant material and information

'Too much information' is a phrase that we often use when we are told more than we want to know. Finding material and information is easy. The crucial skill is knowing how to use it. Decisions about relevance help to focus your ideas and play a large part in determining the quality of your work.

S2 Making and recording measurements or observations

Making your own observations – about your school's recycling habits, the role mathematics plays in your life, or the local amateur performance of *Look Back in Anger* – will give your work an immediacy which examiners will relish.

S3 Deciding which pieces of information are relevant to the solution of a particular problem

This is an extension of **S1**. An essay about attitudes to religion will need variety and balance. A case study of political ideology will need objectivity and focus.

S4 Presenting information in summary form

Writing concise summaries is a vital synoptic skill. Writing 600 words is far harder than writing 2,000. Making what you write imply what you have had to leave out is a skill worth developing.

S5 Integrating knowledge from different domains

General Studies is an integrative subject. A discussion of euthanasia should include scientific, medical, ethical, philosophical, practical, legal and religious elements. This is perhaps the most complex synoptic skill, combining as it does elements of all the others.

S6 Planning an activity and interpreting information from large data sets

This may appear to be two skills. However, if the scope, nature and size of the data set are not planned at the outset, you may end up with data which are unwieldy and difficult to interpret.

S7 Estimating and observing

The time factor is crucial in research. Developing techniques, such as sampling and calculating averages for accurate estimation of data in surveys, saves time and hones the skill of summarising.

S8 Using conventions to label charts, graphs, diagrams

This is the most practical skill, and one in which computers are of great help. Visual summaries of research need clarity and impact.

S9 Drawing conclusions relating to the purpose of the study

Maintaining focus on the purpose of your study is less easy than it sounds, particularly if there is cognitive dissonance between the expected and actual results. Above all, drawing conclusions requires honesty.

S10 Justifying the choice of methods selected

Questionnaire results detailing what people eat at breakfast might suggest dietary virtue – muesli, decaffeinated coffee and fresh fruit. But data harvested from their supermarket loyalty cards might suggest a daily fried breakfast.

TASK

What method would you use to take this research a stage further? Why?

1.1 Political systems, processes and goals

OVERVIEW

In this block of work we will look at

- the British political system: how a government is formed, different roles within government
- political parties and figures in the UK, political controversies and the role of pressure groups
- voting issues: why people vote in a particular way; first-past-the-post versus proportional representation; vote turnout; referenda; opinion polls.
- the European Union: its origins, the Euro and political issues relevant to the EU.

QUESTIONS

1 Is the Royal Family outdated?
2 Does the UK have the fairest electoral system possible?
3 What counts more for a prime minister: policy or personality?
4 Is there any need for local government?
5 Why are pressure groups important in politics today?
6 Why do people vote in a particular way?
7 Should the electorate get to have its say in a referendum?
8 Why are the British people so sceptical about joining the Euro and being 'more European'?

TASK

What do you think are the main advantages and disadvantages of keeping the monarchy in this country? Compare opposing views in your answer – and support your argument with examples. You might be able to have a class debate on this question.

1.1.1 Structure and role of parliament

In the United Kingdom, it is government that holds power. While once kings and queens were in charge of how the country was ruled, the UK is now a constitutional monarchy. A constitution means that there is an agreed way to govern the country – a body of rules and laws about what a government can do. A monarch is a king or queen and the UK has one as 'head of state'. This is a symbolic role: the monarch gives final approval to the government's laws and policies – but could never actually refuse to approve a law or insist on a particular policy.

"This royal throne of kings, this sceptic Isle!"

Figure 1

At the head of government in the UK is the prime minister. Government has executive power, which means it runs the country. As well as the UK government, the UK also has a separate government for Scotland, and Wales and Northern Ireland each have their own executive body.

The ability to make laws is called legislative power – very important for structuring the way a country works. In the UK, legislative power is held by the government and by parliament. Parliament makes laws and the executive – government – is constantly answerable to parliament for its actions. This is the big difference between a parliamentary system and a presidential system – a presidency is an executive power that usually is not answerable to the legislative power. And the UK also has an independent judiciary: a legal system that applies laws made in parliament. It is independent of the executive and parliament so that the way people are judged is not affected by party politics.

Parliaments are often split into chambers or houses. In the UK, parliament is split into the House of Commons and the House of Lords; there is also a Scottish parliament and a Northern Ireland assembly and a Welsh assembly. The House of Commons makes the laws and the House of Lords checks them over and either approves them or sends them back for reworking. Both Houses have a role in keeping the government in check: the House of Commons can dismiss a government by a vote of no confidence. The members of the House of Commons are elected – the people of the United Kingdom who are eligible to vote get a choice of who makes the laws. This is called a parliamentary **democracy**. Voting also decides who runs the country – the government.

The UK has a multi-party system. A political party represents a particular ideology or vision and in a multi-party system the different parties compete for votes from the electorate: those eligible to vote. When an election is called, a date is fixed and each political party begins the process of persuading the electorate to vote for it. An election of **Members of Parliament (MPs)** to the House of Commons takes place in a **General Election**. Once all the votes are counted, the party with the greatest number of elected candidates is invited by the monarch to form a government.

The House of Lords is different to the House of Commons: not all of its members are elected and none is directly elected by the people. Lords and other nobles used to have great power in the UK, as members of the aristocracy and many hundreds of families had the hereditary right to a seat as a peer (a noble) in the House of Lords because of their family history. In 1999 the House of Lords Act cut the number of hereditary peers allowed a seat in the House of Lords to 92. There are 620 life peers: their role is not passed down to their descendants. Debate now centres on what proportion of peers should be elected (a proposal for 80 per cent elected was narrowly defeated in 2003). What do you think? Should the House of Lords be elected like the House of Commons? Or are there advantages to the current system?

The role of the prime minister

The prime minister is a powerful person who can prove to be an influential and prominent force in everyday life and dominate the political agenda of the country. In the UK, the prime minister is usually the leader of the largest party in parliament but parliament doesn't vote on who the prime minister will be. Members of the party in government elect the prime minister. And it is actually the monarch who appoints the prime minister. Sometimes the monarch has a choice – this last happened in 1963.

Prime ministers come from varied family and social backgrounds. In past centuries, high public office was the territory of the rich, titled noblemen of the country, who were usually chosen for office by their

KEY TERMS

In a **democracy** the eligible citizens of a country or state vote to choose people to represent their interests in the way the country is run. Representatives do not have to do what voters tell them to, but they run the risk of not being re-elected if they don't serve the interests of those they represent.

A **Member of Parliament** (MP) is a representative elected by voters to parliament. MPs tend to be members of political parties (though some act independently). Each MP represents a constituency – a body of voters in a particular area: there are around 650 constituencies in the UK.

A **General Election** is the election of Members of Parliament to the House of Commons; these must be held within five years and one month of the last one, but are often held before that time because it is up to the party in government to decide when to call a General Election.

TASK

Research the main differences between the functions of the House of Commons and the House of Lords.

TASK

Consider the three images of past prime ministers and research their greatest achievements. Were they famous for their policy and style of government or for their personality and image?

a **David Lloyd-George** (Liberal)

b **Winston Churchill** (Conservative)

c **Tony Blair** (Labour)

Figure 2

peers according to their family position or wealth. In recent years, a more democratic process has seen prime ministers selected by not only their fellow members of parliament but also by the ordinary membership of the party.

The role of the cabinet

The cabinet is a group of senior members of government who effectively decide government policy and the way in which this can be made into law through parliament. They hold a collective responsibility. This means decisions made in cabinet are binding on all members of the government. Ministers can argue freely in private while keeping a united front when decisions have been made.

Cabinet decisions are taken by consensus. There is never a vote at a cabinet meeting. All members must adhere to government policy, even if they are personally unsure. In practice the decision making process is made easier by the fact that much of the cabinet's business is delegated to many subcommittees who report their findings back to the cabinet with recommendations. Invariably, these decisions are accepted but the prime minister still has the Royal Prerogative (the power of the monarch) for such matters as the declaration of war and the firing of nuclear weapons.

1.1.2 Political parties in the UK

Since 1945 either the Conservative or Labour Party has been the party of government with the majority of MPs in the House of Commons. Labour, the Conservatives and the Liberal Democrats are the largest parties in parliament, but there are other smaller parties and many others in the wider democratic system.

What do the main parties in parliament stand for? See table on page 13.

The website www.direct.gov.uk includes a list of the political parties with members in UK parliaments and assemblies and also in the European parliament. There is a wide range of other parties which campaign in the UK but which are not currently represented in UK or European government. Often, smaller parties focus on a particular issue or linked set of issues, which inform their position on a range of different subjects. So, for example

- the UK Independence Party is strongly against UK integration into the European Union
- the Pensioners Party looks to protect the interests of those currently on a pension, or who will one day rely on a pension
- the Christian People's Alliance promotes Christian social policies.

Name	Number of MPs (2007)	Main principles
Labour Party www.labour.org.uk	355	Originally founded as a socialist party that aimed to improve conditions for the working class, Labour reinvented itself as a party of the 'centre' to win the 1997 election. It still has strong links with trade unions but also now supports big business and cooperation between business and the state to meet social needs. Supports the idea of the UK being more integrated with the European Union.
Conservative Party www.conservatives.com	197	A longstanding party of British politics with a leaning towards tradition and encouraging individuals to make a success of themselves rather than having the state support everyone. In recent years, however, the party has made more commitment to effective state support for health and other services. The party has often been divided in its views on integration with the European Union.
Liberal Democrats www.libdems.org.uk	63	Often called the Lib Dems, this is a relatively new party, formed in 1988. The party is based on the idea of liberalism – freedom from state control. The Lib Dems believe government should give everyone equal opportunities and the freedom to choose their own route through life. This includes clearing state regulation and protection from the way the economy works. The party has always been pro-European. Problems have arisen in the past in relation to the party's commitment to a high rate of tax for the better off – this commitment has now been dropped in favour of lower taxes where possible.
Democratic Unionist Party www.dup.org.uk	9	In UK politics, Unionism means a belief in keeping Northern Ireland a part of the UK rather than being ruled separately. The Democratic Unionists are the larger of the two main Unionist parties in Northern Ireland. Formerly opposed to any dealings with Irish Republican parties, the DUP entered into power-sharing devolved government with Sinn Féin in 2006. (A devolved government means that the UK government has granted governing powers to a smaller kingdom or province, but can take these powers back again if it wants to.)
Scottish National Party www.snp.org	6	This is currently the largest party in Scotland and runs the Scottish government. It believes in full independence for Scotland from the rest of the United Kingdom.
Sinn Féin www.sinnfein.ie	5	The largest Irish Republican party, Sinn Féin believes that Northern Ireland should become part of the Republic of Ireland. The struggle between Republicans and Unionists, which is also broadly a conflict between Catholics and Protestants, has a long and terrible history and the move back to power-sharing between the DUP and Sinn Féin has been seen world-wide as a major step forward.
Plaid Cymru www.plaidcymru.org	3	Plaid Cymru believes in independence for Wales. It currently shares power with the Welsh Labour Party in the government of Wales: the National Assembly for Wales.

Pressure groups

While political parties seek to gain power themselves by being elected into government, pressure groups try to influence those already in power. They may be supporting the interests of a particular group – like teachers, for example – or they may be trying to influence the government on a policy issue – like reducing greenhouse gas emissions, for example.

Figure 3

Here are some examples of pressure groups.

Name of group	Purpose
Animal Liberation Front	To stop and prevent medical experiments on animals
Confederation of British Industry	To advance the interests of companies, mainly manufacturing
Campaign for Nuclear Disarmament	To get rid of all nuclear arms
Hunt Saboteurs Association	To prevent blood sports, especially fox hunting
OutRage!	To challenge homophobia

These are just a few examples of the many pressure groups that exist in society, coming from all walks of life. There are so many groups that they tend to be subdivided.

Figure 4

Sectional	⇨	representing a section of society according to occupation, e.g. The Law Society.
Cause	⇨	representing those concerned with a social or ethical issue, e.g. Greenpeace.
Insider	⇨	members of the group have regular contact with government ministers.
Outsider	⇨	members of the group are not afforded such contact.

TASK

Research a range of protests carried out by pressure groups. This could be locally in your town or city (e.g. a new one-way system), regionally in your county (e.g. the siting of a wind farm), nationally (e.g. demonstrations against fuel costs) or globally (e.g. protesting against terrorism).

The most notable forms of action taken by pressure groups are called direct action. This may include protest marches, boycotts, stunts, blockades, malicious damage, and violence.

Areas of political controversy

As this brief survey of political parties and pressure groups shows, there are many different opinions about how the UK should be run. Some people would like to remain part of the UK; others would like to be independent of it. Some argue for closer links with Europe, others for less. The three largest parties may sometimes experience conflicts between their general principles and a new issue of political controversy and they may have to make quick decisions about their standpoint – which sometimes they have to backtrack on! Some of the most difficult issues relate to clashes of interest between groups of people. For a government that needs to govern for all its citizens this can lead to some very difficult political decisions. For example

- if big business drives the economy how do you convince industries to meet tough pollution targets?
- if immigrants take on jobs no one else will do, how do you deal with problems of integrating different cultures into existing communities?
- if some people object to hunting and some earn their living from it, whom should the government support?
- if people enjoy smoking and drinking, should they still pay the same for health care as people who take care of their health?

Leader   **The Observer**

Coming of age

Sir Menzies Campbell's leadership of the Liberal Democrats was dogged by puerile sniping about his age. His supporters said this reflected a wider culture of ageism. But outside Westminster, advanced years are getting due respect. Tate Modern is currently celebrating the work of sculptor Louise Bourgeois (95). The Nobel Prize for Literature was this year awarded to Doris Lessing (88 tomorrow). Bruce Forsyth (79) still presents – and dances in – prime-time TV. Only in politics is breaching the retirement age taboo.

That will change. By 2025, one-third of the population will be over 55. There will be more over-60s than under-25s. That makes the silver-haired voter a force to be reckoned with. We look forward to Sir Ming recast as the Lib Dems' comeback kid.

Sunday 21 October 2007

Source 1: Ageism

TASK

Consider Source 1. Outline the main themes of the passage. Discuss three areas of concern which politicians may have in relation to older people.

Britain can now be said to be a truly multi-ethnic, multi-cultural society. The population is growing and could hit 65 million by 2020. Yet despite all of the efforts of government, special interest groups, religions and individuals, racial tension is still very high on the political agenda as an area of controversy.

Disintegrating Britain
18 September 2007 1:30 PM

The Commission for Racial Equality (CRE), which will wind up its operations later this month, to be replaced by the Commission for Equality and Human Rights, will publish a report tomorrow analysing the state of race relations in Britain.

The report, *A Lot Done, A Lot More to Do, Our Vision for an Integrated Britain*, claims that 30 years after the Race Relations Act and the creation of the CRE, segregation and extremism are growing as bonds of solidarity across society reduce and tensions increase.

While signs like 'no blacks, no Irish, no dogs' are now considered unacceptable, the report says: 'an ethnic minority British baby born today is sadly still more likely to go on to receive poor quality education, be paid less, live in substandard housing, be in poor health and be discriminated against in other ways than his or her white contemporaries.'

A *Guardian* news report this morning summed up the findings of the bleak report, saying: 'Britain is still a place of inequality, exclusion and isolation.' Do you think this is the case?

http://commentisfree.guardian.co.uk/open_thread/2007/09/state_of_race.html

Source 2: Racial equality

What are the key political issues of our time? In the 21st century the political parties share much more common ground but there are still issues that produce major differences in policy. The following diagram shows some of these key political issues. Complete the task alongside it. You could use this as the basis of an essay using key thinking skills.

Figure 5 Key political issues

1.1.3 Voting issues

The UK currently has a 'first-past-the-post' system of electing candidates in general elections. This means that on election day, the candidate with the most votes wins the election. There are other systems such as proportional representation where voters have the opportunity to place the candidates in their order of preference. Which is the fairest? Each system has its advantages and disadvantages.

Advantages and disadvantages often feature in examination questions set at A level. The aim is to elicit a balanced argument from you and give you the opportunity to fully examine and exploit a topic in the time allowed. Any question about electoral systems is likely to ask you to compare one system against another. The table looks at this for first-past-the-post.

"If we didn't have a first past the post system, I'd beat you every time!"

Figure 6

Advantages and disadvantages of first-past-the-post

Advantages		Disadvantages	
Idea	Support	Idea	Support
It is a simple to understand system.	On polling day, everyone knows that the person with the highest number of votes wins the election – there is no indecision or confusion.	At every election as many as 70% of the votes can be wasted.	As a result, the number of seats won by a party nationally in no way reflects the number of votes that have been cast for it.

TASK

1 Add three more ideas for each side of the table.
2 Write a conclusion.

Party	Number of seats	% of the vote
Labour	356	35.3
Conservative	198	32.3
Liberal Democrat	62	22.1
Others	32	10

Here are the results of the 2005 General Election. It is worth noting how close the percentage of votes cast for the two main parties was, compared with the number of seats which they gained. How might this come across to those who voted for the individual parties?

Why do people vote in a particular way?

Why do people vote the way that they do? Is it because of a principle, family tradition, national interest, membership of a union or ethnic minority, favouring one leader over another? Could it be that the policies of one party seem more attractive, workable and acceptable than the others? At General Elections in the UK around 70 per cent of those eligible to vote actually cast a vote; in local elections this number reduces to between 30 and 40 per cent and for European elections the number is even smaller. What can be done to encourage people to exercise their democratic right? Should we make voting compulsory as it is in Australia? There, everyone must cast their vote, but is this taken entirely seriously?

One of the most difficult problems to solve is voter apathy. Why do so many people fail to cast their vote on election day? There could be a number of factors.

CASE STUDY

Here are some suggestions from the Electoral Reform Society about how reluctant voters may be tempted to cast their votes.

Postal voting

A proven and popular way to raise turnout, but with postal voting being open to fraud, should its use be so widespread?

E-voting

Voting via the internet is easy, but is it secure?

Compulsory voting

When people won't do as they're told and vote voluntarily, is it time to get tough?

Incentive voting

Bribing people to go to the polls – novel, but is this moral?

Other

Weekend voting, more polling stations, a national holiday and 'none of the above'.

TASK

Discuss each of the suggested ways of encouraging people to vote. Which do you think is best? Is there an alternative?

The use of referenda

'Let the people decide' is a key component of a democracy. In a referendum, a vote is taken on a single question. The answer required is usually 'yes' or 'no'. They are not often held in the UK but they are more common in some EU countries and the United States.

TASK

'There is never a clearer method of carrying out the people's wishes than when there is a referendum.' Discuss this statement.

Advantages of referendum	Disadvantages of referendum
• encourages people to get involved in democracy • gives a simple, clear, irrefutable answer • adds weight to a measure to be taken • provides firm direction for a controversial issue	• undermines the government • there can be problems with the phrasing of the question • issues are too complex for 'yes' and 'no' • the result may not be clear

The value and use of opinion polls

Opinion polls have a margin for error (+/− 4 per cent) and some people, when interviewed, do not tell the truth or change their minds. The number of people saying 'Don't know' can also be a problem. Why?

Table 1
How would you vote if there were a General Election tomorrow? Which party are you most inclined to support?
Base: All naming a party (1,987)

Party	%
Conservative	35
Labour	43
Liberal Democrat (Lib Dem)	13
Scottish/Welsh Nationalist	2
Green Party	2
UK Independence Party	1
Other	4
Labour lead (±%)	**+8**
Would not vote	14
Undecided	10
Refused	1

Voting: Ipsos MORI 28 October 2007

Table 2
What would you say is the most important issue facing Britain today?
Base: 1,004 British adults 18+

Issue	%
Race relations/immigration/immigrants	25
National Health Service/hospitals/health care	13
Crime/law & order/violence/vandalism/anti-social (yob) behaviour	15
Defence/foreign affairs/international terrorism	8
Education/schools	4
Housing	4
Economy/economic situation	5
Drug abuse	2
Taxation	1
Morality/individual behaviour	2
Unemployment/factory closure/lack of industry	2
Pollution/environment	2
Pensions/social security/benefits	1
Common Market/EU/Europe/Euro	1
Inflation/prices	1
Poverty/inequality	2
Public services in general	1
Transport/public transport	1
Other	6
Don't know	4

This sort of information is what party policy designers need to know. Bear in mind that these figures came in the mid-term of a Labour government. Polls are carried out scientifically. They do not involve everyone, but a representative sample of the electorate. In the days leading up to an election, many opinion polls are commissioned, some concerned with the feelings of the whole country and others in the marginal **constituencies** where a party needs to make some ground in order to gain power.

KEY TERMS

A constituency is an area from where voters in an election are drawn. Each constituency elects one MP to represent the voters in parliament.

TASK

You may be offered data to consider in the examination. You would need to consider the trends presented as well as the reliability of the source. It would not be enough to simply 'lift' the figures from the table. Try these questions.

1. The Conservatives have closed the gap on Labour since 1997. Can you suggest *two* reasons for this? [4 marks]
2. Account for *two* reasons why, in Table 1, 14 per cent of the electorate say that they would not vote. [4 marks]
3. Outline and discuss the outcomes suggested by Table 2. How far do you agree or disagree with the opinion poll's findings? [6 marks]

Figure 7

A **ward** is an electoral district within a town or district, used in local politics. It is represented by a councillor who is usually affiliated to one of the major political parties.

1.1.4 Local government

Parish Councils were formed in 1894 to take over the social welfare and civic duties of towns and villages. Before this date a variety of groups based around church parishes had responsibility for these matters, in a system of local government that dated back to the feudal system.

County Councils are councils that govern a county. They are responsible for more strategic services in a region, with smaller Urban and Rural District Councils being responsible for other activities.

Parish and town councils in England, and community and town councils in Wales, are the first tier of local government. They deliver a vast range of services at community level. There are around 10,000 community, parish and town councils in England and Wales, made up of nearly 100,000 councillors.

Local government is run by both elected councillors and a network of departments and professional officers. Councillors are elected in the same way as MPs, though they only serve four-year terms. Some councils elect all their members every few years, but others only elect one council seat per **ward** each year. This system maintains an interest in local issues and encourages voting.

Is there a need for local government? Some people believe that services would be best delivered locally but managed nationally to avoid any unfairness or unevenness in the distribution of services. For example, social security and employment services are delivered through local offices but managed centrally in London.

TASK

1 Find out how local politics are run in your area. What are the names of your local councillors? Which party controls the council? Research and outline what the council's major areas of concern are at the moment.
2 Hold a debate on the motion *This House believes that local government should be abolished in favour of central, national government control from London.* One third of the group should speak FOR the motion, one third should speak AGAINST the motion, the remainder act as judges to decide whether the motion is carried.

1.1.5 The origins of the EU

The Treaty of Rome was signed in 1957 and the European Economic Community (EEC) officially launched on 1 January 1958. The UK did not join the EEC at first as it felt itself independent, a strong world power that did not need to call upon the benefits of the EEC. French President de Gaulle doubted that Britain was serious about joining and vetoed the applications of 1961 and 1967. It was not until 1973 that the Conservative prime minister, Edward Heath, took Britain into the EEC.

The European Union (EU) is the result of a process of cooperation and integration begun in 1951 after World War II. The urge to safeguard peace and build up economic prosperity gave birth to the idea of close and firm cooperation between the war-weary countries. Since then, this cooperation has extended to new areas. The EU of today is now an important forum for solving problems that can no longer be solved by individual countries.

The overriding aim of the EU is to

- promote economic and social progress and high levels of employment
- assert the European identity in international forums
- introduce EU citizenship
- develop an area for freedom, security and justice
- maintain and expand the community.

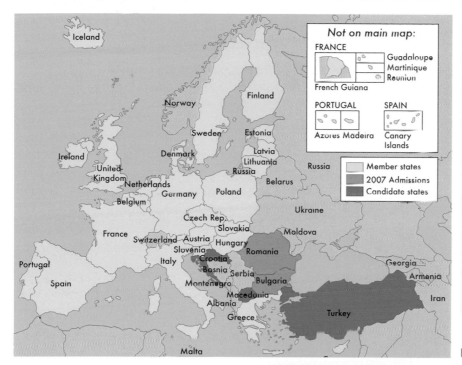

Figure 8

The Euro

Why are the British people so sceptical about joining the **Euro** and taking a more solid step towards becoming part of the community?

Figure 9

KEY TERMS

Euro A single unit of currency common to most EU countries. So far some countries, including the UK, have not adopted the Euro.

One of the most critical issues is the relative cost of goods after the change. Some business people used the currency change as a stealth measure in order to 'hike' prices. In some countries, the conversion rate to the old currency still remains on till receipts!

Item	Portugal Euro	£	Spain Euro	£	Germany Euro	£	Italy Euro	£	France Euro	£
1.5 litre Coke	1.37	.88	1.42	.86	1.12	.68	1.20	.73	1.18	.71
1 litre fresh milk	.78	.47	1.17	.71	.61	.37	1.21	.73	1.08	.65
6 large fresh eggs	.70	.42	1.65	1	1.25	.76	1.34	.81	1.28	.78
10 Bic comfort twin razors	6.28	3.83	4.74	2.89	N/A		2.50	1.52	4.26	2.59
1l Tropicana Orange Juice	2.09	2.66	2.98	1.81	N/A		1.54	.93	2.56	3.41
250g Lavazzo Gran Coffee	4.76	2.90	4.74	2.89	3.99	2.43	2.37	1.44	2.84	1.73
Nescafe Selection Instant coffee	4.48	2.73	3.96	2.41	3.99	2.43	N/A		3.10	2.94
25 Liptons yellow label tea bags	1.42	.85	1.65	1	N/A		1.71	1.04	1.39	.84
1 kilo rump steak	8.48	5.17	10.25	6.25	15.29	9.33	10.60	6.46	14.43	8.80
1 kilo oranges	.74	.45	.19	.11	1.99	1.21	1.54	.93	2.12	1.29
Heinz tomato ketchup (342g)	1.42	.86	1.29	.78	1.69	1.01	1.58	.96	1.23	.75
Veuve Cliquot champagne (orange label)	26.32	16.05	27.92	17.03	22.99	14.64	27.10	16.53	24.72	15.07
Johnny Walker red label (70cl)	8.94	5.45	9.61	5.86	12.16	7.41	8.80	5.37	13.53	8.25
M&M peanuts (200g)	2.29	1.39	2.05	1.25	1.45	.88	1.90	1.16	1.59	.97
1.5 litre bottle Vichy mineral water	.94	.57	.82	.50	N/A		.48	.29	.55	.33
Peugeot 206 XR 1.4i 5 door	17,468	10,655	11,740	7,161.40	12,020	7,332.20	11,650	7,105.50	11,740	7,161.40

Figure 10

Standard VAT rates in Europe	
Belgium	21%
Denmark	25%
Germany	16%
Greece	18%
Spain	16%
France	19.6%
Ireland	20%
Italy	20%
Luxembourg	15%
Netherlands	19%
Austria	20%
Portugal	17%
Finland	22%
Sweden	25%
UK	17.5%

TASK

Consider Figure 10 and discuss where the major price differences lie. Try to account for these changes and discrepancies.

WHAT NEXT?

Examine the key aims and objectives of the three major political parties in the UK.

To what extent are their philosophies **left wing**, **right wing** or a mixture of the two? Refer to the party's website for clarification.

www.labour.co.uk
www.conservatives.com
www.libdems.org.uk

KEY TERMS

Left wing politics are usually associated with the working class, civil rights, gender and racial equality.

Right wing politics are usually associated with capitalism and the creation and maintenance of wealth.

Examiners often ask you to interpret data in order to outline the main features. This involves looking at variations as well as consistencies. In the case of the data that follow, some geographical knowledge may also be helpful. In tackling question 1 (page 24), a *developed reason*, perhaps including some *exemplification*, would score three marks. The simple naming of a reason would only score one mark.

Command words are very important elements in any examination question. They indicate the extent and depth expected in response to a question. Question 2 uses the command words *outline* and *discuss*.

- *Outline – the main features, the general ideas, plan, draft*, these indicate a short section of the essay which sets the scene and introduces the main themes.

- *Discuss, an examination and consideration of information*, this is the main body of the work where there is an opportunity to score many marks through a *logical and balanced* examination of several viewpoints in a *rational and fair-minded way*.

A typical Section C question (such as question 3) uses source material to uncover the meaning or truth behind an issue. So for question 3, your answer to the first highlighted word might be: Reform, a change (one mark) which is brought about in order to effect some improvement (one mark), in this case the overhauling of an outdated system (one mark). For the second part of the question, also worth three marks, examiners would be looking for either *three individual points* or *two points with some exemplification* or *one point that is fully developed and secure*.

Comparisons feature a lot in General Studies lessons and examinations. They promote argument and thereby reveal strengths, weaknesses, flaws and contradictions, which are many of the key elements found in Assessment Objective 3 (different kinds of knowledge). Here is an example.

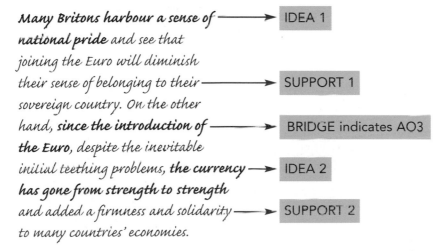

Many Britons harbour a sense of national pride and see that joining the Euro will diminish their sense of belonging to their sovereign country. On the other hand, since the introduction of the Euro, despite the inevitable initial teething problems, the currency has gone from strength to strength and added a firmness and solidarity to many countries' economies.

IDEA 1

SUPPORT 1

BRIDGE indicates AO3

IDEA 2

SUPPORT 2

EXAMINATION PRACTICE

1 Consider the following data. Suggest *three* reasons for some of the regional variations in voter turnout. [9 marks]

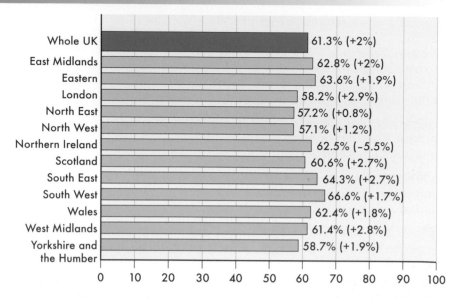

Whole UK	61.3% (+2%)
East Midlands	62.8% (+2%)
Eastern	63.6% (+1.9%)
London	58.2% (+2.9%)
North East	57.2% (+0.8%)
North West	57.1% (+1.2%)
Northern Ireland	62.5% (−5.5%)
Scotland	60.6% (+2.7%)
South East	64.3% (+2.7%)
South West	66.6% (+1.7%)
Wales	62.4% (+1.8%)
West Midlands	61.4% (+2.8%)
Yorkshire and the Humber	58.7% (+1.9%)

Figure 11: Voter turnout

2 Briefly outline the contribution made by one of these prime ministers and discuss the extent to which they have had a positive influence on the country's history. [10 marks]

Figure 12   a **David Lloyd-George** (Liberal)   b **Winston Churchill** (Conservative)   c **Tony Blair** (Labour)

3 Read the passage carefully. Briefly outline the meaning of the highlighted phrases, as used in the passage. [3 marks for each phrase]

How would these changes 'substantially reduce the prime minister's powers'? [3 marks]

4 Consider the advertisement for Cancer Research UK in Figure 13. Outline two strengths and two weaknesses of its impact on the viewer. [10 marks]

5 Consider the advantages and disadvantages of a first-past-the-post electoral system. [30 marks]

Ending patronage

Lords **reform** is seen by ministers as unfinished business after they removed all but 92 **hereditary peers** from the House of Lords in 1999. But both MPs and peers failed to agree on seven options for the second stage of reform, ranging from a **completely appointed second chamber** to an all-elected one. On Wednesday, the Queen said: 'Legislation will be brought forward to reform the House of Lords. This will remove hereditary peers and establish an independent Appointments Commission to select **non-party members of the Upper House.**' Whitehall officials say the bill would end centuries of **government patronage** and substantially reduce the prime minister's powers. The plans to rid the Lords of the remaining hereditary peers will face stiff opposition.

Figure 13

www.bbc.co.uk/politics
23 November 2003

1.2 Social and economic trends and constraints

OVERVIEW

In this block of work we will look at

- the public sector: national systems like the British state education system and the National Health Service and problems in providing these services
- the private sector: private enterprise, privatisation and problems of private provision
- work and leisure, including changing employment patterns, unemployment, the world of work and changing patterns of leisure
- the distribution of wealth: how wealth is distributed within society
- transport issues: including transport services, commuting and congestion.

TASK

Examiners sometimes use headlines from newspapers as a 'hook' to focus your attention on to a particular topic. Which of these headlines are about social and economic **trends** or **constraints** – or both?

Research each headline and write a summary passage which includes the main issues and arguments. *Limit yourself to 300 words.*

KEY TERMS

A trend is the direction that our social and economic lifestyle and world is taking.

A constraint is a social condition that restricts progress.

Still waiting at hospitals?

www.channel4.com/news

Pupils' exam success earns praise

BBC News, 8 Aug 2006

Teacher shortage cuts timetable

BBC News, 21 Sep 2004

Herceptin improves some breast cancer survival rates

Guardian Unlimited, 5 Jan 2007

QUESTIONS

1. What factors push society in one direction but then, for another reason, halt its progress?
2. Why do we need school?
3. If you pay for your higher education, should you be able to say how you want to be taught?
4. To what extent does the NHS still maintain its original aims?
5. What effect does immigration have on the UK economy and society?
6. Why do people want to come to the UK?
7. Why are people paid such different amounts for different jobs?
8. Is transport in the UK in crisis?

DEFINITIONS

Public school A fee-charging school, which may or may not set academic or other standards for entry.

Entrepreneur A person who identifies a possible market opportunity and uses available resources to exploit the opportunity as effectively as possible.

Casual unemployment For example, in tourism and agriculture where the working season is only part of the year.

Structural unemployment Whole industries (like coal and steel) are shut down due to decline.

Frictional unemployment Where the workforce will not move from one area to another e.g. for family reasons.

Deregulation When transport is no longer controlled by government and anyone can bid to operate a service.

1.2.1 Introduction

Social and economic trends are dependent upon people, their standards of living and their lifestyle. Each one may vary from year to year, country to country, culture to culture. Each one of us is likely to come into contact with the essential social services in the course of our lives, most notably health and education.

To find out about the underlying social issues of our times it is useful to consult government-produced documents which are reliable sources of statistics, such as the *UK Census 2001*. Other trends and constraints that might be explored would involve study of: leisure activities, work patterns and hours, class distinction, travel preferences, and housing market patterns.

TASK

Read the passage. What are the key social trends and constraints of 2007, according to government statistics?

The underlying theme in 2007 is children and young people. Children are living in an increasing range of family structures and participating more in education. They are also very much in touch with today's digital age of mobile phones and the internet. However, today's young people are still not flying the nest and considered [in the full report] are some of the issues which may be influencing these decisions. The population of the UK is still growing but family sizes are shrinking. Homes with fewer bedrooms are being built but increases in housing density are placing increasing pressure on the land and environment. More years are spent in poor health, and obesity is rising, but our attitudes towards our lifestyles may be changing. More opportunities for sport are being provided through schools and we are taking more holidays abroad than ever before.

www.statistics.gov.uk

1.2.2 The public sector: education

The public sector is the delivery of services or products by the government rather than by private companies. Education is a good example of a public service – in the UK every child is entitled to an education that would cost thousands of pounds in the private sector. Yet privately funded schools still exist and are popular: why would anyone pay for something that they could get for free? What are the trends and constraints in public sector education?

Education has changed a great deal over the last few decades. Here are a few points to consider.

- Children attend school at a younger age and stay longer.
- Teachers are more accountable for children's progress (there are performance **league tables**).
- Most go to comprehensive schools at 11.
- Further education has expanded dramatically.

KEY TERMS

League tables are a way of measuring schools against each other in terms of examination success.

This passage is typical of the sort used in Section C of the examination. There are several bullet points. A question might be:

Briefly outline the key points raised in the passage. [12 marks]

There are six bullet points and 12 marks; therefore, there are two marks for each bullet point to be awarded as follows:

A single fact: 'In the last 35 years the number of under-fours enrolling for school has tripled.' *(1 mark)*

Support: possibly due to the increase in pre-schools being available or built/because more mothers want to get back to work sooner after pregnancy/the increased availability of skilled teachers. *(1 mark)*

- The proportion of three- and four-year-olds enrolled in all schools in the UK tripled from 21 per cent in 1970/71 to 64 per cent in 2005/06.
- In 2005, 704,000 children were enrolled in full-day childcare settings in England compared with 539,000 in 2001. The number enrolled for part of the day has fallen, from 589,000 in 2001 to 390,000 in 2005.
- The rate of permanent exclusion among school pupils in England has fallen by 23 per cent since 1997/98 to 12 in every 10,000 pupils of compulsory school age in 2004/05.
- At the end of 2005, a record 76 per cent of 16-year-olds were in full-time further education in England.
- In both 1996 and 2006, girls outperformed boys in teacher assessments in England, although there were improvements in the performance of both sexes at all Key Stages.
- There were 441,000 full-time teachers in mainstream schools in the UK in 2004/05, an overall fall of 10 per cent since 1981/82 despite rises since the late 1990s.

Social Trends No. 37 2007, HMSO

The National Curriculum

The National Curriculum was introduced to ensure that all children in **state schools** receive the same basic education up to the age of 16. For Key Stage 4 the following subjects are compulsory

- English
- mathematics
- science
- ICT
- PE
- citizenship
- religious education
- sex education
- careers education
- work-related learning

The arts, design and technology, modern foreign languages and the humanities are entitlement areas – which means that schools must make these courses available to students who want to study them.

Schools fulfil far more roles than simply teaching young people facts. They are culturally and socially important to the development of contemporary society through their influence on young people's outlook and attitude. It could be a school's influence that instils a sense of *reliability*, *honesty* and *respect* for one's fellow humans and the law, society's values and tolerance.

KEY TERMS

A **state school** is a government-funded school which provides education free of charge to children.

TASK

Divide into groups. Consider the list of subjects from the National Curriculum. Design a timetable for an 11–16 comprehensive school. Compare each group's choice. Which subjects were dropped, which subjects were introduced, and why? Is it a question of abandoning subjects or simply modifying the content of the lessons?

Higher education

When discussing education matters, some consideration must be given to the introduction of tuition fees for higher education courses and the impact that this has had on individuals and families. There are a number of positive and negative views about tuition fees. In addition, students are beginning to get used to the idea of paying for their education and, like any other service, they are considering other aspects such as 'value for money' and 'quality'. Consider this passage.

TASK

What do you associate with the word 'university'? How does this compare with the views of the rest of your group?

What potential students care about can be quite different from what a university thinks they ought to. Figures about student–staff ratios and added value don't hit the spot in many cases. Minor luxuries can seem more important. Applicants shouldn't be blamed for this. The rise in tuition fees has made people feel that they deserve something tangible for paying £3,000 a year, even if payment is no longer demanded upfront.

Working out what really matters can be particularly tough for kids without family experience of higher education. Since going to university can be a form of going away, many apply holiday standards. Like airline passengers, they do not just want to arrive at their goal, but do so in comfort. Asked what they associate with the word university, teenagers I spoke to mentioned an end to early morning starts, to parental interference and to homework. "No more pressure" was a common phrase.

What do students want?, Elfi Pallis, *The Guardian*, 8 May 2006

1.2.3 The public sector: health

The work of the National Health Service began in 1948 when The National Health Service Act 1946 became law thanks to the work of Labour health minister Aneurin Bevan. All treatment was to be free and, with a budget of over £100 billion in 2007–2008, the NHS is one of the top three employers in the world. To what extent does the NHS still maintain its original aim? Public sector finance is dominated by demands to develop and improve healthcare. In some cases investment is needed to maintain services at an acceptably safe level, but there are other demands on the public purse too. The responsibility for this lies with the government and, finally, the taxpayer. As people live longer and technology becomes more complex and expensive, what is the solution? The National Health Service prided itself in caring for everyone 'from the cradle to the grave'. Can it go on without private investment and assistance?

"Have no fear on that account, Mrs Old, the NHS will honour its pledge to care for everybody...from cradle to grave(ly ill)."

Figure 1

TASK

Consider the cartoon caption above carefully, notably the last two words. Then consider the quotation (right) by a prominent Health Authority executive. What are the contrasting messages being conveyed?

It is important that we continue to work with the public to demonstrate that we can improve the services on offer and in turn improve personal health, families' health and, in some cases, increase life expectancy.

Jo Cubbon, Chief Executive of East Lancashire Hospitals NHS Trust

1 The social and cultural domains

How the NHS works

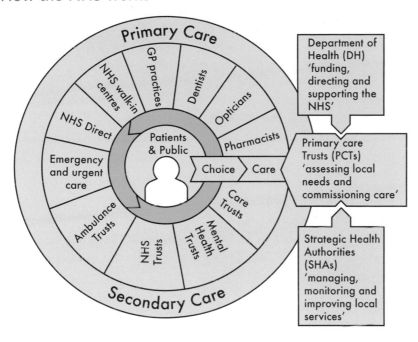

Figure 2

Assessment Objective 3: *demonstrate understanding of different types of knowledge, appreciating their strengths and limitations.*

This is the most challenging area in which to pick up marks. One way this can be done is by examining *dilemmas* and *contradictions*:

Figure 3

1 The government faces a *dilemma*; to balance its books it cannot fund the NHS as well as it should do. Lives are lost at the expense of cost-cutting, but how does this measure against the concept of caring for people 'from the cradle to the grave'?

2 The first caption says 'cares for everyone' which is contradicted by the second one which suggests 'tries to care for everyone'. This subtle difference results in a major change of attitude and policy.

Which statement is the truth? Which statement is the most reliable? It is likely that both are true to some extent, whether historically correct, or contemporary fact. The examiner will be looking for your ability to examine and analyse each one based on your personal knowledge, views and experience.

A further question arises: what should doctors do when they are faced with the decision 'to treat or not to treat'?

> 'Doctors have many rights, but in civilised countries they have not had the right to kill their patients.'
>
> Clergyman

> 'Cuts in care, staff shortages, a lack of beds, nurses doing doctors' jobs, poor hospital food and MRSA infections have left me deeply concerned about the service my patients are receiving. When I hear their complaints about the care they have received at the hands of the NHS, it leaves me wondering about how it will care for my own family.'
>
> GP

TASK

Consider the views above. They provoke ample controversy for a group discussion and debate.

Doctors are taught to abide by an ethical code, which informs the way they care for their patients – but is this always practical? In the 21st century other factors come into play, such as sustainability of resources and profitability of services. Should our National Health Service run at a profit or loss? This was not what was envisaged when the service was set up.

Emergency services

Figure 4

At their best in times of crisis, the UK's emergency rescue services are second to none, praised for their courage, loyalty, skill and dexterity. Once the emergency passes, politicians, press and public seize upon their shortcomings, most notably

TASK

Choose *one* of the emergency services. Research and outline its provision in your area. How is it funded?

- when there is a dispute for additional pay
- when there is a delay due to shortages of personnel and equipment
- when there is a big public bill to fund services such as the Air Ambulance, which benefits only a few
- when there is a reliance on charity funds to save a service from being curtailed (such as the Royal National Lifeboat Institution).

1 The social and cultural domains

There are variations in provision in different parts of the country, for example in the time it takes to get from rural locations to an urban hospital unit. How effectively and strategically are the services placed in order to operate efficiently? Is there a need for local rescue services coordinated at local level as opposed to a regional or national service?

Here is an alternative approach by the people of the Channel Island of Guernsey.

What are the **advantages** and **disadvantages** of this scheme if it was to be brought into use on the mainland?

Ambulance service calls for funds

Guernsey's ambulance service is making its annual appeal for funds. In return for signing up to a subscription scheme people will not have to pay for emergency ambulance journeys next year. The scheme gives islanders a chance to support the service and protect themselves against any charges they may incur from ambulance journeys in 2008.

Islanders can pay a subscription of £19.50 for a single person or £39 for a couple. Both schemes also cover children living at home who are still in full-time education. There is also a reduced rate available for subscribers aged over 65. Anyone who does not sign up to the scheme and needs an emergency ambulance will have to pay £160.

1.2.4 The private sector

In the private sector, services and products are produced for profit, without state control. Rather than the state deciding what should be done and in what way, private enterprise drives production. There is a story that when a senior official from the USSR visited London at the height of the Cold War, he asked who was in charge of ensuring that bread reached the millions of London citizens each day. In the USSR every aspect of production was controlled by the state and these sorts of logistical challenges were very important. He was told that no one was in charge of this. Instead, the **market economy** meant that the demand for bread was met by enough people looking to make a profit from being bakers, delivery people and shopkeepers.

Such are the problems and expense of state provision of services that many governments today are finding them impossible to continue – at least at a level that meets customer demand. As a result, national, state-run services are often a target for **privatisation**. In a capitalist economy, it is often felt that private companies provide a better and more efficient service than the public sector. Because private companies compete against each other they need to offer a better service for less or they will go out of business. If a public sector service has no competitors, it has no incentive to improve its service or be more efficient.

The modern economy demonstrates some very efficient companies. Consider mobile phones, for example. The huge level of competition between companies means an incredible rate of innovation and levels of service. Do you think that if there was one government mobile phone producer we would have the models and features available today? Another example is supermarkets: here the private sector shows a level of control over demand, pricing and delivery that would make the USSR official of the Cold War green with envy.

KEY TERMS

Market economy This means that the producer gets to decide what to produce, how much to produce, what to charge customers for those goods and what to pay employees – not the government.

Privatisation is the process by which governments transfer ownership of an industry or service from the public sector to the private sector.

TASK

The National Health Service is run by the state. What would be the advantages and disadvantages of a private sector health service?

However, is the private sector and privatisation always the best solution? The technological development of mobile phones is amazing, but do we really need a new mobile every six months – and what is the environmental cost of all that production? Cheap food all year round is very convenient, but what is the cost to society and the economy of all the smaller grocery stores that have to close down near every giant supermarket? Is a privatised nuclear industry as concerned with safety as a nationalised one where profits are not the be all and end all?

Employment

The development of big business has meant increasing numbers of jobs. However, in many cases, the domestic employment market fails to meet this demand because of the low wages being offered. This has resulted in massive surges of new workers from the EU descending on the UK to fill the gaps in the job market. Two and a half million foreigners have moved to the UK to work since 2002.

> 66 *We have found migrant workers to have a very satisfactory work ethic, in many cases superior to domestic workers.* 99

Submission by Sainsbury's to Lords' Committee

TASK

What are the consequences of high unemployment? Look back at historical evidence from the 1930s and the 1970s.

People born overseas account for one in eight of the UK's working age population, an official report says.

The Home Office paper says economic immigration has 'clear benefits' for the UK – but it adds that the lowest paid can experience falls in wages.

Recently-arrived workers from Eastern Europe have not led to British people losing their jobs, the report says.

The paper has been published before a meeting of a government body looking at the regional impact of immigrants.

The report into the economic impact of immigration draws together a comprehensive range of research from across government and the academic world.

It quotes official labour market statistics which reveal that in the final quarter of 2006 people born overseas accounted for 12.5% of the working age population – up from 7.4% a decade earlier.

BBC News, 17 October 2007

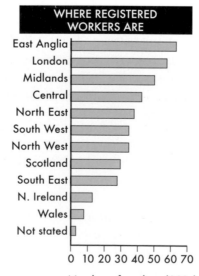

NATIONALITY OF APPLICANTS

Number of applicants (000s)
Source : Home Office

WHERE REGISTERED WORKERS ARE

Number of workers (000s)
Source : Home Office

Figure 5

TASK

1 What are the main causes of unemployment?
2 What are the advantages and disadvantages of a large migrant workforce? Using Figure 5, account for the countries of origin of recent applicants to enter the UK and where they have settled.

1.2.5 Work and leisure

People's whole attitudes and approaches to work and leisure have changed in recent years. No longer is it the case that a job is for life or a career stretches 40 years or more. The changing dynamics of the employment market and the differing demands for skills are bringing about new trends in the job market. There has been a tremendous growth in the service sector and a move away from traditional manufacturing, but one thing remains constant. The workforce needs to be better skilled and trained to meet the changing demands of the 21st century.

EXAMINATION PRACTICE

British people work some of the longest hours in Europe. Yet due to stress and fatigue, productivity is one of the lowest.[1] With levels falling far behind France, Britain's long hours culture is not only affecting our opportunities for a social and family life but is also seriously threatening our physical and mental health.[2]

Britain currently stands as the only EU country to include an opt-out in the **Working Time Directive**, allowing employees to sign away their right to a cap on their working hours. While many do not truly volunteer but sign under pressure or simply do not know they can refuse, it comes as no surprise that we are experiencing record levels of employee sick leave, due to long hours and stress, and an increasing number of people opting to take jobs less skilled than their ability in order to access flexible or less stressful work.[3]

With more than four million people in the UK already working over 48 hours per week, the long hours culture has encroached on our society. A cultural revolution is now needed if we are to achieve the work life balance we want for both men and women.[4]

More than half of British workers say they have experienced symptoms of overwork and burnout and 30% believe that they have suffered exhaustion. Sadly the British work culture is such that stress is seen as a weakness[5] and instead of changing our approach makes our workforce even more vulnerable. With indirect results of long hours, such as tiredness on the roads, being particularly damaging, and symptoms of stress and fatigue often worse than being under the influence of alcohol or drugs, cutting the UK's long hours and introducing flexibility will protect all of society in so many ways.[6] It may help to solve other problems the government is concerned about such as increased alcohol consumption and weight gain.

Today's communication tools, which offer the possibility of greater flexibility, can also lead to the expectation that people will always be available on the end of a phone or computer. It is essential that we establish an 'off' time to diminish the blur between our working and personal lives.[7]

The UK government is talking about flexible working but continues to do its utmost to keep the Working Time Directive out of our lives – propping up the long hours culture. It is time the government accepted that long hours are damaging to us as individuals, economically, and to society in general.[8]

This passage can not only be used to research the subject of work and leisure by using its content to trigger ideas, but also to provide some General Studies question practice, especially in relation to *Assessment Objectives*. Study each of the points indicated (in red, 1–8) and, for each one, work out an explanation (*AO1* and *AO2*), a personal reaction or experience or a contradiction (*AO3*). Write in clear sentences using appropriate vocabulary and phrases (*AO4*).

Must I work harder?, Jean Lambert, *The Guardian*, 14 February 2007

The **unemployment rate** is used as a guide to how well a country is doing economically and politically. High unemployment usually signals that there is something going wrong somewhere!

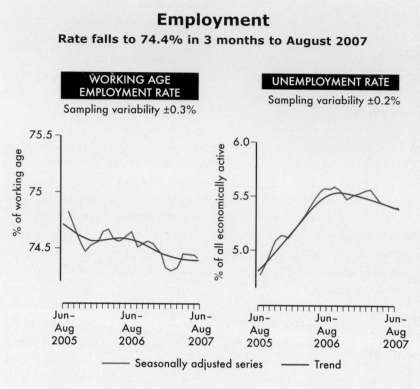

Employment
Rate falls to 74.4% in 3 months to August 2007

Figure 6

The trends in the employment and unemployment rates are falling. There has been a further fall in the number of people claiming Jobseeker's Allowance benefit. The rising trend in the inactivity rate appears to be levelling off. The number of job vacancies has increased. Growth in average earnings, both excluding and including bonuses, has increased.

The employment rate for people of working age was 74.4 per cent for the three months ending in August 2007, down 0.1 from the previous quarter and down 0.3 over the year.

The number of people in employment for the three months ending in August 2007 was 29.10 million, up 22,000 over the quarter and up 82,000 over the year. Total hours worked per week were 935.5 million, up 5.3 million over the quarter and up 5.6 million over the year. These figures for employment and hours worked are the highest since comparable records began in 1971.

The unemployment rate was 5.4 per cent, unchanged over the previous quarter but down 0.2 over the year. The number of unemployed people fell by 5,000 over the quarter and by 47,000 over the year, to reach 1.65 million.

www.statistics.gov.uk

Ageism

Ageism is becoming a big issue in the world of work, even though, legally, people can no longer be discriminated against because of their age. Organisations that represent older people are making efforts to redress this situation with education and publicity drives.

Common sources of ageism are
- being refused interest-free credit, a new credit card or car insurance because of your age
- finding that an organisation's attitude to older people results in you receiving a lower quality of service
- age limits on benefits such as Disability Living Allowance
- a doctor deciding not to refer you to a consultant because you are 'too old'
- losing your job because of your age.

www.ageconcern.org.uk

On 1 October 2006, The Employment Equality (Age) Regulations 2006 came into force in England, Wales and Scotland. The Regulations provide protection against age discrimination in employment, training and adult education, for people of all ages.

Leisure

What do we mean by leisure? The time when we are freed from work or any other commitment which stops us from relaxing? Leisure also means some enjoyment and pleasure, not necessarily relaxation because some people enjoy energetic leisure to improve their stamina and fitness. Leisure is undoubtedly good for the population's health as well as its business. The growth in the fitness industry, where leisure is sold as a health product, has been astronomical in the last ten years.

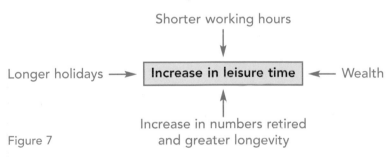

Figure 7

Some of the other factors that affect an aspect of leisure – tourism – are outlined in the following passage. It is clear that the UK is a popular place for tourists to visit. Why do you think this is?

KEY TERMS

Social class A division of the population into groups according to factors such as wealth, education, birth.

For Britain's tourism industry, the bank holiday weekend this year is more crucial than ever. All eyes are on the weather forecast in the hope that a spell of sunshine will help save what has so far been a miserable summer. With some of the wettest weather on record, a surge in the strength of the pound, stockmarket turmoil and scares over an outbreak of foot and mouth disease, the industry has been fighting a series of battles.

The Office for National Statistics said last week that in the three months to June this year, 8.1 million tourists came to the UK. This was 3% fewer than in the winter months of January to March. Numbers of American visitors in particular were down for the second consecutive quarter. Visit Britain, the national tourism agency, said that last year the number of French visitors overtook Americans for the first time.

The year British holidays were rained off, Angela Balakrishnan, Pui-Guan Man and Laura Valdez, *The Guardian*, 21 August 2007

1.2.6 Distribution of wealth

Every society has its share of rich and poor people. Top incomes today, particularly in sport and entertainment, are exceedingly high, whereas at the other end of the scale there are older people and single parents who may have to survive on minimum wages or state benefits. How can the wealth gap be evened out? Increased tax on the rich? A more efficient pension scheme?

Figure 8

TASK

Research the spending profile of three people: a salaried professional, a shop worker, a retired person. Design a questionnaire to discover how they manage their weekly/monthly income. Aim to discover priorities and difficulties. Examine their ability to save money.

Earnings
Weekly pay up 2.9% to £457

The results of the 2007 Annual Survey of Hours and Earnings (ASHE) show that median weekly pay for full-time employees in the UK grew by 2.9 per cent in the year to April 2007 to reach £457. Median earnings of full-time male employees was £498 per week in April 2007; for women the median was £394.

The top 10 per cent of the earnings distribution earned more than £906 per week, while the bottom 10 per cent earned less than £252. Between April 2006 and 2007 the distribution of gross weekly pay narrowed, with a 3.5 per cent increase at the bottom decile, and a 2.8 per cent increase at the top decile.

Median gross weekly earnings for full-time employees were highest for 40 to 49-year-olds at £516 for this age group. Male employees reached their highest earnings in this age group at £575, whereas women reached their highest earnings for 30 to 39-year-olds at £460. Earnings increased until employees reached these age groups and steadily decreased thereafter.

Median full-time weekly earnings in London were £581, significantly higher than in other regions, where they ranged from £402 in Northern Ireland to £481 in the South East.

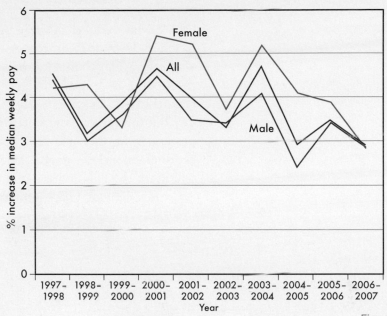

Figure 9

The occupations with the highest earnings in 2007 were 'Health professionals' (median pay of full-time employees of £1,019 a week), followed by 'Corporate managers' (£702) and 'Science and technology professionals' (£670). The lowest paid of all full-time employees were 'Sales occupations', at £264 a week.

The monetary difference between the median level of full-time earnings in the public sector (£498 per week in April 2007) and the private sector (£439 per week) has widened over the year to April 2007, following annual increases of 3.0 per cent and 2.9 per cent respectively.

Annual Survey of Hours and Earnings (ASHE)

EXAMINATION TALK

It would be quite easy to explain the trends to be found in the information above, but what about the differences? Why are there gender and regional differences? Why are male and female profiles moving closer together in 2007? You need to speculate and hypothesise sometimes in order to extract an argument which may well be inferred, but displays advanced thinking and analytical skills in manipulating the information. You need to provide a detailed analysis.

The wage levels for different jobs vary tremendously, though the UK now has a minimum wage policy. The minimum wage from 1 October 2007 is £5.52 per hour for workers aged 22 and over. This contrasts with the amount of money paid to sports professionals and entertainers who are able to supplement their income through the use of their name. Factors which influence wage level are

- skill level
- specialist ability
- uniqueness and availability
- risk and danger
- location.

TASK

Discuss the relative significance of each of these factors.

1.2.7 Transport issues

On 18 May 2006, the Airbus A380, the world's biggest airliner, touched down at Heathrow Airport for the first time. With a wingspan wider than a football pitch it dwarfs the traditional Jumbo, the Boeing 747, and can carry up to 800 passengers, nearly 400 more than the 747. Despite its size it can land on the same runways as the 747 but few airports currently have the capacity to handle so many passengers at once. However, once in service it will be the most economical airliner in the sky, with a range of nearly 10,000 miles. It will mark the culmination of a unique partnership between four EU countries: France, UK, Germany and Spain.

Figure 10

The project has created employment in many industries both directly and indirectly involved in the production process. It has also brought about a fierce, transatlantic competition between Airbus and the world's other major plane-maker, Boeing. However, there are those who see it as a cause of more pollution and increased danger for air travellers.

Better public transport

Governments believe that the best way forward is to have a modern and reliable public transport service. This would involve less travel by car and more use of bus and train services. Ideally, there would be an **integrated transport system** created so that people living in outlying areas would be able to travel by bus to a centrally located **interchange**. This system has been successfully implemented in other European countries such as Holland, Belgium and Spain for many years.

However, the cost to the taxpayer of creating a system such as this in the UK would be enormous. In fact, in some cities, such as Manchester, money from private investment has been used to support the development of the successful Metrolink tram system.

> **KEY TERMS**
>
> An integrated transport system is where trams, buses and trains link together.
>
> An interchange is where it is possible to change from one mode of transport to another.

Big transport problems facing society are *increasing numbers of cars, fuel costs, pollution* and *congestion*. Here are some questions to which the public might need answers.

1 Why don't we build more roads to ease congestion?
2 What needs to be done to make public transport more reliable?
3 How can the rise in the number of cars on the road be stopped?
4 Are measures such as road pricing and congestion charging the answer?

Many policies have been put forward aiming to improve public transport and to persuade drivers to leave their cars at home. Figure 11 looks at some of the issues involved. The key points are in bold, the supporting points follow the arrows.

politicians	• **increases in taxation**	⇨ will enable investment in the infrastructure such as the introduction of new light railways.
	• **financial support for new projects**	⇨ from private investment ⇨ will reduce the burden on the Treasury ⇨ this would include help to research and develop energy-efficient modes of transport.
transport operators	• **run a system that generates high profits**	⇨ but will stimulate further expansion and development of existing services and routes.
	• **lower taxes on fuel by the government**	⇨ and subsidies for expansion plans to routes ⇨ would encourage expansion.
transport users	• **cheaper fares**	⇨ and more reliable timetables ⇨ would generate confidence by users
	• **safer journeys**	⇨ in clean and modern conditions ⇨ would encourage more people to leave their cars at home.

Figure 11

EXAMINATION TALK

In your exam, you can gain marks by developing and supporting your ideas.

Congestion

The Environmental Transport Association defines congestion as a vehicle being unable to pass a set of traffic lights in one go, or vehicles on motorways being unable to travel faster than 50 miles per hour. Congestion causes pollution and makes journeys longer and more miserable. Here is a list of concerns about congestion. Place them in order of rank, giving reasons for your choice.

- Journey times are uncertain
- Pollution and health problems
- Noise
- No concerns
- Big impact on business
- Need for more roads
- Increased global warming
- Causes accidents.

It is clear that improving and developing transport will continue to dominate everyday life for many years, and will be high on the agendas of governments. There will need to be great investments of finance, time and patience if the UK is ever likely to reach the state of being a 'green' country where happy commuters leave their polluting motors at home and jump onto one of the regular, clean and reliable buses or trains that whisk them to work.

This is how the pressure group Transport 2000 sees the situation.

Few people would disagree that transport in the UK is in crisis. Road traffic is growing by the day, leading to congestion, pollution, safety concerns, health problems, climate change and for many a reduction in the quality of life. The total distance travelled by all motor vehicles in Britain is almost 500 billion kilometres, more than 40 round trips from Earth to Pluto. Meanwhile, if all the cars in Britain were lined up head to tail they would go twice round the world. These figures are frightening but things are set to get even worse. The latest figures show that traffic is rising by 2 per cent annually, enough to make a big difference in just a few years.

www.transport2000.com

WHAT NEXT?

1 Here are some terms, ideas and topics to research and discuss in class:
   - the effect of low budget airlines on the travel industry
   - the reactivation of rail lines closed in the 1960s
   - the reintroduction of street trams
   - the inclusion of transport issues in the school curriculum.

2 Consider the case of the Airbus A380 super jumbo (page 38). Form three groups: one supporting its introduction, one against its introduction, and a third group that will act as judge. Each of the opposing groups must consider their case and present at least three points of evidence. The judging group must research the case fully and remain neutral. The judgement must be made on the balance of evidence presented.

3 Investigate the transport systems in your area. How would you develop services to improve and expand what is in place?

4 Analyse the following headlines. In each case, what is the key issue that you think the editor is trying to convey? Work in a group to carry out some research.

1,000 New carriages to ease rail crushes

Daily Mirror, 14 March 2007

European dogfight for budget airlines

Times, 9 May 2004

Trams fail to cut jams

Manchester Evening News, 23 April 2004

1 The social and cultural domains

Examiners recognise that private and public enterprise are very big topics in their own right and that the General Studies specification cannot cover them in great depth. One way in which your knowledge and understanding may be discovered is through a passage to trigger and stimulate the release of information: as in questions 1 and 3 below. These are typical of the questions used in Section A of the examination.

It is also common for examiners to offer you a piece of source material to stimulate your interest and then ask you a related question, rather than making a direct reference to the source. So for question 4, the source material might be anything to do with ageism and employment. The essay question here does not refer to the source at all: it would just be to get you thinking. Can you think of a good source to put with a question like this?

Look at questions 5 and 6. Marks can be gained by the inclusion of *different kinds of knowledge* (Assessment Objective 3). This works well for questions when you are asked to discuss issues and dilemmas. There are many *dilemmas* surrounding the development and provision of transport, such as

- the increase in the size and efficiency of aircraft means more people can travel further *but* at the cost of increased pollution and the exhaustion of fuel sources
- the running of trains at high speed between cities enables quicker journey times *but* the rail network remains outdated, decaying and in need of massive investment
- the improvement of bus services may encourage people to use public transport *but* at the cost of increased congestion and concerns for road safety.

Much is already being done to break the **cycle of educational disadvantage**. Efforts to raise standards in all schools and to allow good schools to expand will pay dividends. So will the measures in the new Education and Inspections Act. And in particular city academies, by focusing new effort, leadership and resources in the poorest areas, are **spreading educational opportunity**.

But today there are less than 50 city academies. In the next few years that will grow to 200. Even then some will be **over-subscribed**. Many disadvantaged parents will find themselves stuck in the **old educational ghetto** by having to send their children to less successful schools. It is for this reason I believe we now need to go further to complement the reforms already being put in place.

At present, any parent can state which school they would prefer their child to attend. To break the cycle of educational disadvantage we need to give parents in the most disadvantaged areas more than preference. They should have choice. Many better-off parents already exercise such choice through **indirect market mechanisms** – most notably the buying of homes near good schools. Poor parents need a more direct mechanism. Countries as diverse as Denmark, Sweden and the USA have all in recent years pioneered different forms of parental choice. The evidence suggests both that choice programmes helped raise standards across all schools and that the most disadvantaged pupils benefited most.

Credit where credit's due: Alan Milburn, *The Guardian*, 23 November 2006

1a Briefly explain the highlighted phrases, as used in the passage. [15 marks]
 b Outline two ways in which schools can raise standards. [4 marks]
 c Suggest two ways in which parents could exercise more choice. [4 marks]
 d Milburn mentions 'the cycle of educational advantage.' How should the government best tackle this important problem? [7 marks]

[Total 30 marks]

2 Outline and discuss a range of advantages and disadvantages of higher education tuition fees. To what extent should students have some say in the quality of service offered to them? [30 marks]

TESCO rang up a record £2.55 billion in pre-tax profits last year, a rise of 13.2 per cent.

- The store accounts for £1 in every £3 spent on food and £1 in every £8 that is spent on the high street on all goods.
- The company makes £5,000 a minute. It has more than 2,000 stores in Britain with plans to open even more. It is also big overseas with stores in Hungary, Thailand, Czech Republic, Turkey, Slovakia, Malaysia and South Korea.
- It intends to break into the United States this year too and is looking at going into India.
- It employs 400,000 staff globally.
- In the UK it controls 31.2 per cent of the grocery market, nearly double that of its closest rival, Asda.

Coventry Telegraph, 6 November 2007

3 By considering the facts given (Assessment Objective 1), outline the *key positive and negative characteristics* of a massive private enterprise such as Tesco in terms of

- the country: cities, towns and country areas
- competition between retailers
- choice and variety
- small businesses. [30 marks]

4 What do you understand by the term ageism? Discuss a range of reasons why older people may wish to continue working over the government retirement age. [30 marks]

Figure 12

5 Outline and discuss how the introduction of super jumbos like the A380 will change the way we travel in the future. [30 marks]

6 Outline and discuss the issues facing government in providing public transport to rural areas in the UK. [30 marks]

1.3 Explanation and evaluation of human behaviour

OVERVIEW

In this block of work we will look at

- influences on human behaviour: how far social conditioning affects individuals and communities

- how people can effect change in social, political and economic life within the local, national and global communities
- tension and harmony within communities.

QUESTIONS

1 What influences our behaviour?
2 What things have been most influential in your life?
3 How do people make change happen?
4 How do organisations help change human behaviour?
5 What things cause tensions between people?
6 Why is there so much more tension than harmony?
7 How can people live in harmony – what works?

1.3.1 Influences on human behaviour

People are influenced by many different things in the course of their lives. It might be the environment, their background, their social class.

Figure 1

Figure 2

Compare the living conditions in these two photographs. They might suggest something about the background of the area where they were taken or the people who live there. People's life experience, particularly as children, may have a profound and formative effect on their futures.

TASK

1 Write a list of words or phrases which you may connect with these two places; use words that are directly evident from the photographs and others that are implicit.
2 How far can we rely upon our own interpretation of what we see?
3 What are the flaws in our evidence?

EXAMINATION TALK

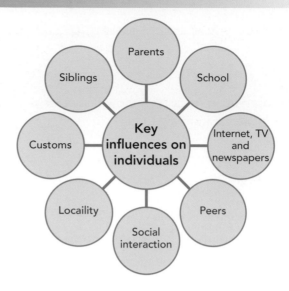

Figure 3

Figure 3 forms the basis of a searching question which would test thinking and analytical skills.

> Consider the information contained in the figure about key influences on individuals. Choose *three* sources which you consider to be the most influential and for each offer reasons for your choice. [10 marks]

AO1	(Knowledge)	3 marks
AO2	(Analysis)	3 marks
AO3	(Different kinds of knowledge)	3 marks
AO4	(Communication)	1 mark

Candidate response

I consider parents to be the most influential on individuals. It is they who bring the child into the world and are responsible for the most important stages in a child's life, at a time when they are very impressionable. On the other hand, some children are neglected and left to fend for themselves at an early age causing them to miss out on basic life skills. Secondly, locality is has a powerful and lasting influence on people. It is difficult to shrug off a local affinity or accent and there is always a sense of pride and belonging when people talk about their home area. Some areas are left forgotten as their reputation is so bad, some members of the community cannot wait to settle elsewhere. Finally, I think that the media have a very strong influence on forming people's opinion. After all, it is the only source of news that we have and an important resource for learning and education. But are the media too powerful? It is possible that media influences on individuals could result in unrest and disquiet rather than peace.

Examiner's comment

Three excellent choices each with a useful supporting statement whilst at the same time indicating a note of caution or contradictory remark. Written with accuracy and fluidity. 3+3+3+1   MARK 10/10

1.3.2 How people can effect change

With so many differing and contrasting groups in our communities, there is plenty of scope for individuals to become involved in projects and organisations that can make a difference to people's lives. Many groups, some of which are regarded as pressure groups, rely on committed enthusiasts and non-professionals to make up their membership. It could be said that people trying to effect change are a form of pressure group, mentioned earlier, but in this context the groups are there to make a difference to the environment or locale by raising awareness and seeking the support of like-minded volunteers, rather than taking direct action.

TASK

Consider the activities of the following four organisations.

- Victim Support
- The Salvation Army
- RSPB (Royal Society for the Protection of Birds)
- Rotary International

1 In what ways do they make a difference to our communities and the world around us?
2 What are their aims and objectives?
3 Who makes up their number?
4 How are they funded?
5 Make a list of other organisations and groups that aim to make a difference. Assess how successful you think they are.

1.3.3 Tension and harmony

The racial, religious and social tensions brought about by challenges to local and national norms and behaviours have become a symptom of modern-day life in some localities. Friction between groups of different racial backgrounds and religious beliefs frequently fills our newspapers and television screens, and questions are asked about why age-old conflicts between groups still exist in a free world.

There are many examples of tensions in our world. People often come into conflict for a mixture of reasons: economic, cultural and social. Poverty and **deprivation** make groups of people look at what others have and ask: 'why them?' and 'why not me?'. Sometimes the reason appears to be 'because they are different': different ethnic groups, different religions, different social class etc.

In the UK there are, unfortunately, many examples of tensions within communities from which to choose. For example, the conflict between Protestants and Catholics in Northern Ireland began many centuries ago and was linked to the control of political power. Sometimes global events may cause such tensions to escalate. An obvious example is the way many Muslim people have been made to feel within British society following the actions of a terrorist group that justified its political actions against the USA on 9/11 with references to Islam.

KEY TERMS

Deprivation is the condition of having little money and few material possessions, and a lack of basic needs such as shelter and water.

Immigration into the UK is always a hot social topic, with people already living here worried about who will live next door to them, who might take their job from them, or who might be getting more than them in benefits from the state.

Increasing levels of unemployment can often cause tensions to escalate within communities, because the economic importance of how people live, or are perceived to live, takes on a greater significance. For example, which people get to keep their jobs and why? Which people are given better council housing than others, perhaps because they come from an ethnic background where large families live together? Which people join strikes and which break them – and so on. Unemployment highlights the fact that much tension in society has its roots in fear, ignorance and jealousy.

TASK

In the 1990s two successful films were made in the UK which both featured unemployment: *Brassed Off* and *The Full Monty*. *Brassed Off* was based around unemployment and the coal industry, *The Full Monty* around unemployment and the steel industry.

Figure 4: *Brassed Off* (1996)

Figure 5: *The Full Monty* (1997)

Watch some excerpts from the films and discover some of the main tensions and issues which affected people during the decline and collapse of these two major British industries.

The opposite of social tension is social harmony. Some might say there is much more tension around than harmony, so where people live in harmony this is often treated as a shining example for others to emulate and celebrate. Harmony tends to develop in situations where information is freely available to all sides, where there are no special rules for one group that do not extend to others, where sharing is equal and tolerance is respected.

1 The social and cultural domains

CASE STUDY

The Birmingham Community Network brought together so many different community groups in the city. The b:cen network ended in November 2007 but the networks it organised then continued as grassroots organisations.

Here is a sample of its achievements

- organising 11 district networks with a membership of more than 8,000 groups and active citizens
- communications including websites, pocket books, online communities, briefings, bus tours, Networker newsletters, grassroots stories, video, audio CD, teleconferences and podcasts as well as the programme's magazine – b:cennected
- organising and funding more than 30 Real Time Community Change projects involving several hundred grassroots groups in the city
- providing small grants to several hundred community groups and small voluntary organisations in the city
- supporting the city's Coalition of Disabled People and the development of city-wide networks for refugees, women's groups, ethnic minority groups, and older people in partnership with other voluntary organisations in the city.

TASK

Study the Birmingham Community Network case study (left). How has this scheme tried to work out solutions to community problems? Could this sort of approach work in your community? Find out what sort of community organisations already exist in your area.

Though most tension erupts into confrontation, harmony is achieved by seeking alternatives to this, such as **b:cen**. In shared events like London's Notting Hill Carnival there is clear evidence of cultural harmony and genuine understanding. This is achieved through the joint effort of communities and their leaders to form groups, forums and committees where mutual understanding and respect can be gained. Most areas of the UK have established police liaison committees where, through regular meetings, members of communities can air grievances and work out solutions to problems.

TASK

Here is a tension and harmony table. See if you can add further examples in each column. Examine **the extent** to which there is complete tension and harmony. This could be done by researching the topic on the internet. Look back at pages 45–47 for more help.

More tension than harmony	Harmony developing out of tension
Iraq and the Middle East	Post-apartheid South Africa
Gun crime in the inner cities	Northern Ireland peace process

Figure 6

WHAT NEXT?

Use these headlines as a basis for further research on national and global issues of tension.

A bitter cocktail of racial tension and gang culture

Daily Telegraph, 24 October 2005

Religious tension rises in holy city after bomb blasts

The Independent, 9 March 2006

EXAMINATION TALK

In some questions, there is a trigger within the wording which, if pulled, will unlock marks and dramatically improve performance. Here is an example of an essay question.

> In what ways can ordinary people, through their work and commitment, make a difference to communities *locally*, *nationally*, and *globally*?

The essay is asking for three perspectives. By providing these, it will be easy for an examiner to award marks from Assessment Objective 3 (different kinds of knowledge).

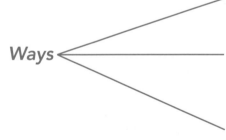

Ways

locally – keeping public spaces clear of litter – a group of people in my town meet each Sunday afternoon and try to improve the appearance of green spaces.

nationally – people regularly give to many charities to support their work – each year my school organises many events to support Children in Need which is specifically intent on making life better for children in the UK.

globally – the Scout Association was set up to support young people in their physical, mental and spiritual development, so that they may play constructive roles in society. I have been a scout and travelled to France to share in activities with scouts from all over the world. It has become an important and influential global organisation for young people.

Figure 7

EXAMINATION PRACTICE

1 In what ways can ordinary people, through their work and commitment, make a difference to communities *locally*, *nationally*, and *globally*? [30 marks]
2 Choose two areas of the world where you consider there is tension. Outline and discuss the chief sources of this tension and suggest ways of improving the situation in the future. [30 marks]
3 Identify and discuss examples where two previously opposing factions can now live in harmony. [30 marks]
4 Sports like football display extremes of tension and harmony between fans. Discuss two contrasting examples which confirm this suggestion. [30 marks]

1 The social and cultural domains

1.4 Beliefs, values and moral reasoning

OVERVIEW

In this block of work we will look at

- knowledge, belief and unbelief: including instinct, indoctrination, personal experience, reason, faith and revelation

- the individual's moral response to matters of conscience such as: abortion, euthanasia, drugs and animal rights.

QUESTIONS

1 What is the truth?
2 Is something true because you believe it?
3 Why is religious belief in decline in some countries?
4 Why is religious fundamentalism increasing in some countries?
5 Would you know if you were being indoctrinated? Are you?
6 Can revelation be proof of a religion?
7 What is your conscience and why does it tell you things?

1.4.1 Knowledge, belief and unbelief

What can we believe that we know to be true?

To believe something means you think it is true, but what does is mean to say you know something? Can you know something that isn't true, or are you only then comparing what you believe to be true with something you believe not to be? It is possible that what was thought to be true would later appear to be false. As we discover new truths about the world around us, previously held beliefs are found to be false. There are truths that cannot be believed. We may not know enough to believe them to be true, or we may be sceptical of the reliability of proof. **Belief** involves what we either cannot know (e.g. whether God exists) or do not know, but personally believe.

KEY TERMS

Belief The psychological state in which an individual holds a proposition or premise to be true.

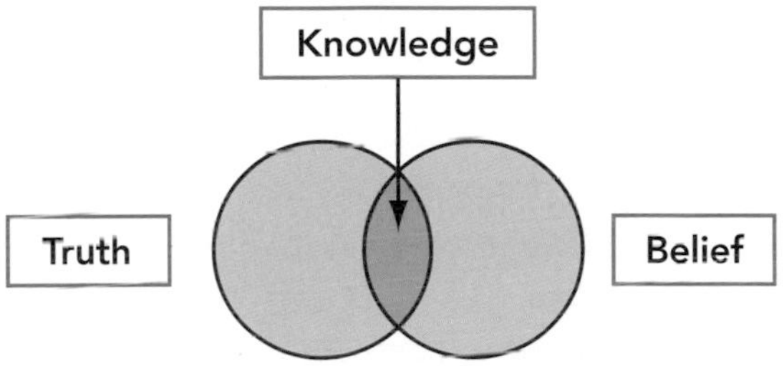

Figure 1

Why is religious worship declining in some countries? There could be a number of reasons for this, not least people's reluctance to believe in a god that they can neither see nor hear, allowing acts of terrorism or the force of a tsunami. Younger generations have inherited a lot of their beliefs from strong family traditions, but there is an increasing number of non-believers and the number of people worshipping regularly is at an all-time low.

TASK

Consider Figure 1: do you agree with this explanation of knowledge as being where truth and belief overlap? Would everyone agree that there is a 'truth' out there to be discovered?

Fundamentalism

This extreme form of belief is becoming more prevalent in today's society. It has been defined as a passionate, unquestioning and unwavering commitment to religious teachings, coupled with intolerance of other views including a total opposition to **secularism**.

> [Fundamentalism] is like viewing the world as being black and white, with little, if any, grey between that which is good and that which is evil. Accompanying this is a tendency toward literalism. If scripture says that Noah built an ark, put two of each type of animal throughout the world on it, and sailed on that boat while the entire earth was flooded, then it happened. No questions need be asked; it happened, regardless of whether it is logically consistent with what we know about animals, floods, ancient ships or the geological record.
>
> www.slowleadership.com

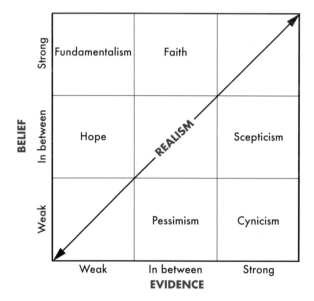

Figure 2

Some might say that to maintain a realistic viewpoint, the relationship between evidence and belief should always be a balanced one. Too much doubt leads to cynicism and the unwillingness to believe anything, even when the evidence for it is strong. Too much dogmatic belief, despite weak or non-existent evidence, leads to fundamentalism: the unwavering attachment to a single point of view regardless of all evidence to the contrary. What do you think of this view?

1.4.2 Instinct, indoctrination, personal experience, reason, faith and revelation

Instinct

This piece, written about Spielberg's Oscar-winning film *Saving Private Ryan*, exemplifies one of the central facets of instinct: acting or responding without thinking. Whether this turns out to be the right or wrong thing to do is open to debate and further examination because some people's instincts are more reliable than others'. Can instinct be measured or scrutinised? Is there such as thing as good or bad instinct? This is an area where people may debate and examine at length and never reach a consensus because the issue is so reliant upon personal experience.

> Kids in combat are simply fighting to survive, fighting to save the guys next to them… When they became heroes it wasn't because they wanted to be like John Wayne, it was because they were not thinking at all. They were acting instinctively, from the gut. These dogfaces who freed the world were a bunch of decent guys. It's their story that now should be told.

Steven Spielberg in an essay published in *Newsweek*, 1998

Indoctrination

Often the word indoctrination implies a negative context as the process involves unquestioning adherence to a set of learned rules and principles. In an historical context there are several cases where indoctrination has proved dangerous. From the early part of the 20th century, the Nazi party strengthened its hold on Germany to the extent that people's lives became endangered if they did not toe the party line. Another extreme example of indoctrination can be seen in Japan, as young *kamikaze* pilots flew to their deaths for glory and victory.

Figure 3

In the state education system today, children in England and Wales are protected by the provisions of the 1996 Education Act, part 406.

Political indoctrination

(1) The local education authority, governing body and head teacher shall forbid—
  (a) the pursuit of partisan political activities by any of those registered pupils at a maintained school who are junior pupils, and
  (b) the promotion of partisan political views in the teaching of any subject in the school

HMSO

TASK

Why do you think the state education system protects children from indoctrination?

The principles of science, the rules governing some professions, and the strictness of behaviour and appearance required in some areas of life might be described by some as indoctrination – but is that reasonable in these contexts?

KEY TERMS

Values describe the beliefs of an *individual* or *culture* – ethical, moral or social.

EXAMINATION TALK

Personal experience

Beliefs and **values** are soundly tested and amended by life experience and changing daily circumstances. Who and what may dictate these changes?

Examiners like to offer choice in questions. The chances are there will be at least one alternative which you can tackle with some confidence.

> Choose one of the following and discuss the extent to which they are influential in the ways we believe and how we act.
> - Family
> - Friends and colleagues
> - Teachers
> - Neighbours
> - Employers
> - Celebrities
>
> [25 marks]

If you consider family, you might include

- strong religious belief and background
- successful education and career to emulate
- family members can be positive or negative role models
- strict family upbringing may make or break a person.

TASK

Develop each of these points with analysis (AO2) and some deeper and varied questioning or a case study (AO3), thereby building up the main supporting section of the essay.

Reason

Reason is objective and is connected to truth. It links consciousness, language and logic together and forms the basis of our way of thinking. Considering any set of ideas or premises together should always lead to a conclusion = TRUTH. In this way reason cannot account for religious beliefs as, for some people, there is insufficient evidence to believe that a god (or gods) exists and acts in the world.

Faith

However, faith is something quite different. It involves confidence, feeling part of something special and unquestionably secure. Sometimes the word conviction is used in the context of faith as it does not require knowledge or reason. Faith can be so strong that it enables people to face up to and get through some of life's greatest traumas.

TASK

Science is based on logic, reason and proof. Yet many scientists believe in God. How might a scientist explain their faith?

> There are those who scoff at the school boy, calling him frivolous and shallow. Yet it was the school boy who said, Faith is believing what you know ain't so.
>
> Mark Twain, *Following the Equator*

Revelation

Faith often comes from or is reinforced by a religious experience or revelation. There are many examples of dramatic revelations in the sacred texts of the world's religions: the Angel Jibril revealing Allah's message to his Prophet; apparitions of the Virgin Mary; Teresa of Avila's passionate experiences of God; St Paul's conversion on the road to Damascus.

But for most religious believers the experience of revelation comes through less dramatic events – although the effect can appear just as powerful – through worship and reading the sacred texts of their religion. Most religions believe that their sacred texts are inspired by God (or in the case of Buddhism contain universal truths) and so revelation comes as this sacred truth is revealed to them. The experience of sharing worship with others has also been the source of revelation for many millions of people.

Different people would take different views on whether these experiences are God speaking directly to them or whether it is something in what they are doing that touches a part of them that is uninspired in other parts of their lives. There are also other non-religious explanations for religious experience, which are about physical and psychological conditions and states of mind.

1.4.3 Matters of conscience

Discovering conscience involves the revelation of a person's sense of right and wrong. Our sense of conscience allows us to tolerate or not to tolerate attitudes and behaviour which we witness in everyday society, first-hand or through the media. Conscience is an important **moral principle** that each person deals with in their own way.

TASK

Can the fact that so many people have had religious experiences be used to prove that God – or some other spiritual presence in the universe – exists? We take many things in life on trust without being able to prove it scientifically, for example that love exists. Should God be any different?

KEY TERMS

Moral principle A code of conduct which is respected and regarded in matters of right and wrong, In all areas of life.

TASK

Consider the following situations and put forward your response as your conscience would dictate. Also consider how far you could rely on your conscience as a guide to what you would do.

1 You find a £20 note on the floor in the school corridor. What do you do?
2 Your best friend tells you she is considering having an abortion. What is your advice?
3 You hear that your elderly neighbour is ill and cannot get to the shops. What is your reaction?
4 A young person is being bullied by members of his class.
5 Persistent vandalism is taking place in the local churchyard.
6 You are called to serve in the armed forces at a time of war.

There is also a strong link between conscience and tolerance.

Some issues may challenge us to examine our conscience and the limits of our tolerance, such as those on page 54.

Abortion

Why abortion is always wrong	Why abortion is not always wrong
Human life begins at conception so a foetus is a human and it is wrong to kill a human	Human life does not begin at conception – the foetus is just a collection of cells
A foetus is a person with rights: it has all the capacity to grow into someone just like you or me	A potential life does not have rights, only an actual life has rights
A foetus can feel pain at 18 weeks: it is wrong to cause pain through abortion after 18 weeks	The ability to feel pain is shared throughout life on earth: this does not stop humans killing other non-human organisms
Abortion is legalised killing – the law should not allow this	When a choice has to be made between a foetus' life and its mother's life, abortion to save the mother is justified
Abortion is seen as a quick solution to an awkward problem instead of life and death – this is bad for society	Women have rights and should be allowed the right to choose what happens to their bodies and their lives

Euthanasia

Why euthanasia is always wrong	Why euthanasia is not always wrong
Human life is sacred and should not be ended for any reason	Dying is part of life and the right to choose in life is what makes it special
Euthanasia suggests some lives (the sick, the disabled) are less valuable than others	Insisting that those sick and disabled people who want the right to choose euthanasia cannot have it devalues them more
Voluntary euthanasia could lead to involuntary euthanasia – getting rid of people society think are undesirable	Euthanasia is happening anyway – it is better to regulate it than let it carry on unregulated. Then proper safeguards could be built into the law
Euthanasia gives too much power to doctors	Doctors have tremendous power over patients anyway – e.g. the power to do nothing, – but few use it badly
Vulnerable people could feel under pressure to end their lives, e.g. to free up medical resources or to save their family the trouble of caring for them	Controls would ensure that no one would die without very careful assessment of their condition and situation
Pain relief techniques now mean that no one should suffer so much that they want to die	Pain relief techniques should always be used – but what if a patient still wants to die?

Drugs

Pop singer George Michael has admitted his marijuana use can be 'a problem' and said he is 'constantly trying' to smoke less of the drug. But he added he did not think his habit was 'getting in the way of my life in any way'. 'I'm a happy man and I can afford my marijuana so that's not a problem,' he told BBC Radio 4's *Desert Island Discs*. Michael has previously said the world would be an 'easier place to live with' if cannabis was legal.

news.bbc.co.uk

Animal rights

It is very easy to confuse the many animal rights and anti-hunting/anti-vivisection campaigns with the issues of conservation and endangered species.

While this confusion is understandable, it is important to be able to separate the main issues involved namely ANIMAL RIGHTS (which covers all forms of cruelty to animals) and CONSERVATION which deals more specifically with endangered species and the protection of wildlife habitats and natural resources. The following areas all contribute to the animal rights problem: hunting, shooting, poaching, culling, the circus, vivisection, cruelty.

www.ypte.org.uk

TASK

Explain what your moral response is to matters of conscience on abortion, euthanasia, drugs and animal rights.

TASK

Using the resources above on matters of conscience, construct a series of questions in the form of either essays or structured answers to use for practice revision.

WHAT NEXT?

Try to answer the following questions through discussion and research on the internet.

1 Why do so many people go to church in the United States?
2 There is a growth in the numbers of Muslims and Sikhs. Why?
3 What is the attraction of new-style religions or 'people's churches'?

EXAMINATION TALK

- Examiners select from a list of command words in order to trigger a response from you such as:

  Examine..........Outline........Explain........Discuss..........
  To what extent........

- Sometimes these words are prefaced by the word 'briefly' which indicates that the response should not be an extensive one.

EXAMINATION PRACTICE

The interpretation of data or numerical information is an essential skill in General Studies. One of the issues which may be covered in this part of the specification may be church attendance.

1 Consider this table and then offer three reasons for the decline in church attendance over recent years.

Year	Average weekly attendance	Average Sunday attendance
2000	1,274,000	1,058,000
2001	1,205,000	1,041,000
2002	1,166,000	1,002,000
2003	1,187,000	1,017,000
2004	1,186,000	1,010,000
2005	1,169,000	988,000

www.churchsociety.org

2 How can reason exert power and influence but also present dangers to us? [25 marks]

3 What does faith mean in the following contexts?

Religion   Relationships   Professional persons' abilities

[10 marks]

Write down *three or four points* for each question, *developed* with some *analysis* and *supported* with *examples*. Aim to provide *nine or ten pieces of information* in four or five sentences.

1.5 Media and communications 1

OVERVIEW

In this block of work we will look at

- current developments within the media and communications
- the strengths and weaknesses of the media and their ability to communicate.

You should consider a range of media including magazines, periodicals, film, video, TV and the internet when working on these topics.

QUESTIONS

1 What is the media?
2 Whom do you trust from the media? What makes you trust them?
3 How different was life before the internet?
4 Is too much information dangerous?
5 Is it fair that not everyone has internet access?
6 How influential is the media on the way your country is run?
7 Should people be protected from the media?

KEY TERMS

Media are ways in which information is communicated to many people.

1.5.1 Current developments

What do we mean by **media**?

- **Recording media** are devices used to store information.
- **Print media** are communications delivered via paper or canvas.
- **Electronic media** are communications delivered via electronic or electromechanical energy such as **multimedia** (communications that incorporate multiple forms of information content and processing).
- **Published media** are any media made available to the public.
- **Broadcast media** are communications delivered over mass electronic communication networks.
- **News media** are mass media focused on communicating news.
- **Media for advertising** (also media-buying) involves choosing and buying TV airtime, radio airtime, newspaper space, etc. for advertising.

TASK

Choose one type of media from the list above. Explain how they have developed so far and suggest where they might go in the future. How effective are your chosen media in transmitting information?

What is digital broadcasting?

Digital Television (DTV) is an advanced broadcasting technology that will transform your television viewing experience. DTV enables broadcasters to offer television with better picture and sound quality. It can also offer multiple programming choices, called multicasting, and interactive capabilities.

Converting to DTV also will free up parts of the scarce and valuable broadcast spectrum. Those portions of the spectrum can then be used for other important services, such as public and safety services (police and fire departments, emergency rescue), and advanced wireless services.

The changeover from analogue to digital broadcasting began in October 2007. This represents a major programme of investment by both the broadcasting industry and the consumer.

www.dtv.gov

You may be asked to speculate about the outcome of an initiative or change – in this case digital broadcasting. In General Studies, you are not expected to have expert knowledge but it is possible to suggest possible outcomes and effects using logical reasoning.

> Outline two advantages and two disadvantages of changing from analogue to digital broadcasting. [25 marks]

PLAN

Definition of terms	Analogue/digital (in terms of audio and visual broadcasting)
Key point 1 – advantage	Increasing choice, variety and range
Key point 2 – advantage	Improvement in quality of sound and vision
Key point 3 – disadvantage	Cost of the changeover to companies and consumers
Key point 4 – disadvantage	Improvement in broadcast quality does not mean that the actual programmes will be better
Balancing statement	Discussion outlining which side has the most solid support
Conclusion	Expression of a personal preference or some speculation about how digital television may develop and/or expand.

The power of the broadcaster

Much of today's media success is reliant not simply on content but also on presentation. The public learns to trust and revere some broadcasters and writers who then possess the power to influence large numbers of people. In some cases, this trust and confidence is misplaced.

Sir Terry Wogan commands the biggest morning radio audience in Western Europe and is very highly regarded and trusted through his long, unblemished career and his association with *Children in Need*.

Michael Fish, former senior weatherman, was trusted implicitly for his weather advice. However, despite all the trust he had built up, his career will always be associated with a remark he made just before the worst storm in living memory hit the UK in October 1987: 'Earlier on today, apparently, a woman rang the BBC and said she heard there was a hurricane on the way; well, if you're watching, don't worry, there isn't.' This was actually in reference to a hurricane in the Caribbean but it has always been associated with the storm in Britain.

Figure 1: Terry Wogan

Figure 2: Michael Fish

1 The social and cultural domains

The internet

The internet is an integral part of our everyday life. It continues to expand its range and influence to every part of the world. It remains an important and incisive communication tool, but in recent times people have had much more personal input and influence over what is posted on the internet with the introduction of blogs and the development of podcasting.

What is a blog?

A blog (web log) provides **commentary or news** on a particular **subject**; others function as more **personal online diaries**. A typical blog combines text, images, and links to other blogs, web pages, and other media related to its topic. **The ability for readers to leave comments** in an interactive format is an important part of many blogs. Most blogs are primarily textual, although some focus on art (artlog), photographs (photoblog), sketchblog, videos (vlog), music (MP3 blog), audio (podcasting) and are part of a wider network of social media.

www.wikipedia.com

What is podcasting?

Podcasting is delivering audio content to **iPods** and other portable media players on demand, so that it **can be listened to at the user's convenience**. The main benefit of podcasting is that listeners **can synchronise content to their media player and take it with them to listen whenever they want to**. Because podcasts are typically saved in MP3 format, they can also be listened to on nearly any computer.

www.podcastingnews.com

Podcasting has opened up the world of broadcasting to everyone because making a podcast involves only a small amount of equipment and minimal technical skills. It enables people to post their personal 'take' or outlook on life on the internet, available to be downloaded by anyone. In addition, the major radio broadcasters are posting podcasts of their major shows on their websites so that those who miss a broadcast can download it to their own personal player to play back at their convenience.

EXAMINATION PRACTICE

Briefly explain the following.

a) Blog. [3 marks]

b) Podcast. [3 marks]

In the boxes above, the key points have been highlighted in bold. You should try to provide three pieces of information and will be awarded one mark for each piece of information communicated in a coherent way.

The internet continues to pose a danger in the way that information can be spread throughout its community with little or no censorship or control. It allows dangerous, sometimes illegal groups to advertise and promote their activities. Censorship control over the whole web is almost impossible, though it is possible to exercise some control at a local level by using parental guidance controls activated by a responsible adult or using filtering mechanisms downloaded from service providers.

However, not everyone has access to the internet. In fact, some parents are unhappy about their children using the internet at home because of the access it gives to every possible kind of information and material.

TASK

Do you think the internet should be used for homework, or is such a huge amount of information too confusing to be useful?

How could teachers make using the internet for research easier and more productive?

1.5.2 Strengths and weaknesses of the media

The media's influence can be displayed in many ways.

Christmas Swizzler!
The rising price of Christmas grub will send us all crackers!

UK tabloid headline

EXAMINATION PRACTICE

What do you understand by the headline and subtext above? [5 marks]

Candidate response

The headline is taken from a tabloid newspaper, renowned for playing on words [1 mark]. *Reference here is to 'swizz' or paying more than something's worth* [1 mark] *but also linking to turkey twizzlers which is a form of fast food* [1 mark]. *The author uses slang to hit the right register with readers (grub)* [1 mark] *and driving someone crackers hints at the annoyance and frustration about the issue but also links with the Christmas theme (Christmas crackers)* [1 mark].

Photography can produce some memorable and priceless moments which capture the mood of the artist without any words. This is the strength of the media which can exert immense power and influence over people. For example, consider this photograph. What is the photographer trying to communicate?

Figure 3

TASK

How can a newspaper influence how people vote in an election? Think of as many ways as you can.

KEY TERMS

Discrimination is focusing on qualities and differences among people such as skin colour or religion and treating people differently because of these.

The instant availability of media coverage of a world event is synonymous with 21st-century daily life. However, the media's power can also be a weakness in that the need to be the 'first on the scene' or win the 'exclusive report' sometimes crosses the bounds of privacy and is shamelessly intrusive. Owners and editors of newspapers and television channels have the power to exert their own pressure and put their own particular bias and spin on a story or sequence of events, particularly when politics is the issue.

Censorship and regulation

Here are some of the organisations whose job it is to censor and regulate the media.

The **Press Complaints Commission** deals with complaints from the public about editorial content of newspapers and magazines. Complaints are investigated under the editors' **Code of Practice**, which binds all national and regional newspapers and magazines, and was drawn up by editors themselves. The code covers the way news is gathered and reported, and provides special protection to particularly vulnerable people such as children, hospital patients and those at risk of **discrimination**.

The **Advertising Standards Authority** (ASA) ensures all advertising, wherever it appears, meets the high standards laid down in the advertising codes. Its website details the rules for advertising, lets you complain online, and explains how the ASA works to keep UK advertising standards as high as possible.

The **Teenage Magazine Arbitration Panel** is the magazine industry's self-regulatory body which ensures that the sexual content of teenage magazines is presented in a responsible and appropriate manner.

Perhaps the most serious problem to deal with is the intrusion of journalists and photographers (sometimes known as the paparazzi).

Figure 4

There is little that can be done to protect the privacy of an individual; many would say that the intrusion has been brought about by the person(s) whose actions have resulted in press and public interest. If more powerful laws are needed to protect individuals, what form should these take? To what extent should the media be morally responsible for their actions?

1 The social and cultural domains

WHAT NEXT?

1 Produce a questionnaire. Construct questions about censorship and intrusion that would apply to a variety of age groups. Obtain a representative sample, say 100 in total. Present your findings as a chart or graph. What are the main conclusions?

2 Obtain copies of a variety of newspapers, both broadsheet and tabloid (and daily and weekend). Compare their style of reporting. Do this by making a direct comparison between the way the same news story is reported in different newspapers.

3 Compare the websites of the main UK national newspapers (such as *The Guardian*, *The Daily Telegraph*, *The Sun*) with those of regional newspapers (*The Birmingham Post*, *The Liverpool Echo*, *The Evening Standard*, *The Manchester Evening News*). What are the main differences in their style and appeal?
Use **www.thebigproject.co.uk/news** for your research.

EXAMINATION PRACTICE

What is the internet used for?

For users aged 16 and over the most common location to access the internet was at home. In 2006, 85 per cent of internet users aged 16 and over who had accessed the internet in the three months before interview had gone online at home. The proportion of households in Great Britain with an internet connection increased from 50 per cent in 2003/04 to 57 per cent in 2006: a total of 13.9 million households. During this period the use of broadband in households increased dramatically from 11 per cent to 40 per cent.

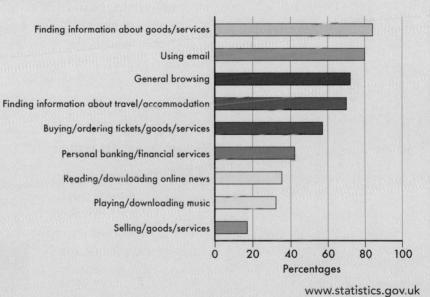

www.statistics.gov.uk

Figure 5: What people use the internet for

For those who did not have household access to the internet, the most common places to go online were at work (46 per cent) and at another person's home (also 46 per cent).

Consider the information entitled 'What is the internet used for?' Outline some of the main reasons for the trends displayed in the bar chart.

1.6 Creativity and innovation

OVERVIEW

In this block of work we will look at

- the creative process
- the development of styles, forms and techniques adopted by artists
- the role of the arts and their benefits to people.

QUESTIONS

1 What is art?
2 What influences artists?
3 Should politics use art for its own aims?
4 Is art a waste of money?
5 Can art help anyone?

1.6.1 The creative process

What is art?

Art is

- a way to be creative and express ourselves
- something that makes us more thoughtful
- both functional and pleasing to the ear or eye
- in a constant state of change
- subjective and means something different to each person.

TASK

What is meant here by elements, principles and physical materials? Try to distinguish between the three parts.

Art is

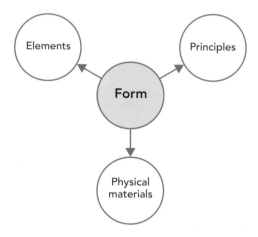

Figure 1

TASK

Apply these points to any work of art with which you are familiar and see how far you think they work as a definition.

Art is

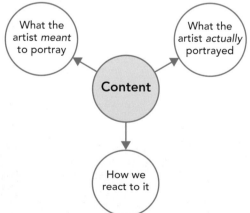

Figure 2

1.6.2 The development of artists' styles

Artists' styles might change for a number of reasons which bear no relation to their craft. These might include the discovery or invention of new materials (for example, the Industrial Revolution changed the way buildings could be built; the invention of the clarinet in the 18th century allowed whole new styles of music) and all manner of minor changes and events that take place. One thing is clear. One style did not end and a new one begin. Art is constantly changing and evolving, sometimes quickly, other times slowly. The development and establishment of a style can take many years or, indeed, the old and the new can live happily side by side as in the case of the old and new Coventry Cathedral (Figure 3). The shell of the old cathedral, bombed in the Second World War, is now symbolically rejoined to the new cathedral, which opened in 1962.

The past century has seen the cinema industry scale new heights and the resurgence of interest in live theatre, most notably the stage **musical**.

Figure 3

KEY TERMS

A musical is a stage play which includes songs sung by the principal characters and the supporting cast.

TASK

1 Make a list of stage plays and musicals currently performing to audiences. Find out the key elements of the most successful ones: what is their appeal and why they are playing for so long? Is it the songs, the choreography, the story, the performers, the staging?

2 Make a list of ten films which have enjoyed major success in the past ten years. Find out what has contributed to their success. Is it storyline, actors, special effects, 'cult status'? What do you count as success: millions at the box office, critical acclaim, cult following?

Art has always been influenced or manipulated by politics and projected some powerful images to the rest of the world. Take for example these two propaganda posters.

By looking at various styles in relation to different influences such as period and historical events, you can get an insight into the politics, beliefs and public opinion of a particular time and how these can affect style and changes in taste.

Figure 4

Figure 5

TASK

What can you tell about the politics behind these two posters from the way they are designed? What political points are they trying to get across? How successful are images like these in making people do what politicians want?

1.6.3 The role of the arts

What is the role of the arts? To comment on life in an historical or contemporary context? To document events and landmarks in history? To serve as an amusement, hobby or pastime? To challenge or agree with society? Any one of these is possible. In addition there is the concern that many people consider the arts to be an extravagance and a waste of money.

EXAMINATION PRACTICE

Here is an interesting role for the arts in an ever-changing metropolis. Read through the passage and the questions that follow. Consider what a student would need to put in their answer to get top marks. Draw up your own mark scheme for the questions.

The role of the arts in regeneration

- The arts could have a **pivotal role** to play in regenerating areas of **social and economic exclusion**. They are seen to be able to operate in a number of different ways. They can attract people who otherwise might not be attracted to participate in arts activities; increase individuals' personal development; improve an area's image; attract economic investment; they can help in the process of community development; and they can lead to training and employment.

- It is important that arts projects and programmes are an integral part of an overall regeneration programme. If not they will remain on the periphery of the development process and their full potential will not be realised. This will require a change in attitudes for local people, regeneration specialists, **arts practitioners** and policy makers.

- Community involvement is essential as arts projects specialise in the people development aspect of regeneration.

- The arts have a particular role to play in encouraging young people into training and employment; supporting volunteers and participants in gaining confidence and a variety of personal development attributes; improving the image that residents and outsiders have of an area; **social cohesion and active citizenship**; local people recognising their own cultural identity and the part they can play in developing it; improving the quality of people's lives through individual and collective creativity; attracting people to come and visit an area thereby bringing direct economic and social benefits.

Alan Kay and Glenys Watt, Blake Stevenson Ltd, Consultants in Social and Economic Development, October 2000

The passage above would form the basis of a typical Section A question 1. Questions might be constructed as follows.

1 What are the meanings of the following phrases as used in the passage?
   a (i) pivotal role [3 marks]
      (ii) social and economic exclusion [3 marks]
      (iii) arts practitioners [3 marks]
      (iv) social cohesion and active citizenship [3 marks]
   b Outline two ways in which the arts could enhance someone's personal development. [6 marks]
   c Outline and discuss two arts activities that could be successfully initiated in an inner-city area and consider what the benefits might be to the community. Where appropriate make reference to your own experience in the answer. [12 marks]

[Total 30 marks]

Mark scheme instructions

The four phrases in part a would require three points to be made or two points with some extension of one to gain full marks. List all possibilities.

In the case of parts b and c, two items are needed for completion of the task. In b each point needs some supporting statement or exemplification to gain full marks. In c more detail is required and hence more marks (and more time). Construct a list of possible arts activities followed by benefits to the community. Give credit for personal experience. Design the mark scheme with four levels for this part of the question (Level 4: 10–12 marks, Level 3: 6–9 marks, Level 2: 3–5 marks, Level 1: 1–2 marks) with clear descriptors for each level.

Arts Council England's ambition for 2006–8 is to put the arts at the heart of national life and people at the heart of the arts.

Our aim is for everyone in the country to have the opportunity to develop a rich and varied artistic and creative life. We will ensure that more high quality work reaches a wider range of people – engaging them as both audience and participants. We will support artists and arts organisations to take creative risks and follow new opportunities.

By 2008 we hope to see:
• a more confident, diverse and innovative arts sector which is valued by and in tune with the communities it serves
• more active participation in the arts by adults and young people across the country.

Bury College
Millennium LRC

www.artscouncil.org.uk

One way in which the arts can be maintained in the UK is through the support and funding of the Arts Council. The work of the Arts Council crosses other borders and sees the arts as an important link to other areas of community concern such as crime prevention, well-being, and how people feel about the communities they live in.

The funding of the arts by the public purse has long been a source of controversy for successive governments. For the electorate to see thousands of pounds spent on works of art or performances which attract poor support seems to go against the need for a better education and health service. In some European countries such as France and Germany, the arts are more heavily subsidised which encourages members of the public of all ages to go out to see works of art 'live'. Consider the following points about arts funding.

1 The National Theatre's turnover is £50m a year. It receives £16m from the Arts Council and £1m from the private sector.

> Does money matter in the arts? Absolutely. Should the state help pay for the arts? Of course it should; it always has. State support for the arts is a great European tradition. The great patrons of the performing arts and the visual arts have always been rulers or monarchs. Now they are governments. There is not much difference between the patronage bestowed on Mozart by Emperor Josef II and what the Arts Council and the Department for Media, Culture and Sport do for arts organisations like the National Theatre today.
>
> **Nicholas Hynter**
> Director of the National Theatre

2 The Menier Chocolate Factory opened for business in 2004 as a 200-seat theatre and 60-seat restaurant on a budget of £10,000. It receives no public funding.

> Not being publicly funded has liberated us. We are not impeded by red tape, nor do we waste man-hours filling out reports. The theatre and the restaurant support each other. And the theatre alone now has a turnover of £1m a year.
>
> But we are time-poor and time is even more important than money. Because we lack staff and man-hours, we work ridiculously punishing schedules. I do wish we didn't have to be bogged down, say, in ordering cleaning supplies. I dream of sleeping eight-hour nights. But I can't afford them.
>
> In America, they've got it right when it comes to money and the arts. The government gives hardly any money to the arts, but tax breaks for sponsors are immense and so advantageous that, in the arts, it's the survival of the fittest. British arts-funding strategy, with its emphasis on establishment (you need to have been running for at least four years before the Arts Council will consider you for a grant) is ridiculously cautious.
>
> In the end, theatre is an act of faith. It's like that line from the movie *Field of Dreams*: 'If you build it, they will come.' Or: 'If you give people what they want, they will continue to be loyal to you.'
>
> **David Babani**
> Director of the Menier Chocolate Factory, London

Extracts adapted from *Does money matter?* on the *Guardian* artsblog
5 November 2006

WHAT NEXT?

Debate the two approaches to funding. Is there room for both or should funding end and the system become 'every man for himself'? Consider arts projects in your area. Contact your local arts association and find out what funding is available for different arts projects.

You need to be familiar with *two out of nine* areas of the arts

- architecture
- fashion
- photography
- painting
- sculpture
- stage
- screen
- music
- the written word.

As there are *nine areas* available to study but only *two* need to be covered in detail there may be general questions on art for which you can relate your answer to one of your chosen areas.

Example 1

It was the best of times, it was the worst of times, it was the age of wisdom, it was the age of foolishness, it was the epoch of belief, it was the epoch of incredulity, it was the season of Light, it was the season of Darkness, it was the spring of hope, it was the winter of despair, we had everything before us, we had nothing before us, we were all going direct to Heaven, we were all going direct the other way – in short, the period was so far like the present period, that some of its noisiest authorities insisted on its being received, for good or for evil, in the superlative degree of comparison only.

A Tale of Two Cities, Charles Dickens

Example 2

Figure 6

Example 1 What does the opening of this Dickens novel tell us about the era it was written in?

Example 2 What was music like in the era when this band was performing? Why were this group also considered as fashion icons?

2.1 Characteristics of the sciences

OVERVIEW

In this block of work we will look at

- greenhouse gases and global warming
- energy
- space and its exploration
- population dynamics and fertility control
- genetic engineering and biotechnology, organ transplantation
- health and fitness, disease control
- pollution and its management
- conservation and environmental management.

2.1.1 Introduction

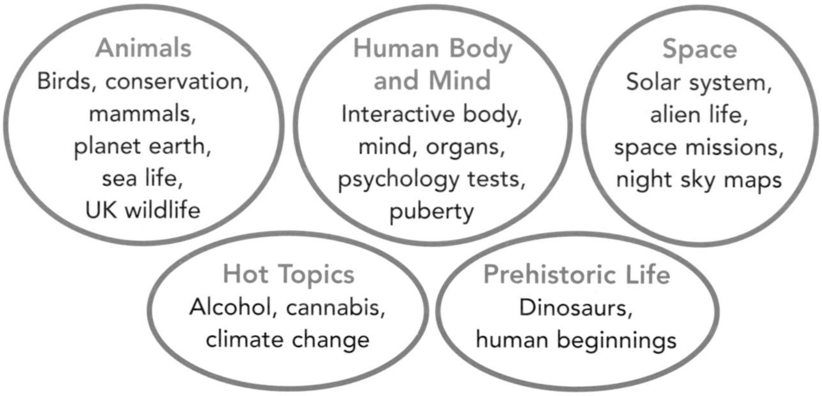

Animals
Birds, conservation, mammals, planet earth, sea life, UK wildlife

Human Body and Mind
Interactive body, mind, organs, psychology tests, puberty

Space
Solar system, alien life, space missions, night sky maps

Hot Topics
Alcohol, cannabis, climate change

Prehistoric Life
Dinosaurs, human beginnings

Figure 1

Figure 1 shows the breadth of the BBC's programmes on science and nature. Such programmes, along with everyday references to the sciences in newspapers and magazines, lend real and visual support to the science learned in lessons. Though the BBC's science and nature programmes might appear comprehensive, what contribution does science make to technology, education and the media?

QUESTIONS

Global warming
1 What is it?
2 What contribution have humans made to it?
3 Does it explain freak weather events?

Energy
1 What is it?
2 How is energy used and transferred?
3 How do we produce electricity?
4 To what extent will we become dependent upon alternative energy?

Space
1 To what extent is space the final frontier?
2 Why might people be fascinated by our solar system, our galaxy and deep space?
3 How do we prioritise the costs of space exploration with needs on Earth?
4 What do the names Copernicus and Stephen Hawking mean to you?

Population dynamics
1 What will the Earth's population be in 2050?
2 Why are some countries overpopulated whilst some are underpopulated?
3 What can be done to manage population growth?

Genetic engineering
1 Why was unravelling the DNA code important?
2 Why does Greenpeace say no to GM crops?
3 How has biotechnology benefited agriculture, food science and medicine?

Health and fitness
1 How do you measure fitness?
2 Does diet influence health?
3 What are nandrolone, testosterone prohormone and creatine?
4 Why use health clubs when we are living longer?

Pollution and its management
1 Who pollutes, and how?
2 What's so bad about CO, NO_X, SO_2, $CFCs$?
3 What is it to be: nuclear power, thermal energy or renewable energy?

Conservation and environmental management
1 Why do we have National Parks?
2 What are SSSIs?
3 How do you reconcile economic growth with environmental conservation?
4 What can be done about threatened species?
5 What is the debate on non-renewable versus renewable resources?

TASK

Construct diagrams similar to Figure 1 to show what each of the following includes

- Science and technology
- Science and education
- Science and media.

Compare your diagrams. Is there any overlap between the three diagrams? If so, why?

KEY TERMS

CO is carbon monoxide.
NO_x is nitrogen oxides.
SO_2 is sulphur dioxide.
CFCs are chlorofluorocarbons.

2.1.2 Global warming and greenhouse gases

The Stern Report of March 2007 stated that while action now to curb emissions would cost some 1 per cent of world economic output, delay could push the price up to 20 per cent.

The Earth's climate has been unstable for most of the past two million years. Ice ages have given way to warm periods. We are currently experiencing an unstable, but warm, climatic period. Research using ice-core samples has related these temperature changes to various **greenhouse gases**, notably carbon dioxide (CO_2). Warm periods occur when there are higher amounts of CO_2 in the atmosphere and cold periods occur when there are lower amounts. The controversial issue is the extent to which the temperature rise of the past 100 years is a product of human activity or a natural change.

KEY TERMS

Greenhouse gases are gases such as carbon dioxide which trap heat radiation from the Sun in the Earth's atmosphere (as glass in a greenhouse traps heat from the Sun), leading to a rise in global temperatures.

TASK

1 Using data from sites such as the Hadley Centre for Climatic Change or NASA, collect data on changes to the Earth's temperature.
2 What are ice ages and interglacial periods?
3 What temperatures did England experience during the 14th and 17th centuries?

Greenhouse gases and the greenhouse effect

Greenhouse gases are vital to the Earth and, without them, average global temperatures would be about 33 °C lower. Carbon dioxide and water vapour are important greenhouse gases. They are stored in seas and oceans, vegetation and fossil fuels, then transferred through processes such as evaporation, burning and plant transpiration, and circulate between land, sea and air. In the atmosphere they effectively trap heat energy from the Sun and keep us warm. Other greenhouse gases such as methane (CH_4), nitrogen oxides (NO_x) and CFCs would be many times more effective in trapping this energy, but these occur in small quantities.

Greenhouse gases allow radiation from the Sun to heat the surface of the Earth. The Earth's surface then reflects radiation back into the atmosphere. This is trapped in the lowest part of the atmosphere by the gases and warms the atmosphere, which leads to global warming (Figure 2).

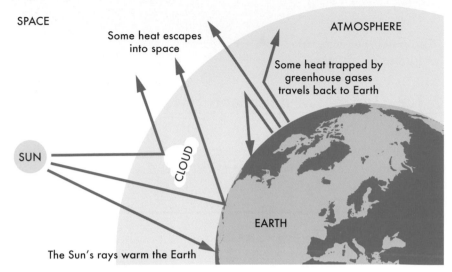

Figure 2

The global warming issue

Current concerns are with the sudden and rapid increases in temperature of the past 100 years. The greenhouse gases thought to be responsible for recent global warming have a variety of sources

- carbon dioxide (CO_2) from burning fossil fuels, evaporation from oceans and lakes, clearing forests (particularly rain forests)
- water vapour (H_2O) from evaporation of lakes, seas and oceans, evaporation and loss of water vapour from plants
- methane (CH_4) from melting of land that is usually permanently frozen, agriculture
- nitrogen oxides (NO_x) from emissions from industry, cars, power stations
- CFCs from refrigerators, volcanic activity, aerosols.

Many scientists think that the increases in the rate of global warming are a result of the release of these gases into the atmosphere. Others think they are caused by natural occurrences, such as increases in sunspot activity (dark cool patches on the Sun's surface). However, Figure 3 suggests that human activity has had an impact on global temperatures. It shows that, in the period 1910 to 2005, average global temperatures rose by 1.6 °C. A doubling of the amount of CO_2 in the atmosphere might cause average global temperatures to rise by between 1.5 °C and 4.5 °C. There is still much debate on how significant such rises could be.

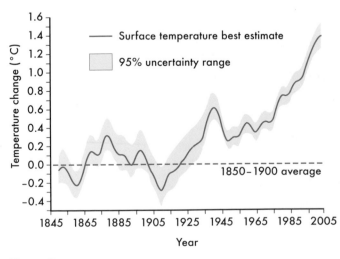

Figure 3

2 Science, mathematics and technology

Some effects of global warming

Global warming is something we all have to face, whatever its cause.

Event	Possible effects
Heat waves and periods of unusually warm weather	Drought, fires, famine, loss of ecosystems, population migration
Climate change	Early spring, 'freak weather', changing crop patterns, disease
Ocean warming	Warmer atmosphere, more severe hurricanes, rising sea levels
Glacier and ice-cap melting	Sea level rise, flooding, the Chinese are worried that, after glaciers melt, there might be reduced water supplies

Table 1: Possible effects of global warming

For people in the UK, it could lead to warmer summers, the ability to grow crops that are currently grown in the Mediterranean region, and lower energy costs. For Canada, it could mean growing wheat further north; some areas, such as Eastern Asia, might even receive more rainfall. The results of global warming are uncertain.

What can be done?

It is now generally accepted that it will take a lot longer to solve the problem than it took to cause it. We could

- ignore it, after all it might be a natural process and may go away
- develop international agreements that everyone should abide by
- let nations do their own thing.

Most agree that an international response is the only real option for achieving change, with nations meeting agreed targets by developing their own strategies.

International responses so far have involved meetings between nations and moderate agreement on various protocols. They have met with mixed success.

Kyoto 1997: 55 nations agree to reduce carbon emissions by 5.4 per cent by 2012. Some nations opt out.

Buenos Aires 1998: 160 countries agree a deadline of late 2000 for establishing rules to enforce the Kyoto Treaty.

Bonn Conference 2006: delegates from 165 countries seek to strengthen international cooperation

Figure 4

Many nations are now seeking, and adopting, measures to cut greenhouse gas emissions, targeting various elements of the economy.

- Energy: how it is produced and conserved, using renewable energy.
- Industry: reducing emissions and making them less polluting, efficiency, changing manufacturing (e.g. less packaging), recycling.
- Transport: emission reduction, fuel efficiency, biofuels, changing modes of transport.
- Agriculture: managing fertilisers, less burning of vegetable matter, which releases greenhouse gases, more efficient use of energy.
- Forestry: regenerate forests and reforest, reduce burning, use wood fuel instead of fossil fuels.

These measures add up to an effort to make economic activity more **sustainable**. While governments and big companies had once seen nothing wrong in racing to extract as much timber, oil, gas, etc. as they could from natural reserves, it is now more and more recognised that a global economic collapse could be right around the corner if global warming fuelled by reckless plundering of non-renewable resources is not controlled. It is largely up to governments to highlight issues and provide the incentives, planning and, possibly, the finance needed to do the job. And big companies are beginning to see that there is money to be made from cleaner, more sustainable technologies.

KEY TERMS

Sustainability means that a process can be continued at a certain level indefinitely. It is used to refer to processes that allow people to meet their immediate needs without compromising the ability of future generations to meet their needs, too.

TASK

Discuss the following points.

1 Should poor nations be expected to do the same as rich nations to reduce greenhouse gas emissions?
2 India and China have vast reserves of coal. They would argue that this is the time for their industrial revolution; countries in the west had theirs 100 years ago.
3 Global warming is a natural process, so why change?
4 Recent weather events have not been unusual.
5 Nature has its own way of reminding humans of their mistakes.

EXAMINATION PRACTICE

1 Outline *three* reasons for recent increases in the amount of carbon dioxide in the atmosphere.
2 Briefly explain the terms *greenhouse gases* and *global warming*.
3 Why is it possible that, in the near future, methane will become a more important greenhouse gas?
4 It is thought that, in the next 100 years, average global temperatures are likely to increase by between 3 and 5 °C. Describe and explain three effects this may have upon the Earth's environment. [30 marks]
5 Describe and assess the strategies that could be adopted to prevent further increases in the carbon dioxide content of the Earth's atmosphere. [30 marks]
6 Global warming is a major issue of today and in the future. Why is the reduction of greenhouse gases proving to be difficult? [30 marks]

2.1.3 Energy production

The term **energy** is part of everyday life. Active people are energetic, a light bulb uses electrical energy, plants use sunlight to make energy in **photosynthesis**, energy is stored in fossil fuels and we complain about the size of our energy bill. What do we mean by energy?

Natural energy

In photosynthesis the green pigment chlorophyll in plants is able to capture light energy from the Sun and convert it to food energy by manufacturing carbohydrates (energy-storing chemicals). The food produced allows plants to grow. Green plants, which trap the Sun's energy, form the start of most food chains.

In any **ecosystem**, energy is transferred along food chains. Food chains can interconnect to form a complicated network of pathways known as a food web. In a food web the direction of the arrows describes a transfer of energy between levels, from one organism to another. The energy transfer is not efficient, because only 10 per cent of the energy stored at one level is transferred to the next, with 90 per cent being lost as heat energy during **respiration** and as faeces to the detrivores (animals that feed on decayed matter, such as worms), and decomposers (organisms that break down dead animals).

> ### KEY TERMS
>
> In science, energy is the ability to do work. Energy cannot be created nor destroyed, although it can be changed from one form to another.
>
> **Photosynthesis** is a series of chemical reactions by which green plants make their food.

> ### KEY TERMS
>
> **Ecosystems** consist of producers (green plants), consumers (herbivores and carnivores), detrivores (e.g. worms) and decomposers (e.g. bacteria).
>
> **Respiration** is the breakdown of organic compounds to release energy and produce carbon dioxide and water.

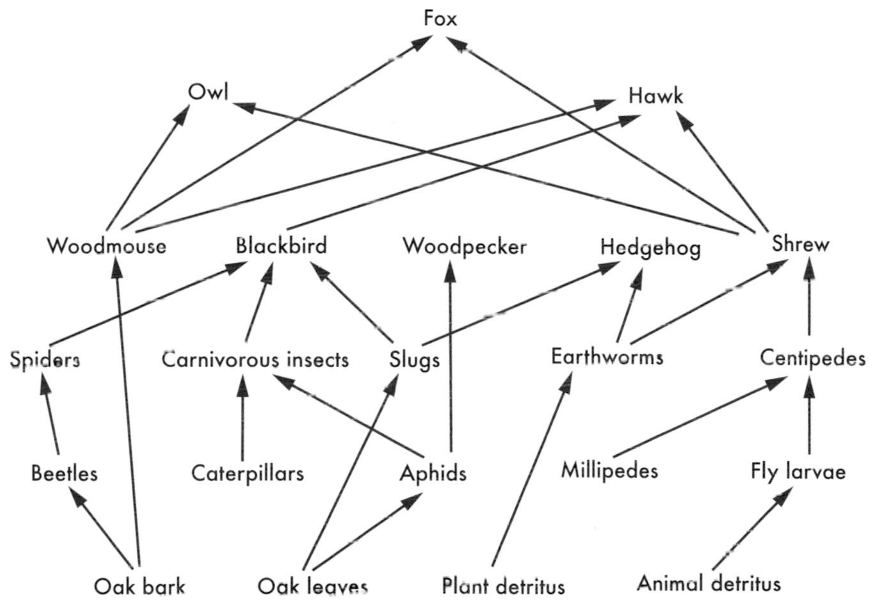

Figure 5: a woodland food web

> ### TASK
>
> 1 Find examples of two-, three-, four- and five-stage food chains in Figure 5. Where appropriate, identify the producers, primary consumers, secondary consumers and predators.
>
> 2 Discuss the ways in which energy is transferred and lost in the woodland ecosystem.
>
> 3 What would be the effects of clearing the woodland for agriculture upon both the food web and the energy stores in a woodland? Think about all levels within the web, biodiversity and species population.

People consume various foods in order to supply their body with energy which is released in respiration in every cell of the body. The human muscle system relies upon the glucose, fatty acids and oxygen supplied by the blood. Before the energy can be used it is first changed into a form that the organism can handle easily. This special carrier of energy is the molecule adenosine triphosphate (ATP). The ATP molecule acts like a chemical battery. It stores energy when it is not needed, but is able to release it instantly when the organism requires it. When oxygen is consumed faster than it can be supplied, there is muscle fatigue as the muscle cells carry out anaerobic respiration (respiration without oxygen).

The human body uses and transfers energy during exercise. Imagine you have just completed a physical workout and are drenched in sweat. Why? The body has worked and released energy in the form of heat; you warm up. When sweat evaporates from the surface of your skin, it removes excess heat and you cool down.

Renewable and non-renewable energy

There are two basic types of energy source: **renewable energy** and **non-renewable energy**.

There is an increasing demand for energy. Whether it is fuel for transport and power or electricity for homes and businesses, this demand has traditionally focused on the non-renewable fossil fuels: coal, natural gas and oil. Thermal power stations use these resources to heat water in the production of electricity; petrol comes from crude oil, and all three fossil fuels are used to heat our homes. There are, however, two major problems with using fossil fuels

- they are sources of pollution
- once used they cannot be replaced.

Renewable sources of energy (wind, water and solar) are seen to be the solution. Hydro-electric power stations have been used for a long time, we are now seeing wave and tidal schemes coming into operation and, although controversial, wind farms are now familiar features on our landscape. Nuclear power has been with us for some time and some nuclear power stations are now being decommissioned. There is strong opposition to increasing the number of nuclear power stations but perhaps fast-breeder reactors or even fusion reactors may become more common.

Table 2 (page 75) shows that non-renewable and renewable resources have their advantages and disadvantages.

KEY TERMS

Renewable energy is energy that is generated using renewable sources, such as wind and water.

Non-renewable energy is energy that is generated using resources that are finite, such as coal or natural gas.

TASK

Research fusion or fission reactors.

TASK

Why not develop geothermal energy, biofuels, wave and tidal energy? They are all in plentiful supply.

Table 2

Energy source	Advantages	Disadvantages
coal	cheap, easily mined, high electricity output, can use current technology, 220 years of supply	dirty, burning emits SO_2, NO_2 and CO_2, ugly power stations
oil	strong current demand, flexible usage in cars, power stations and oil by-products	may run out in 30 years, releases SO_2, NO_2 and CO_2
natural gas	cleanest of the fossil fuels, easily and cheaply transported, widespread usage	may run out in 50 years
nuclear energy	high electricity output, considerable reserves of uranium, clean, can be reprocessed	accidents, waste storage, radioactive discharge
wind	pollution-free, reduced dependence on fossil fuels, does not interfere with farming	inefficient, unreliable, visual intrusion, possible effects on wildlife
hydro-electric power	established technology, supplies local demand, plenty of rainfall, reservoirs for recreational use	reservoirs have environmental impacts, relatively low output
solar energy	no pollution, once installed cheap with little maintenance	initially expensive, locations are restricted

The future

Current trends in energy consumption show oil, coal and gas well ahead of renewable and nuclear energy (Figure 6) However, fossil fuels will soon run out. How will **developed countries** and **developing countries** cope?

KEY TERMS

A **developed country** is a country with high standards of living and an advanced economy (MEDC).

A **developing country** is a term often used to describe a less economically developed country (LEDC).

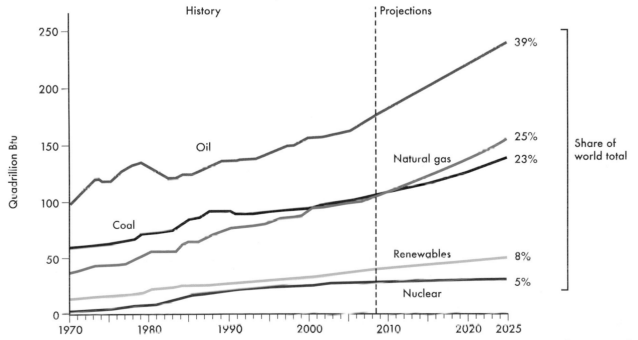

Figure 6: Global shares in use of energy sources, renewable and non-renewables

EIA International Energy Outlook

There are pressures on all nations to cut down their use of fossil fuels and develop alternative sources of energy. Many developing nations already use solar power, biofuels and hydro-electricity and some see the need to continue to use their fossil fuels. Some developed countries are accused of excessive consumption of fossil fuels and ignoring pressures on their use. Developed nations are sometimes accused of bullying developing nations.

TASK

1 Using examples of rich and poor nations, to what extent can the opinion stated in this cartoon be justified?

"I blame the billions in the 3rd world, wanting to get what we've got!"

Figure 7

2 Is nuclear power the only viable solution to meeting our future demands for electricity?
3 Should all road transport use biofuels?
4 Should airships and sail replace current forms of aircraft and shipping?
5 Is there no need to panic? Should we carry on as we have always done?

WHAT NEXT?

Investigate the contribution that NASA, Google Earth, Greenpeace, the Medical Research Council and the Open University might make to your understanding and use of science.

1 Describe and explain how energy is transferred though a food web.
2 Using examples, distinguish between renewable and non-renewable energy.
3 Outline *two* arguments for and *two* arguments against the further development of nuclear energy in the UK. [30 marks]
4 Outline and justify the important components of an energy-efficient building. [30 marks]
5 The UK has a dilemma: how to meet its growing energy demand and at the same time reduce carbon dioxide emissions from cars, industry and power stations.
Describe the advantages and disadvantages of *two* possible solutions to this dilemma. [30 marks]

2.1.4 Space and its exploration

Throughout history humans have wondered at the scale and beauty of the universe. On a clear night, go out and have a look at the night sky. Use a night sky map from the internet or a newspaper and try to find the planets Jupiter or Saturn, the summer triangle Deneb, Vega and Altair; or wonder at the brightest star Sirius (the name for which comes from the Greek word *Seirius*, meaning 'searing' or 'scorching'). If you use binoculars or a telescope you will see even more.

A matter of scale

The Earth is a small planet in an outer spiral arm of a large galaxy called the Milky Way, which is often clearly visible as a white belt extending across the night sky. As we look at it sideways on, it appears like a disc. Because of the vast distances involved, **light years** are used as a unit of measurement when talking about features of the universe. Light travels at 186,000 miles a second (more accurately expressed as 3×10^8 metres a second). The Sun is eight light minutes away, Neptune is four light hours away and our nearest star, *Proxima*, is four light years away. Part of *Monty Python's Galaxy Song* sums up the scale of our galaxy.

> 'Our galaxy itself contains a hundred billion stars.
> It's a hundred thousand light years side to side.
> It bulges in the middle, sixteen thousand light years thick,
> But out by us, it's just three thousand light years wide.'

> *Is the universe actually infinite or just very large? And is it everlasting or just long lived? How could our finite minds comprehend an infinite universe?*
>
> Stephen Hawking

KEY TERMS

A **light year** is a unit of measurement used for space exploration and is the distance light travels in a year.

Origins

The origins of the universe, our galaxy and the solar system have been debated for a long time.

Scientists now believe the universe formed about 15 billion years ago in a single event called the Big Bang. At the Big Bang moment (only a fraction of a second long), the universe was small, dense and infinitely hot: only energy existed. After one second the temperature fell to about 10^{10} °C, equivalent to 1,000 times the temperature at the centre of our Sun. In the new universe, particles and energy were unevenly distributed and some concentrations of matter formed into clouds which condensed into stars. A cloud 300 light years across has sufficient mass to produce over 10,000 stars.

Some 500 million years after the Big Bang, galaxies began to form and took a further 700 million years to evolve. Our galaxy (the Milky Way), the second largest of the local galaxies after Andromeda, is a concentration of millions of stars in the shape of a spiral. Our solar system lies in one of the outer arms of this spiral.

Galaxy facts
1 The centre of the Milky Way lies in the direction of the constellation Sagittarius.
2 There is a galactic equator.
3 Our galaxy is currently eating a smaller neighbouring galaxy.

Our solar system started to form about nine billion years ago and took its present form about 4.5 billion years ago. According to the nebula theory, the solar system formed from the collapse of a giant cloud of matter (or nebula). As the cloud rotated faster, particles collided, it became hotter and flattened into the flat disc shape we see today. Eventually the Sun formed and the remaining dust and gas became the planets.

KEY TERMS

Dwarf planets are a new category of bodies that orbit the Sun – they have a round shape produced by their own gravity but they aren't large enough to have pulled in and so cleared smaller bodies around them. Not all scientists agree that this category should exist.

TASK

1 Use the NASA website to discover more about our solar system and beyond.
2 Why has what used to be planet Pluto now been demoted to a dwarf planet?
3 What are the rings around Saturn? Does Jupiter have rings?
4 Is Venus an extreme example of the greenhouse effect?
5 Research the constellation Orion. Is there anything odd about how distant its stars are from us?
6 Investigate some colour images of galaxies and nebulae: they are interesting and beautiful art forms. The Hubble telescope website has a gallery of space photography.

A research frontier

Our knowledge of astronomy comes from a wide variety of data-collecting sources. We see stars and planets with the naked eye, use telescopes, record noise and use satellites: it's an expensive, highly technical and fascinating business.

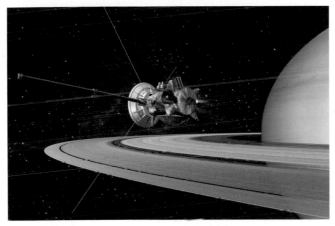

Figure 8: the Cassini-Huygens mission to Saturn. Launched 1997, reached Saturn 2005

Figure 9: Hubble Space Telescope, launched 1990

Cassini-Huygens mission The Cassini spacecraft was the first to explore Saturn's rings and moons from orbit. Seventeen nations were involved in building it and 250 scientists are working on the data sent to Earth. It did a Jupiter flyby and discovered three new moons. It cost about $3.26 billion.

Figure 10: International Space Station

Hubble Space Telescope This is named after Edwin Hubble. It orbits the Earth at a height of 366 miles (589 km) every 97 minutes. Its views of space are not blurred by the Earth's atmosphere and there is no light interference. It can view distant galaxies and has provided information on nebulae and **black holes**. It has produced clear pictures of the collision of a comet with Jupiter in 1994. It has cost approximately $2.5 billion since it was launched.

KEY TERMS

Black holes are objects with gravity so strong that even light cannot escape its pull. Einstein showed that mass bends space and time, and gravity is the pull that exists along these curves in the universe. So a truly massive object, such as the singularity formed when a star collapses in on itself, could create such a gigantic pull that even light is sucked in.

International Space Station A research facility being assembled in space, continuously inhabited since 2000. It is serviced by Russian *Soyuz* and *Progress* spacecraft with US Shuttle craft. Its main areas of research are biology, biomedical research, physics, astronomy and meteorology. It is solar powered. Estimated cost from 1994 to the end of its life is $53 billion.

Costs and benefits

What are the benefits of spending such vast sums on space technology? We have increased our knowledge, but are there any other benefits? They are largely technological and wide-ranging. The Cassini project has contributed radio transponders, new gyros that can be used in aircraft and refinements to communication systems. Not only is the International Space Station seen to encourage cooperation between nations, but it has enabled observations of the Earth's environment, improved communication systems and developed water and air quality technologies.

However, whilst space technology can provide such things as computer equipment, enriched baby food, golf ball aerodynamics, smoke detectors, cool suits and protective clothing, what about needs on Earth? Arguments for spending on supporting the needs of developing countries, disaster relief and climate change, etc. are equally convincing. In 2007 the World Food Programme faced a $157 million shortfall to feed 9.7 million people. In 2005 it cost $5,000 to deliver a load of corn, beans, mosquito nets and blankets to northern Uganda: how many loads of corn, beans and mosquito nets would the money spent on the Hubble Space Telescope have paid for?

TASK

To what extent can spending on space technology be justified?

WHAT NEXT?

Visit the Hubble site for great resources on space exploration.
http://hubblesite.org

NASA's site also contains lots of useful information.
http://www.nasa.gov

EXAMINATION PRACTICE

1 Distinguish between the terms nebula, galaxy and solar system.
2 Outline *three* benefits of using orbiting space satellites.
3 Outline *three* reasons why, with the naked eye
   • it may be possible to observe a small number of planets in the night sky at the same time
   • the planets appear to travel across the night sky at a faster speed than stars.
4 Describe and explain how investments in space technology have been of technological benefit to people on Earth. [30 marks]
5 Can space exploration be justified? Prepare cases for and against the funding of further space exploration. [30 marks]

2 Science, mathematics and technology

2.1.5 Population dynamics

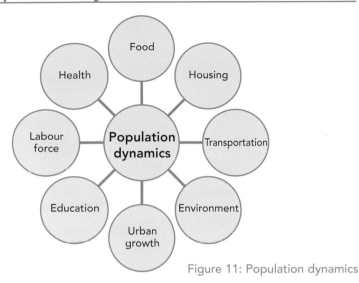

Figure 11: Population dynamics

Population issues generally focus on population growth. This is understandable, because the Earth's population is set to rise from about 7 billion in 2007 to 8.9 billion in 2050: 76 million per year. Planning for such growth places a strain on economies at both a global and a country scale. To focus just on numerical growth, however, tends to mask other important issues. What about

- variations in birth and death rates or **immigration** and **emigration**
- whether a nation has too many young or old people to cope with
- the balance between males and females
- the countries that are overpopulated, underpopulated or can balance their population with available resources?

TASK

Discuss the following

1 Unmanaged population growth will affect housing, education, the environment and employment.
2 Populations are growing most rapidly where such growth can be least afforded.
3 What will be the effect of a shrinking labour force having to support an increasingly larger and older population?
4 Every country would benefit from an environmentally sustainable population policy.
5 What factors affect the retirement decisions of older men and women?
6 If towns and cities are unable to accommodate their future populations, more building will have to be done in the countryside.

Population change

Figure 12 is a model that shows the inputs and outputs that determine the total population of a country. Generally, changes to the birth rate and death rate have a stronger impact than immigration and emigration.

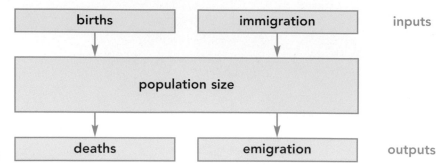

Figure 12

An early study of population dynamics by the Reverend Thomas Malthus painted a very pessimistic scenario. He viewed population growth as constantly placing pressures upon food production. In this model, checks on population growth such as famine, war and disease will occur once the population exceeds food production. An alternative model proposed by Esther Boserup takes an optimistic scenario whereby if 'necessity is the mother of invention' is held to be true, then improvements in technology will enable nations to cope with problems of population growth.

Trends, predictions and reasons

Based on current data, the pattern of global population growth for the period 1750 to 2100 almost suggests a Malthusian pattern, but it is a complex issue.

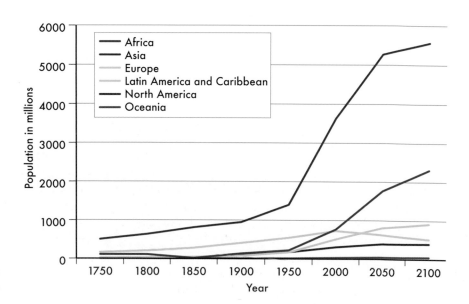

Figure 13: World population growth 1750 to 2100, based on UN data

With the exception of Europe, each continent shows high (Asia and Africa) or gentler (South America, Oceania and North America) population growth until 2050 before slowing down. Europe's population actually decreases. The reasons for these trends are varied and are summarised in Table 3.

Continent	Reasons
Asia	Rapid development will mean higher standards of living, career-oriented families, later marriages and fewer children. The effects of stringent birth control strategies might also be noticed. Japan has an ageing population and low birth rates.
Africa	Currently drought, famine, Aids and low standards of living affect sub-Saharan Africa. High birth rates maintain the working population and high infant mortality means child replacement is seen as necessary. Current difficulties might continue.
Europe	Very high standards of living mean high life expectancy but low birth rates contribute to an ageing population. Decreases in population are possible.
Latin America and the Caribbean	A region with room for expansion. It is possible that continued socio-economic progress and full utilisation of its vast resources will allow for continued population growth. However, there are variations, e.g. Argentina is relatively rich whilst Paraguay is less wealthy.
North America	Highly developed and rich with high standards of living. Family planning and career-oriented families ensure slow population growth. However, immigration and large cultural differences might distort birth and death rates, since some cultures encourage large families while others encourage small families.
Oceania	Although there are vast expanses of land available not all is easily settled. High standards of living in Australia and New Zealand ensure that family size is small and life expectancy high.

Table 3: Global population dynamics: some reasons

The importance of resources

The level of provision of resources such as food, water, effective health care and technology go towards setting the **carrying capacity** of a country. These resources are taken for granted in most developed countries. However, for many developing countries the size of the population now exceeds the carrying capacity. India has a rapidly expanding economy but with a population of over one billion to feed, it could be classed as overpopulated. Some sub-Saharan countries with very small populations are so poor they cannot feed themselves and are also overpopulated.

KEY TERMS

Carrying capacity is the maximum number of people a country or area can support.

TASK

1 To what extent are countries within the six regions in Table 3 overpopulated or underpopulated? Use the concept of carrying capacity to make your assessment.
2 What problems are caused by
   • high life expectancy and an ageing population
   • low life expectancy and a high birth rate?

A sustainable future

At the moment the Earth is a closed system and, until we build submarine cities, lunar waste dumps or Martian overspill cities, there is nowhere else to go. The future largely depends on two factors

- successful management of the global population
- the provision of resources for the growing population.

Population management

For developing countries, population management does not necessarily mean the imposition of a one-child policy or compulsory sterilisation. Family planning, a success in the developed world, is less successful in developing countries. It needs to be accompanied by education, family planning services and free contraception, and perhaps tax incentives to encourage smaller families. In developed countries there are different issues. Here family planning and high standards of living have already contributed to low rates of population growth. The concern is with the impact of low birth rates and **ageing populations**; some nations are even experiencing a decrease in their population. In the UK there are concerns about the size of the pensionable sector of the population (the grey economy). The cost of health care and welfare rises but the size of the work force reduces, so there is not as much money raised through taxation to pay for the services.

Fertility

To manage population change successfully, indicators of fertility such as birth rates are used. Fertility indicators can be expressed in three ways

- the crude birth rate is the number of births per 1,000 of the population
- the general fertility rate is the number of births in a year per 1,000 women of normal reproductive age (i.e. the 15 to 45 age group)
- the child–women ratio is the ratio of children under five years old to women of child-bearing age.

Appropriate measures for managing birth rates can range from strict legislation through to encouragement, advice and incentives. Table 4 summarises some of the issues and measures that might be adopted.

> ### KEY TERMS
>
> **Ageing population** is where the average age of a nation's population is increasing.

> ### TASK
>
> 1 As a group, discuss the measures that are being used in the UK to manage its population. You might need to consider: education (in schools and colleges), family planning and social habits.
> 2 To what extent is the problem of an ageing population solved by encouraging immigration?
> 3 Investigate the population issues of two contrasting countries. Assess the measures they have adopted to manage these issues. Examples for research could be Italy and China; Germany and Singapore; the UK and India.

Population issues	Broad objectives	Measures
Overpopulation, high birth rates, large numbers in the 0–15 age group and increasing life expectancy. e.g. sub-Saharan Africa, 1980s China, India	To stabilise population growth; reduce family size; improve standards of living	Legislation such as China's one-child policy has succeeded in reducing birth rates but created social problems. Many developing nations offer family planning services, advice and free contraception
Too few children and an ageing population	To increase the birth rate and provide for a better balance between age groups, a future working population, and to ease, via taxation, the cost burden of an ageing population	Introduce incentives to increase the birth rate, e.g. time off work during pregnancy; salary and employment protection for working mothers; tax incentives
Social issues such as unwanted pregnancies and general birth control	To enable 'safe' sexual activity as well as managing the birth rate	Contraceptive measures: the pill, condoms, injections, sterilisation, etc. Family planning and education
Childlessness	To enable couples to conceive children	The use of IVF, fertility drugs, surrogacy and sperm donation

Table 4

WHAT NEXT?

The following links provide more information on population dynamics and how population growth and changes are measured.

www.statistics.gov.uk/census

www.census.gov/ipc/www/idb

www.un.org/esa/population/publications/WPP2004/wpp2004.htm

www.wri.org/powerpoints/trends/index.htm

www.population.com

EXAMINATION PRACTICE

1 Describe how the size of a country's population would be affected by changes to birth rates, death rates, immigration and emigration.

2 What is meant by the term *carrying capacity*? Why is it important that the carrying capacity of a country keeps ahead of population growth?

3 How can governments influence the rate of population growth in their countries?

4 Why are some governments attempting to reduce rates of population growth when others are trying to increase theirs? [30 marks]

5 Describe and explain how and why developed countries (MEDCs) have different policies relating to managing population change than developing countries (LEDCs). [30 marks]

2.1.6 Genetic engineering and biotechnology

Human trials of GM drugs could be five years away

Untested GM rice found in food, says Greenpeace

Oil Eaters Slurp Up Spills
'Bacteria consume the oil until there is no residue left'

Skinny gene could become weapon in fight against obesity

Developments in biotechnology and genetic engineering are controversial. Whilst one group would see them as a vital and important development, another would see them as a human-made disaster. What is it all about and what is the controversy? In 1990 *New Scientist* editor Bernard Dixon said 'What is the scientific evidence for the public's apparent fear of biotechnology?'. This drew the response that 'if indeed the public were afraid, it was far from clear what they were afraid of or on what grounds their reservations were based'.

Biotechnology has been with us for a long time. It can be described as the use of living organisms and their products to produce food, drink, medicines and other benefits to the human race, animals and the environment. **Genetic engineering** has emerged as a modern biotechnological development. Here is a simplified timeline for biotechnology.

KEY TERMS

Genetic engineering means the deliberate alteration of the DNA in a cell nucleus with the objective of altering an organism or group of organisms.

1750BCE The Sumerians brew beer
250BCE The Greeks use crop rotation to maintain soil fertility

1590 CE Jannson invents the microscope
1797 Jenner inoculates a child with vaccine against smallpox

1863 Mendel, in his study of peas, discovers that certain traits are passed on from one generation to another His studies are the groundwork for genetics
1888 Waldeyer discovers the chromosome

1914 Manchester sewage is treated using bacteria
1919 A Hungarian engineer is thought to be the first to use the term 'biotechnology'

1943 Avery shows that DNA is the material of genes

1961 The genetic code is first understood

1981 Mice are cloned
1986 First field tests on genetically engineered tobacco
1993 It is announced that genetically engineered foods are 'not inherently dangerous'
2001 *Science* and *Nature* (scientific journals) publish the sequence of the human genome

Figure 14

Early humans employed biotechnology by using yeast to make bread and ferment alcohol, by selecting seeds for cultivation and by breeding animals. The cross-pollination of plants and cross-breeding of animals were used to improve the quality of food. Today biotechnology is used in industry in the form of biodegradable packaging and the treatment of industrial waste; in agriculture for pesticides and treating contaminated land; and in medicine, for example in developing therapeutic drugs.

Genetic engineering or modification (GM)

Genetics is concerned with the passing on of characteristics from one generation to another. Chromosomes, present in the nucleus of all cells, are long thin strands that store this information. Chromosomes are made up of a special chemical called DNA (deoxyribonucleic acid). It is here the genetic information is stored. A DNA molecule consists of two chains twisted round each other to form a double helix. Each DNA molecule contains about 1,000 genes, and each gene has a different code relating to a particular characteristic or trait.

Here are some simple rules of genetics.

- Organisms get their traits or characteristics from their genes.
- A pair of genes, one from each parent, controls particular characteristics.
- Genes may be dominant or recessive; dominant genes generally decide characteristics over recessive genes.

In a human there are 46 chromosomes in each cell, of which two are sex chromosomes called X and Y. Males carry XY and females XX. A human baby's gender is determined by the sperm that fertilises the egg cell. The baby will be a girl if the sperm carries the X chromosome and a boy if it carries the Y chromosome.

Genetic engineering enables the genes in a chromosome to be altered. This forms a vast and controversial area of current scientific research. Five examples are given overleaf.

> **TASK**
>
> Apart from genetic engineering, investigate four different contributions biotechnology has made to modern society.

> **TASK**
>
> Research Mendel's two laws: the law of segregation and the law of independent assortment.

Example	Benefits
Improved rice Rice is a staple crop of Asia but it is low in vitamin A. Such a deficiency can lead to early blindness. By transferring genes from other species into rice, a new strain of rice that is rich in vitamin A has been produced.	Incidence of blindness has been reduced and normal vision is being restored to many people. Plants are now being cross-bred with other varieties of rice. This 'miracle rice' was tried and tested in the Philippines. A similar technique can be used to produce iron-rich rice to cure anaemia.
Virus-resistant crops Viruses infect people and animals and can be spread by insects. Plants can be protected by copying the gene from the virus into the plants' DNA, which ultimately stimulates the plants' natural defences. This technique is used in tomatoes, potatoes, papaya.	As plants now have natural defences against viruses there is less need for pesticides and insecticides that can pollute the ground, rivers and lakes. These are environmental benefits.
Insulin production Genetic engineers are able to insert the gene for human insulin into a common bacterium called *E. coli**. When this bacterium was grown in cultures it produced vast quantities of high-quality human insulin.	Used in the treatment of diabetes. Insulin produced in this way is more effective than insulin from cows, to which people had allergies. It is produced in vast quantities and can be isolated easily in a pure form.
Reproductive cloning This needs a living cell and a human egg. The nucleus of the egg which contains DNA is removed and replaced with the nucleus and DNA from the cell of the person or animal to be cloned. An electrical impulse then stimulates the egg to fertilise. The embryo is then implanted into the womb of the person or animal, where it develops into the clone.	Reproductive cloning is seen by some to assist with infertility; the replacement of a lost child; creating 'donor' people; and saving endangered species. However, there are strong religious and ethical concerns about this technique, and the success rate is uncertain.
Therapeutic cloning and stem cells Stem cells can reproduce and become one of many different kinds of cell, e.g. skin, liver, hair, blood. Stem cells are extracted after the embryo starts dividing in the first 14 days after fertilisation.	This technique allows the replacement of organs and tissues. There is the possibility of new skin for burn victims, brain cells for those with brain damage, spinal rod cells for the paralysed, and complete new organs (hearts, liver, kidney and lungs).

* *E. coli* can be very dangerous in an unmodified form.

Table 5: Examples of genetic engineering and their benefits

TASK
As a group, discuss the moral and environmental issues linked to • biotechnology in general • genetic engineering.

There are objections to various aspects of biotechnology: in particular genetic engineering raises moral and religious concerns. Are the upsides outweighed by the downsides? There are moral objections to the use of animals by humans, generally as well as for genetic modification: what are the consequences and what harm may be caused? What about GM crops? There are concerns that they are grown in a way that reduces biodiversity. There are fears that a GM crop trial may release a pathogen (disease-causing agent such as a virus) that could adversely affect the microbes in a soil. Wind can enable the cross-pollination of GM crops with non GM crops.

Organ transplantation

An organ transplant involves transferring a whole or partial organ from the body of one person to another: a working organ replaces a damaged or failing organ. The success of this biotechnology relies on donors. In the UK registering as a potential donor is currently voluntary. Organ donors can be living or dead and the transplants are classed as life-saving (e.g. of heart or liver) or life-enhancing (e.g. of skin). This time line shows both the extent and history of medical transplantations. It is worth noting the transition from single organ transplants from dead donors through to double organ transplants, to successful transplants from living donors.

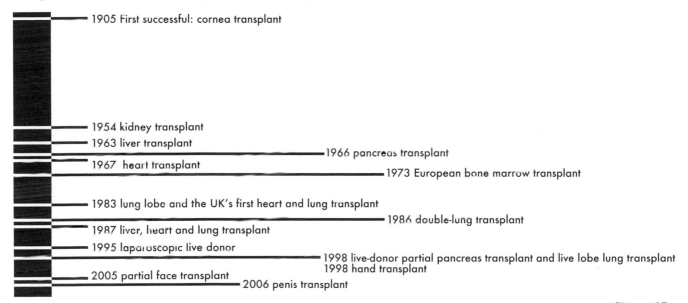

- 1905 First successful: cornea transplant
- 1954 kidney transplant
- 1963 liver transplant
- 1966 pancreas transplant
- 1967 heart transplant
- 1973 European bone marrow transplant
- 1983 lung lobe and the UK's first heart and lung transplant
- 1986 double-lung transplant
- 1987 liver, heart and lung transplant
- 1995 laparoscopic live donor
- 1998 live-donor partial pancreas transplant and live lobe lung transplant
- 1998 hand transplant
- 2005 partial face transplant
- 2006 penis transplant

Figure 15

Concerns about organ transplantations

Many concerns have been expressed about this area of biotechnology.

- Ethical concerns range from objections to transferring organs from one body to another, to the harm caused by the trade in organs found in many developing nations (e.g. a kidney may cost $1,000 in Manila and $20,000 in South Africa).
- In some nations there is the risk of diseased organs being transplanted. In some poor nations donors have been unable to receive regular health care and organ dealers may evade the disease-screening process.
- Transplant rejection is a major issue and concern for many. This occurs when the immune system of the recipient attacks the transplanted organ or tissue. Rejection occurs at three levels: hyperacute rejection means the organ must be removed within minutes of the transplant; acute rejection requires the taking of drugs to suppress the immune system; and chronic rejection describes the long-term loss of organ functions, causing a gradual deterioration in performance of the organ.

TASK

1 Assess the use of organ transplants in treating organ failure.
2 Should organ donation be compulsory or voluntary?

• There are not enough organs available to meet demand. Some believe consent for organ donation after death should be assumed (which removes the need to ask grieving relatives for permission to remove organs) unless a person 'opts out' and carries a card to say they do not wish to be a donor in the event of their death.

WHAT NEXT?

1 Biotechnology has supporters and opponents. Summarise Friends of the Earth's opposition to biotechnology. What would its supporters say in its defence?
www.foe.org/
2 Research UK Transplant's new My Life, My Gift campaign, which is inviting around 11 million homes in England and Northern Ireland to join the NHS Organ Donor Register.
www.uktransplant.org.uk

EXAMINATION PRACTICE

1 Using examples, distinguish between biotechnology and genetic engineering.
2 Outline *three* ways in which genetic engineering can be beneficial to humans.
3 In a recent advertisement, a genetics research group stated that 'using our state-of-the-art technologies, you can quite possibly ensure that your child's life will be free from such diseases as cancer, Alzheimer's and heart disease – as well as conditions like obesity, aggression and dyslexia'.
To what extent do the advantages of genetic engineering outweigh its dangers? [30 marks]
4 Organ transplantation is being used more and more.
Discuss whether you think scientists should continue to research and develop organ transplant techniques in order to improve people's lives. [30 marks]

2.1.7 Health and fitness: disease control

Every time I get the urge to exercise, I lie down until the feeling passes.

I don't like going to the doctor's and the dentist scares me.

The advantage of exercising every day is that you die healthier.

It is possible to trivialise health and fitness, but these three statements have a serious side to them. Some have a negative attitude toward diet and fitness, others are fearful of visiting the doctor or dentist. Some people simply do not take their personal health seriously.

2 Science, mathematics and technology

What do we mean by 'health and fitness'? The World Health Organization (WHO) describes good health as *'a state of complete physical, mental and social well-being and not merely the absence of disease or infirmity in order to lead a socially and economically productive life'*. Fitness, although important, is just one contributor to good health.

TASK

Discuss the contribution each of these makes towards good health.

1 Lifestyle: diet, exercise, habits
2 Mental health: emotional and psychological well-being
3 Nutrition: a balanced daily diet
4 Exercise: jogging, gym, school PE, sports clubs
5 Hygiene: brushing teeth, washing, cleaning food
6 Health care: prevention, treatment and management of illness

How healthy are you?

Can we successfully take control of our own health, or do we need help? The current problems with obesity in the UK and other developed countries suggest the answer may be that many people cannot look after their own best interests for long-term health. Obesity is now regarded as a serious and growing public health problem that can lead to cardiovascular disease, type II diabetes, strokes, osteoarthritis and some cancers. Furthermore, some obese people are more likely to suffer from problems such as depression, social discrimination and low self-esteem.

Here are some UK statistics:
- By 2010 it is expected that 22 per cent of girls and 16.7 per cent of boys will be obese.
- 22 per cent of the adult population are classed as obese.
- Over 30,000 deaths a year are linked to obesity.
- It is estimated that obesity costs the National Health Service in excess of £1 billion per year.

Part of the government's commitment to reducing obesity is to have a record of the body mass index (BMI) of the population. Body mass index relates body height to weight, with the results placed into healthy and unhealthy bands.

$$\text{BMI} = \frac{\text{weight in kg}}{(\text{height in metres})^2} \quad \text{or} \quad \frac{\text{kg}}{\text{m}^2}$$

A person 1.75 metres tall with a body weight of 80 kg would have a BMI of 26.1.

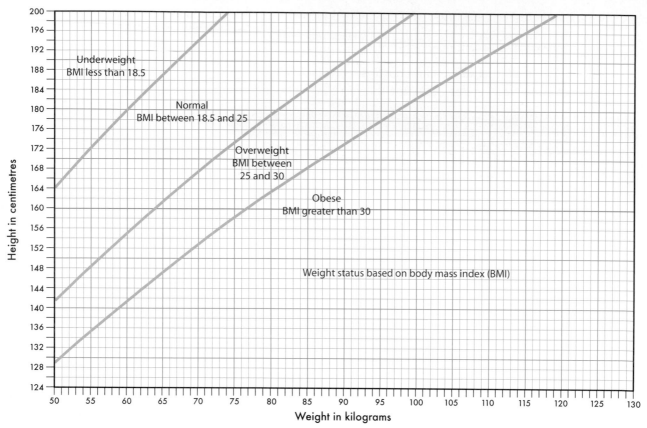

Figure 16: The BMI bands

Height and weight can be tied to BMI bands. A BMI of less than 18.5 is not unhealthy but is regarded as low. Although a BMI of over 25 is regarded as high, this could be due to muscle rather than fat. An athlete may be muscular with very little body fat. A precautionary note is that this BMI scale is not suitable for pregnant women and young children.

Testing for fitness is more specific and important. Although a traditional part of training in sport, it is now a common feature of school and college life and there is plenty of advice in books and health centres and on the internet. Some tests involve groups whilst there are others that you can do yourself.

Testing for fitness

A **heart recovery test** is where the pulse rate is measured before and after strenuous exercise. H, the index of fitness is determined by:

$$H = \frac{P_4 - P_6}{P_4 - P_{10}}$$ where

P_4 is the pulse rate after 4 minutes of rest
P_6 is the rate again after 6 minutes of rest
P_{10} is the pulse rate after 10 minutes of exercise
The closer you are to 1 the healthier you are.

The popular **beep test** needs some equipment and is best done in groups. It involves running repeatedly between two lines set 20 metres apart. The aim is to reach the line before the beep. The time between recorded beeps reduces as you go through the levels. You drop out when you can no longer keep up with the beeps. Keep your score so that you can see by how much you have improved.

2 Science, mathematics and technology

Do people abuse their health?

- Are we too busy to prepare healthy meals?
- At the end of a day, are we too tired to take exercise?
- Are fatty foods, chocolate, etc. more attractive than fruit and vegetables?
- Is smoking that hard to give up?
- Are weekends a great time to party and get drunk?
- Do people enjoy their food too much to diet?
- Diet pills, a drastic diet, and not eating all cause rapid weight loss, but what are the dangers?
- Would you rather play computer games than take exercise?

Tobacco and alcohol are classed as recreational drugs and, unless you are under age, they are legal. Health abuse by using illegal drugs has become a common feature of many towns and cities. Whilst there has been considerable debate (e.g. health benefits for multiple sclerosis sufferers) over cannabis's legal status, it is still illegal, along with class A and B drugs such as heroin or cocaine.

Drugs in sport

The use of drugs in sport has a high profile in the media. Drugs have been introduced to enhance performance. Athletes take enormous risks in taking drugs, all for a few moments of glory. Some 1960s and 1970s athletes from Eastern Europe are now suffering the effects of taking performance-enhancing drugs. Over 4,000 drugs have been banned by the International Olympic Committee.

TASK

1 What is the difference between class A, B and C drugs? What strategies should be put in place to reduce their usage?
2 Is it fair that all athletes tested positively for drugs should be banned and have past performances disqualified?
3 Should a professional sportsman or woman be banned for missing a drugs test?

Table 6: Drugs in sport and their effects

Banned substance	Side effects
Erythropoietin (EPO) is produced naturally by the kidneys and taken to stimulate red blood cells.	Extra dosage can lead to blood clotting and heart attack.
Human growth hormone (HGH) promotes physical development.	Too much when young can cause excessive growth in height, or even excessive finger, tongue and lip growth.
Anabolic steroids resemble testosterone and are used to increase muscle strength. **Nandrolone** is in this group.	In female athletes these have caused increased body hair and a deepening of the voice.
Blood doping boosts the concentration of oxygen-carrying red blood cells in order to improve athletic performance.	There are risks of getting infectious diseases (hepatitis B) or severe reactions if the wrong blood type is used.

Controlling disease

Disease means any alteration of the normal vital processes of people, animals or plants. Successful prevention of illness can take place through encouraging awareness, understanding and concern. Thus health and fitness testing, understanding diet and managing our life style all have a part to play.

Unfortunately diseases can be unexpected and, sometimes, seemingly inevitable. Flu epidemics spread from one country to another; HIV/Aids spreads through unprotected sexual activity. Disease comes from unclean water and contaminated food, and also can be spread from animal species to humans.

In the UK we are relatively fortunate. The National Health Service and private health care cover most of our needs. Through these services, both minor and severe illnesses and injuries can be treated using vaccinations, medicines and operations. Government-run organisations are there to oversee the quality of our food, water and waste disposal. It is all about preventing disease and illness.

TASK

To what extent is it possible to control the spread of endemic (present in a local area) diseases?

Outbreak!

Within the past ten years, Defra (the Department for Environment, Food and Rural Affairs) has had to deal with outbreaks of these diseases in livestock, at a huge economic and emotional cost.

avian influenza, brucellosis, BSE, classical swine fever, equine infectious anaemia, foot and mouth disease, blue tongue disease, rabies, tuberculosis, scrapie

WHAT NEXT?

What other tests can be used to measure health and fitness? Think in terms of stamina, strength, weight, lung capacity, and body muscle and fat distribution.

Visit http://drugs.homeoffice.gov.uk/young-people/strategy to see how the UK government is tackling drug use amongst young people. What are the challenges such an initiative faces?

EXAMINATION PRACTICE

1 Identify a sporting activity that would be appropriate for each of the following.
Use a different sport for each and justify your choices.
a an overweight person
b a teenage wheelchair user
c a pregnant woman
2 Outline *three* different reasons why physical fitness can mean different things to different people.

3 At a time when life expectancy is increasing, more people are attending health and fitness clubs. Discuss the reasons for this. [30 marks]
4 An inquiry into the government's drugs policy concluded that 'if there is to be one single lesson from the experience of the past 30 years, it is that policies based on enforcement are destined to fail'. To what extent do you agree with this statement? Justify your answer. [30 marks]

2.1.8 Pollution and its management

Figure 17

Figure 18

KEY TERMS

Pollution is an event which adversely affects the health of organisms or their environment. **Acid rain** is rain that contains pollutants such as SO_2, and is therefore acidic. It causes damage to trees and buildings. **Bio-magnification** is a process by which chemical pollutants such as pesticides are found in higher concentrations as you go up a food chain. **Aesthetic pollution** is pollution such as sewage waste that is visible on the surface.

The definition of **pollution** is one that includes humans as major contributors, but does not ignore natural events such as emissions of CFC gases and sulphur dioxide during a volcanic eruption, peat bogs releasing methane and radon gas from rocks.

Sources of pollution

Humans pollute the environment in many ways. Power stations, transport and agriculture are major sources of pollution, but industry and households also contribute.

TASK

List ways in which land, marine or air pollution can be hazardous to
• human health
• ecological systems
• buildings.

Source	Pollutant	Effects
Power stations burning fossil fuels: coal, oil and natural gas	Carbon dioxide (CO_2) Sulphur dioxide (SO_2) Nitrogen oxides (NO_x)	Greenhouse gases, **acid rain**, respiratory diseases, chemical erosion of buildings, eye and throat infections.
Motor vehicles	Carbon monoxide (CO) Nitrogen oxides (NO_x), Unburned hydrocarbons	Decreased blood oxygen concentration. As above, plus nitrogen oxide contributes to photochemical smog.
Industry, e.g. metals, textiles, paper	Heat, noise, heavy metals, acids, dioxins, smoke	Pollution of groundwater and rivers, food contamination, smells, impaired visibility.
Residential	Fossil fuel pollutants, sewage, organic and inorganic waste	In some countries disease, e.g. cholera and typhoid; river pollution, air pollution.
Agricultural	Pesticides, organophosphates, fertilisers, methane (livestock, rice paddy)	Pesticides can be stored in animals' fatty tissues and can cause **bio-magnification**. Fertilisers can lead to river eutrophication. Methane is a greenhouse gas.
Marine	Pollution from rivers containing chemicals, sewage, nutrients. Deliberate sewage disposal. War relics, nuclear waste. Oil pollution (tanker accidents).	Chemical leakage, red tides containing algal blooms, marine ecosystems disrupted, heavy metals contaminating fish and, often ignored, **aesthetic pollution.**

Table 7: Sources of pollution and their effects

TASK

Discuss the contributions that noise, oil tanker accidents and air transport make to environmental pollution.

Pollution pathways

Many environmental indicators can be used to identify and measure different levels and types of pollution.

- There may be a loss of biodiversity in rivers and lakes, or they may contain algal blooms.
- The stonework on buildings may be corroded.
- Trees might be stunted and have little foliage.

However, identifying a source of pollution can be difficult. Point sources such as sewage outlets or power station chimneys are easy to identify because the pollutants are coming from a specific point. Non-point sources are the result of common and widespread agricultural, industrial and urban activities in which pollutants may have mixed, been transported and appeared somewhere else. Pollutants follow certain pathways, along which they may be altered, change from liquid to gas or arrive at their destination unaltered.

The burning of fossil fuels in urban and industrial areas produces emissions of carbon dioxide (CO_2), sulphur dioxide (SO_2) and nitrogen oxides (NO_x). Some of the sulphur dioxide and nitrogen oxides will return to the ground in dry form and contribute to pollution in the urban area and to the soils and vegetation in the immediately surrounding region. The remainder will be carried into the atmosphere to be converted into nitric and sulphuric acid to form acid rain. Acid deposition occurs when dry deposition of particles or wet deposition of acid rain increases any natural acidity in the soil, water and vegetation.

Ozone depletion

Ozone depletion and the formation of holes in the ozone layer represent another pollution pathway. Atmospheric ozone (O_3) is a form of oxygen that has two effects: at ground level it is a pollutant, and 10–50 km high in the atmosphere it protects us from ultra-violet (UV) solar radiation. Atmospheric ozone is formed when UV radiation splits an oxygen molecule (O_2) into two oxygen atoms (O + O); an oxygen atom then combines with an O_2 molecule to form ozone (O_3). Without this atmospheric ozone shield we would become overexposed to UV radiation, which can cause radiation blindness and cataracts, and decrease photosynthesis in plants. In the 1990s, scientists working in the Antarctic noticed that the concentration of atmospheric ozone had fallen and a hole in the ozone layer had formed. These holes increase and decrease in size according to the season. The damage is believed to have been caused by the release of chlorofluorocarbons (CFCs) from aerosols and refrigerants, bromine from pesticides, halons from fire extinguishers and various cleaning solvents.

This pathway involves CFC molecules ($CFCl_3$) rising into the atmosphere where, as a result of UV radiation, they divide into $CFCl_2$ and Cl (chlorine atoms). Chlorine is the main pollutant that reacts with ozone, and through complex reactions, contributes to the destruction of ozone. Because of this, the concentration of ozone is reduced and the amount of UV radiation affecting the Earth's surface increases.

Urban air quality

The air quality of our towns and cities can be very poor. Heating and air-conditioning systems, motor vehicles and industries release chemical pollutants; noise levels are often high and, in some cities, the absence of parks means there are few places where peace and quiet can be found. The layout of many cities, with their narrow streets and high-rise buildings, makes the problem worse, as it is difficult for polluted air to escape and be replaced with fresher air.

Los Angeles is an excellent example of a polluted city, and another example of a pollution pathway. It is a large city whose major roads carry about six million cars a day, releasing a mixture of nitrogen oxide (NO), carbon monoxide (CO), unburned petrol vapours and hydrocarbons. Sunlight then converts NO and hydrocarbons into nitrogen dioxide (NO_2). This process releases particles that encourage condensation in the form of clouds and photochemical smog, which is a dense yellow cloud that obscures the city in some summer months in a mixture of chemicals that can cause eye irritation, unpleasant smells and bronchial complaints – and can lead to death. Los Angeles is situated in a huge valley that is surrounded by mountains. Sometimes the atmospheric conditions do not allow the pollution to disperse and the photochemical smog lingers for a long time.

Controlling pollution

The control of pollution is not easy. We can each do our bit, but this might seem insignificant when compared to the scale of regional and global pollution. Pollutants are dispersed by wind and water and do not recognise country boundaries. They follow complex pathways where they might disappear or change and become more potent.

Pollution monitoring and management already take place in many British towns and cities. Public awareness is raised via daily information on carbon monoxide, ozone and nitrogen levels. Direct action such as park-and-ride schemes, congestion charges and pedestrian zones help to reduce traffic congestion and pollution from vehicles. Urban planning sometimes includes the provision and protection of parks, in which trees and bushes filter out some of the noise as well noxious fumes. Local authority grants towards house insulation are another example of how both energy conservation and reduction of pollution can take place.

TASK

Investigate the pollution pathways

- that can cause eutrophication in rivers
- produced by the Chernobyl nuclear reactor accident of April 1986.

Industries are also trying to reduce pollution. Nuclear power, wind farms, hydro-electric power and wave energy have the potential to replace thermal power stations, particularly those using coal (see page 75). Emissions of acid gases can also be reduced by intervening during, before and after combustion of fossil fuels. For example, SO_2 emissions are reduced by 12 per cent when coal is washed and by up to 95 per cent when sulphur is removed from waste gases. Catalytic converters in cars reduce NO_x by 75 per cent.

TASK

To what extent would each of these help reduce pollution?

1 use of catalytic converters
2 cavity wall and roof insulation
3 an annual vehicle inspection
4 organic farming
5 hydrogen-fuelled cars
6 high-speed cross-channel rail links
7 improved suburban rail services
8 increasing fuel taxes
9 biofuels
10 public awareness and concern

Controlling or managing pollution at a national or international level is a complex issue. Although the Kyoto Treaty (see page 71) provided targets for reducing greenhouse gas emissions, many countries will not achieve a 5.2 per cent reduction by 2012. Some countries such as Russia fell below this target by 1990, but this was due to industrial decline, not reducing emissions. Other countries can expand their existing areas of forest and offset their commitment to the Kyoto targets. The Montreal Protocol, which came into force in January 1989, with the help of subsequent agreements, has been successful in replacing ozone-destroying chemicals with substitutes; atmospheric ozone is slowly recovering.

TASK

1 Should all nations be compelled by international law to enforce controls on pollution?
2 How could this be achieved?

EXAMINATION PRACTICE

1 Distinguish between ozone depletion and global warming.
2 Outline *three* sources of pollution in cities and describe their effects.
3 Describe how agricultural activity can lead to river pollution.
4 Using examples outline the important strategies which aim to reduce air pollution in cities. To what extent have they been successful? [30 marks]
5 Explain why at international, national and local scales it is difficult to control pollution. Use examples to illustrate your answer. [30 marks]

2 Science, mathematics and technology

2.1.9 Conservation and environmental management

Much of this topic block has been concerned with conservation. The future of the Earth's environment probably depends on how global warming is managed, energy conserved and pollution controlled. The current and future health of humans relies upon the management of population, a healthy diet and medical advances. Should conservation now be extended to the outermost reaches of our atmosphere as it becomes littered with electronic gadgetry?

> ❝ *Conservation is a state of harmony between men and land.* ❞
>
> Aldo Leopold 1887–1962

Figure 19: Ecotourism

Figure 20: Threatened species

Figure 21: Wind farm

Each of these images is linked to conservation. Wind farms are seen as a means of conserving fossil fuels and cleaning the atmosphere, yet they pose a threat to birds and the aesthetics of our landscape. They are also noisy. As human activity threatens habitats through direct invasion or indirectly via climatic change, many species are threatened with extinction. Ecotourism offers a mechanism for viewing, learning about and engaging with natural environments.

What is conservation?

In 1983 the World Commission on Environment and Development was set up to consider the relationship between the environment and **development**.

Conservation refers to the protection and possible enhancement of natural environments and landscapes developed by humans for current and future use.

KEY TERMS

Sustainable development is development that meets the needs of the present, without compromising the ability of future generations to meet their own needs.

TASK

1 Make a list of natural and human-made items, places and environments that you feel are in need of conservation. Try to reach at least 50.
2 Place your conservation items into any of these groups: urban, landscape, ecological, historical, architectural, oceanic, atmosphere and cultural. Explain why some occur in more than one group

Why conserve environments?

Environmental conservation is not new but has become increasingly necessary. Natural environments and habitats untouched by human activity are now extremely rare, thus the need for maintenance and restoration. Reasons for conservation frequently include the following.

- Certain areas are of high intrinsic value: geological importance; landscape beauty; unique ecology; history, architecture.
- Population pressure refers to the growth of towns and cities; high volumes of traffic, pollution, long- and short-term visits.
- Environmental fragility: the extent to which an environment is placed under threat, e.g. footpath erosion, noise and litter pollution, loss of habitats and threatened species.
- Economic pressures such as reservoirs, quarries, manufacturing industry, tourism, theme parks.
- Accidents, sometimes on a large scale such as oil tanker spillage, nuclear reactor explosion, fires.

Conservation strategies

The protection of areas and sites in the UK occurs at a number of levels. It is not uncommon for towns and villages to have their own 'millenium' greens or conservation sites. Run by volunteers and sometimes funded by the lottery, relatively small sites of historical and/or ecological importance have been restored and are maintained as a local amenity. At a national scale, conservation of environments and species involves a wide range of organisations. Here are some of them.

- National Parks. In 2007 there were 15 National Parks in the UK, with the purpose of conserving and enhancing landscapes whilst promoting public enjoyment of them.
- Areas of Outstanding Natural Beauty (AONBs) conserve natural beauty, which includes wildlife, landscapes and features of cultural importance.
- Sites of Special Scientific Interest (SSSIs) protect some of the best examples of the UK's ecology, geology and landforms. Many of these sites are privately owned; others are managed by public bodies.
- Ramsar sites include wetlands of international importance such as the Norfolk Broads.
- World Heritage Sites are recognised as being of global importance. Dorset's Jurassic Coastline is a site of outstanding beauty and unique geological importance that now ranks alongside the Galapagos Islands and Australia's Great Barrier Reef.

National Parks

The UK's National Parks are only a small part of a global total of 6,555 protected areas that cover 1 million km² (12 per cent of the Earth's surface). Our National Parks are part of a European network

---

TASK

Select an area in the locality of your school or college that is either in need of environmental conservation or is currently being conserved. Assess the pressures that human activity have placed upon it and describe the strategies that could be or are used to enable its conservation.

spread across 37 countries. In the UK each Park is administered by its own National Park Authority with two major objectives that are firmly embedded in sustainable development

- to conserve and enhance the natural beauty, wildlife and cultural heritage
- to promote opportunities for the understanding and enjoyment of the special qualities of each National Park.

These objectives can conflict with each other and, should this occur, conservation takes priority. An added complication is that most of the land within these parks is owned by farmers, the Forestry Commission, the Ministry of Defence or private households.

TASK

The case study contains information about the Lake District National Park. Research and construct a similar set of data on two different UK National Parks. The New Forest and Pembrokeshire Coast have some interesting contrasts with the Lake District.

CASE STUDY: The Lake District National Park

Lake District National Park

General details	Fragile natural environments	Planning and use
England's largest park at 2,292 km².	Diverse woodlands with native animals and plants.	Walking/cycling on 3,500 km of public rights of way. Footpath repair and management.
Fourteen lakes and six mountains over 900 metres.	Varied habitats including: freshwater, woodland, limestone pavements, upland heath, screes and arctic–alpine communities, coastal heath and dunes.	Visitor centre and internet advice on walks.
Over 12 million visitors per year of which 89% come by motor vehicle.		Visitor centre advice on birds, wildlife, access and places to visit (including Beatrix Potter's house).
6,000 archaeological sites.		Specified conservation areas.
Twenty-one conservation areas.		Active woodland preservation.
Travel via the M6.	**Fragile human environments**	Advice on car parks and use of public transport.
Finance 2008–09: Expenditure £9,754,000 Income £9,657,000 Probable deficit £97,000	Many conservation sites are in towns and villages such as Ambleside, Grasmere and Ravenglass.	Advertising and enforcement of the Country Code.

The Lake District National Park

CASE STUDY: The National Trust

Unlike National Parks, the National Trust is a charity and completely independent of the government. It raises its funds via its 3.5 million membership and its 12 million paying visitors. Apart from protecting historic houses and monuments it looks after forests, coastlines, farmland and nature reserves. By the 1990s the National Trust had acquired around 20,000 hectares of land and 350 stately homes. The National Trust's Neptune Coastline Campaign involves raising capital to protect and manage our coastline.

TASK

To what extent is conservation a central objective in these case studies of National Parks and the National Trust?

Bedruthan Steps or Carnewas: Cornwall, a National Trust Site

General details	Fragile natural environment	Planning and use
North Cornwall coastline between Newquay and Padstow.	Site of Special Scientific Interest (SSSI) with distinctive fauna, flora and geology.	The Trust has rebuilt the cliff staircase down to the beach and restored footpaths.
Ample car park space.	Coastal beauty and rugged cliff coastline.	A leaflet provides details on circular walks and information on local history, geology and wildlife.
A shop and information centre.	Fragile cliffs that have suffered from landslips and rock falls caused by natural processes and footpath erosion.	
Refreshments.		
Access via road, footpath and local services.		

Conservation of species

A vital feature of any National Park or other conservation area is the preservation of its fauna and flora. Threatened extinction is such a problem that the International Union for the Conservation of Nature and Natural Resources (IUCN) publishes a list of endangered species called the *IUCN Red List of Threatened Species*™. For 2007 it published the following data. (Be aware that for reptiles, fishes, insects, molluscs and plants only a very small proportion of the species in each taxonomic group has been assessed, so the figures are not comparable to those for mammals, birds and amphibians, which have been comprehensively assessed.)

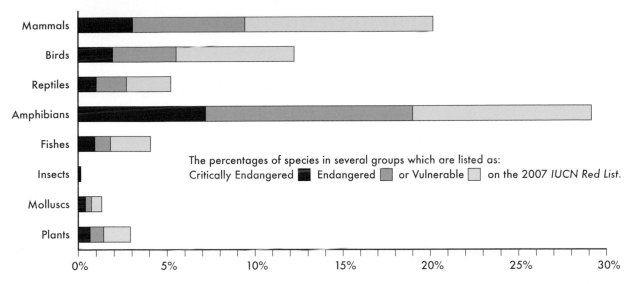

Figure 22: The *IUCN Red List of Threatened Species*™

Strategies to conserve and preserve threatened species often involve organisations such as the Royal Society for Protection of Birds (RSPB) along with places that have a specific responsibility for wild and domesticated animals.

- Zoos are an important example of species preservation in which animals are protected and breeding programmes enable the continuation of the species. Their other responsibilities include education, research and where possible the reintroduction of species into their natural habitats.
- Safari parks have similar responsibilities to zoos but retain their wildlife in more natural surroundings. On a relatively small scale, places such as Longleat and the West Midlands Safari Parks have fewer species than zoos, and animals are viewed in enclosures.
- On a much grander scale, the Serengeti National Park in Tanzania covers an area of 15,000 km². The park offers protection to wildebeest, game, and over 500 species of birds in their natural habitats.

WHAT NEXT?

1 Visit www.nationalparks.gov.uk and put together your own case study on the conservation work of a National Park.
2 Select *one* major group of endangered animals e.g. whales, primates, tigers etc. Investigate why they are threatened and what is being done to enable their conservation. www.wwf.org.uk is a good place to start.
3 Should we be concerned about the numbers of endangered species shown on the *IUCN Red List of Threatened Species*™ or regard it all as part of evolution? www.iucnredlist.org

EXAMINATION PRACTICE

1 Distinguish between conservation and preservation.
2 Outline how sustainable development and successful conservation are linked.
3 Outline *three* different ways in which human activity can damage natural environments.
4 Describe the strategies that have been used in *one* named environmental conservation scheme you have visited and/or studied. To what extent have these strategies been successful? [30 marks]
5 What are the arguments for and against keeping animals in zoos and safari parks? [30 marks]

2 Science, mathematics and technology

2.2 Understanding scientific methods, principles, criteria and their applications

OVERVIEW

In this block of work we will look at

- induction and classification
- hypothesis testing, experimental and investigative design, deduction, theory and law
- modelling, forecasting and reliability
- the role of timescale
- evaluation and limitations of scientific methods.

2.2.1 Investigating science

The familiar subjects of physics, chemistry and biology cover a wide range of scientific areas. Each area contains theories and knowledge of the physical world, obtained and tested using appropriate methods. Scientific method is a tool that scientists use to answer questions such as those listed below.

> **❝** *Science involves more than the gaining of knowledge. It is the systematic and organised inquiry into the natural world and its phenomena. Science is about gaining a deeper and often useful understanding of the world.* **❞**

Multicultural History of Science
Vanderbilt University

Figure 1: Investigating science: physics, chemistry and biology

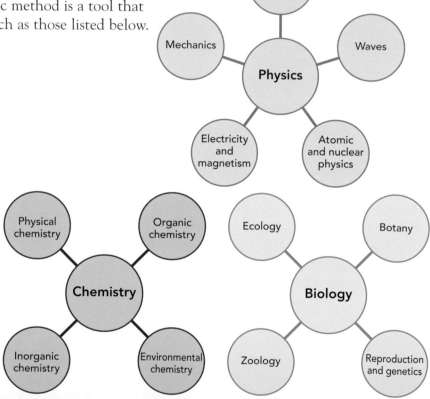

QUESTIONS

1 What is the contribution of yeast in the baking of bread or the brewing of beer?
2 What effect does the brightness of light have on the growth rate of a plant?
3 What effect does the mass of a motor vehicle have upon its stopping distance?
4 Do increases in temperature speed up the rate of chemical reactions?
5 Is global warming contributing to an increase in the number and intensity of freak weather events?
6 Does the 'red shift' provide evidence that the universe is expanding and support the Big Bang theory?

Scientists investigate such questions and then write up their findings in scientific papers. In some ways scientific papers are like a detective's report, saying

- here's what we think
- here's what we found
- how would you interpret what we found?
- what do others feel about our findings?

A scientific investigation starts with a broad area of interest that is narrowed down to a single question or hypothesis but later broadens once the results enable generalisations to be made.

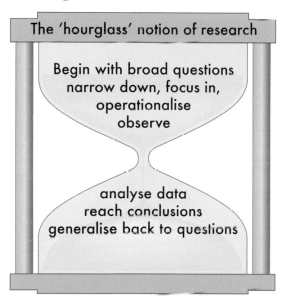

Figure 2· The 'hourglass' notion of research

TASK

1 Is it true that you will never need to show that water (H$_2$O) is made up of one oxygen (O) and two hydrogen (H) atoms because many scientists before you have confirmed the fact? Explain why.
2 A feature of science is that a **theory** or **hypothesis** must be falsifiable: there must be some experiment that could prove the theory untrue. Is this true of Einstein's theory of relativity? Explain why.
3 Why is the statement 'the moon is populated by little green men who can read our minds, hide whenever anyone from Earth looks for them and flee into space whenever a spaceship comes near' not scientific? Is the theory that 'there are no little green men on the moon' more scientific? Explain why.

KEY TERMS

A theory is an explanation of a set of related observations or events based upon proven hypotheses and checked several times through experimentation and observation by researchers.

An hypothesis is a question that has been reworded into a form that can be tested by **experiment**, or an educated guess based on observations that can be proved or disproved by experiment.

An experiment is an examination of conditions or a set of observations performed to solve a problem, answer a question or test a hypothesis.

KEY TERMS

Induction is the process of reasoning from particular instances to general principles.

Research is a process of observing phenomena to learn new facts or test the application of theories and hypotheses to known facts.

A **law** is a statement of fact to explain, in concise terms, an action or a set of actions. It is generally accepted to be true.

2.2.2 Induction and classification

Like nearly all scientific investigations, **inductive reasoning** or **research** begins with a general idea that leads to the collection of data. This research may yield a vast amount of data which needs to be collated (sorted out), classified and presented, perhaps in the form of tables and graphs. It is then possible to observe patterns from which a theory may be developed. Further research may add to the initial investigation and, should this lend sufficient support to it or verify it, the theory can become **law**.

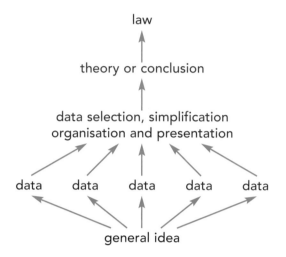

Figure 3

Did Charles Darwin intentionally or otherwise adopt an inductive approach to his research?

'When on board H.M.S. Beagle as naturalist, I was much struck with certain facts in the distribution of the inhabitants of South America, and in the geological relations of the present to the past inhabitants of that continent.' (Charles Darwin)

- Darwin had been impressed by the work of geologists such as James Hutton and was influenced by Aristotle who, like other ancient Greek philosophers, used an inductive approach.
- During his five-year voyage on the *Beagle*, Darwin read Charles Lyell's *Principles of Geology*, which showed that fossils were animals that lived millions of years ago.
- On his visit to the Galapagos Islands, Darwin observed and recorded species that, although similar to those on the distant mainland, had evolved in a different way.
- Back in England, Darwin worked on his observations and proposed a theory of evolution occurring by the process of natural selection.
- After Darwin learnt that the naturalist Alfred Russel Wallace had come to the same conclusions, they made a joint declaration in 1858.

TASK

Research an area of science that has been mentioned earlier in this book. Is there evidence of an inductive approach being used for this research?

2 Science, mathematics and technology

Classification

By putting items, people and even the activities we engage upon into groups, we are involved in classification. In science, classification is an important stage of the inductive method. When observations are made it is helpful to order them by dividing them into groups. For a classification system to be successful it should be simple, easy to remember and easy to use. A good classification system should have the following features:

- there is maximum similarity between members of a group, e.g. all mammals have mammary glands
- there is maximum difference between groups, e.g. vertebrates and invertebrates
- members of groups should fit into one group only, e.g. a mammal is not a bird
- members of groups should be easily recognised
- there should be few groups with only one member.

One of the best known classification systems was devised by the Swedish scientist Carl Linnaeus, whose system for biology forms the basis of much that is used today. The original form of his classification system has been revised to improve consistency with, for instance, Darwin's principles of common descent. Biological classification is hierarchical because it works from the general to the specific. The simplified classification in Figure 4 shows the hierarchy that leads to humans.

Other classification systems commonly used in science include

- The Periodic Table used in chemistry which was originally published by Dimitri Mendeléev in 1869. In this table elements are arranged in order of their atomic number.
- Geological time is divided into eras and periods. For example, the Jurassic period is located within the Mesozoic era. Eras broadly reflect domination by a particular group of animals: the Caenozoic by mammals; the Mesozoic by reptiles and the Palaeozoic by fishes.
- Ecologists divide the Earth into biomes (major ecological communities) such as Tropical Rainforest, Savanna and Tundra. Each biome is identified by distinctive vegetation that has adapted to its climate and soils.

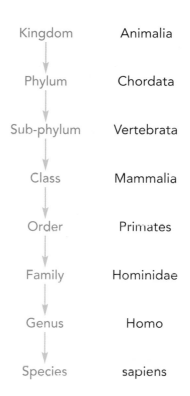

Kingdom	Animalia
Phylum	Chordata
Sub-phylum	Vertebrata
Class	Mammalia
Order	Primates
Family	Hominidae
Genus	Homo
Species	sapiens

Figure 4: Biological classification for humans

TASK

Select *two* different classification systems used in science.
a Describe the main features of each system.
b Does each system satisfy the five conditions that contribute to a good classification system?

2.2.3 Hypothesis testing, deduction and investigative design

A deductive approach to an investigation is something you may have encountered in doing GCSE projects for science or geography. Students are advised to structure their investigations to test a hypothesis or answer a question. You may have received instructions to follow correct scientific methodology.

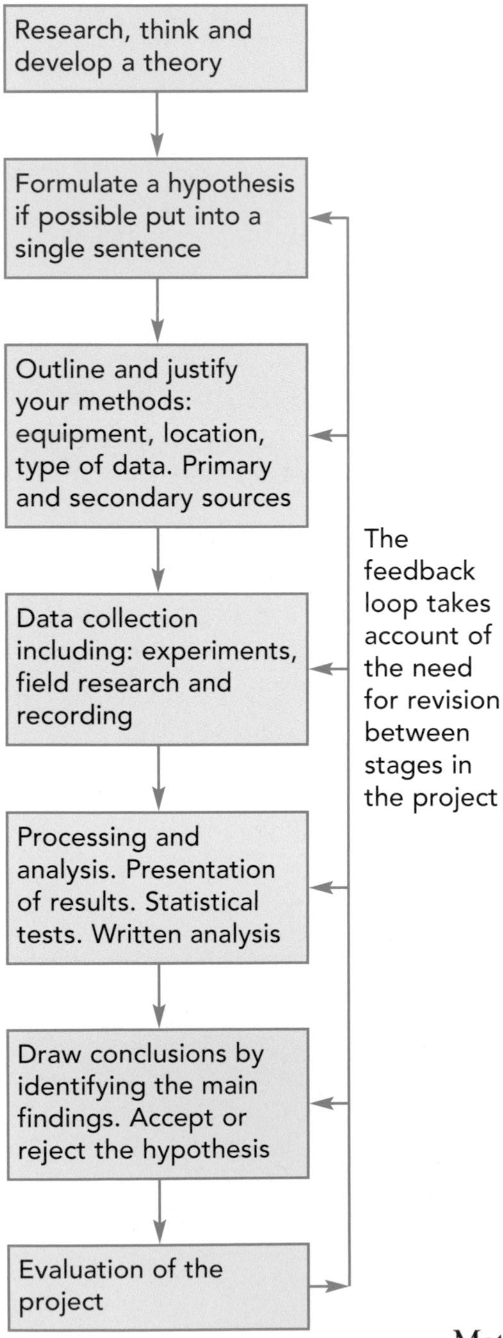

Designing an investigation

A deductive method is different from induction. Here you begin at a very general level and, through a number of stages, become specific. First you think up a theory, which you narrow to a hypothesis that can be tested. The next stage is to test the hypothesis through experiments, observations and measurement and ultimately confirm or otherwise your original theory. A hypothesis-testing model could take this form.

You may begin with a general idea or theory that the rate at which plants grow varies according to the type of fertiliser used. The number of people demanding organically produced food is increasing so you decide to investigate organic fertilisers versus chemical fertilisers.

As it is the effect of the fertiliser you are investigating, there is no need to choose more than one type of plant. You decide to investigate tomato plants because you can relate the three measurable qualities, plant height, foliage and fruit, to each fertiliser. These decisions enable you to set out the questions you will be asking at the end.

1 Which group of plants grew the fastest? Those that had the chemical fertiliser, organic fertiliser, or no fertiliser?
2 Which group of plants produced most tomatoes?
3 Which group of plants grew tallest?
4 Which is the most suitable fertiliser for growing tomatoes?
5 How did the fertilisers affect the soil?
6 Finally, can the best fertiliser be used with other food-producing crops?

This preliminary work enables the construction of a hypothesis

> **although the chemical fertiliser will be more beneficial to tomato plants than the organic fertiliser, it will be more damaging to the soil**

Methods

The plants will be grown in separate pots in the controlled environment of a greenhouse. Pots A–C will be the control plants with no fertiliser. Pots D, E and F will contain the same organic

---

Research, think and develop a theory

↓

Formulate a hypothesis if possible put into a single sentence

↓

Outline and justify your methods: equipment, location, type of data. Primary and secondary sources

↓

Data collection including: experiments, field research and recording

↓

Processing and analysis. Presentation of results. Statistical tests. Written analysis

↓

Draw conclusions by identifying the main findings. Accept or reject the hypothesis

↓

Evaluation of the project

The feedback loop takes account of the need for revision between stages in the project

Figure 5: Hypothesis-testing model

2 Science, mathematics and technology

fertiliser and pots G, H and I the same chemical fertiliser. Calculating the mean for each group of plants overcomes the problem of unusual results. The environmental conditions for all plants will be the same and they will receive the same volume of fertiliser and watering. The plants will be grown from seeds. The project will be run for a period of three months.

Data collection
Measurements of plant height will be taken at one-week intervals; foliage, fruit size and fruit quantity at the end of the project. The date at which the first flowers form will be recorded with the plant height data. *Notice that here we are concerned with the collection of numerical data.* Appropriate data sheets will be used for each plant and the results recorded on an Excel spreadsheet. Soil chemistry (pH and nitrate content) and texture will be observed at the beginning and end of the experiment.

Results and analysis
Plant height will be shown on line graphs, fruit size on bar graphs, and scaled leaf diagrams will show the size of leaves. The number and density of leaves will also be noted. The analysis will consist of a description of the results, emphasising the influence of each fertiliser. Soil data will be shown in tables and comparisons drawn between the soils at the beginning and end of the experiment.

Conclusion
This will compare the control plants with the other groups, giving some indication of whether the original hypothesis should be accepted or rejected.

Evaluation
The evaluation will assess the strengths and weaknesses in the research process and not do the job of the conclusion. A good evaluation will pinpoint the stages where things went well or errors were made. Whilst it is impractical to repeat the whole of the investigation, the feedback loop in the model does suggest that adjustments can be made at all stages.

Do	Don't
Read as many references as you can, using texts, electronic sources, magazines, etc.	Rush into the experiment.
Carry out an exploratory experiment before you start.	Choose a topic that is too broad or general.
Choose a problem that can be solved experimentally.	Assume you are going to prove the hypothesis right or wrong: your results may agree or disagree with the hypothesis.
Write down your hypothesis before beginning the experiment.	Change your hypothesis to suit your findings.
Only have one independent variable, i.e. the factor that can be varied or manipulated in an experiment (e.g. time, temperature, ...)	Leave out results that do not agree with your hypothesis.
If practical, repeat the experiment to check your findings.	Confuse conclusions with evaluations.
Give reasons for any differences between the hypothesis and the results.	
Make certain the evaluation mentions strengths and weaknesses and points out how improvements can be made.	

TASK
Plan an experiment using the hypothesis-testing model. To what extent does this approach form a practical route through an investigation?

2.2.4 Modelling, forecasting and reliability

Figure 6

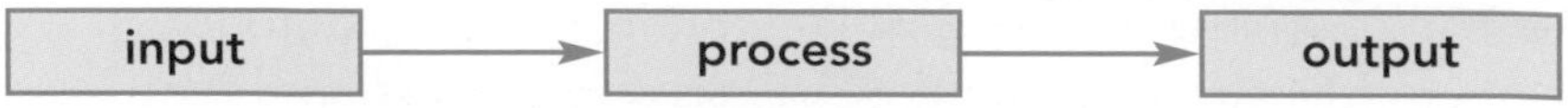

| input | → | process | → | output |

Nearly everything we do in science requires the components of the model above. You need to understand why and use each component correctly. You would not attempt a chemistry experiment without considering the equipment and chemicals needed.

A model can be viewed as a simple version of reality. A scientific model is supported by experiment and may be accurate under certain conditions. For example, Newton's laws of motion are accurate for most everyday applications, but Einstein's theory of relativity is needed when you consider particles that are moving at or close to the speed of light.

A hypothesis-testing model provided a framework for the investigation into the effects of fertilisers on the growth of tomato plants, taking the study through a sequence of research stages. Such frameworks can be modified to suit the needs of the researcher. Once the research has a successful model or framework, it can be used in different situations.

However, modelling in science does not necessarily mean a written statement or diagrammatic plan. Models could be physical constructions, maps or mathematical equations.

Modelling the spread of disease

Diffusion refers to how things spread, scatter or diverge. Diseases will spread across short distances as a result of direct human contact and over global distances when carried by winds, water or migrating animals. Diffusion models try to show different ways in which an infection can spread from a central point. Understanding how contagious diseases such as SARS (severe acute respiratory syndrome) or tuberculosis spread through human networks can be illustrated through a model or map.

In this example, contact tracing (see Figure 7) is used to model or map the spread of the infection so that it can be controlled.

Figure 7: Model of the spread of an infection
Black dots are people with a clinical disease who are potentially infectious.
Pink dots are people with incubating (or dormant) infection who are *not* infectious.
Green dots represent people who have been exposed to the disease, have no infection and are *not* infectious.

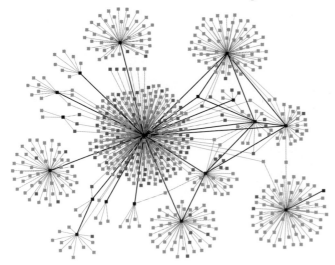

Many people are concerned about the likelihood of a new global flu pandemic. Much of the concern about avian flu is related to its ability to spread, as it recently did from SE Asia into Europe. Tracking the path of avian flu requires the gathering of data on when the disease arrives at a location. The data can be processed by computers and displayed as a detailed layered map via GIS (geographical information systems) to plot how the outbreak spreads. Such maps enable forecasts to be made about the probable spread of a disease.

Using models in design

Have you ever thought about the features that need to be considered in the design of the driver's seat in a car?

- There must be good visibility of the road and instruments.
- Without stretching, all controls should be within reach.
- The body should be supported and muscular effort minimised.
- The shape of the seat should provide good body distribution over the seat.
- Shocks and vibrations should be minimised.
- The seat should be fully adjustable, e.g. seat and back angle, backward and forward adjustment, headrest adjustment, etc.

Figure 8: An **ergonomic** model

A car manufacturer might use a flexible scale model of a person (called an ergonome) to refine the design.

TASK

To what extent do you feel it is possible to accurately forecast the arrival of a contagious disease by diffusion modelling? Consider other examples.

TASK

Use the idea of an ergonome to design a settee, stepladders, or a kitchen.

Do you consider this to be a good example of experimental design?

KEY TERMS

Ergonomics is about the fit between people, the things they do and the objects they use.

In this context it is only possible to offer a brief summary of the use of models in science. The world is complex and to understand its processes and events scientists need to simplify and resort to modelling. The effects of greenhouse gases and global warming (page 69) have been modelled in order to forecast future weather events and climate change. The ecology of an oak woodland is sufficiently complex to warrant the use of simplified food webs and nutrient cycles (page 73).

2.2.5 The role of the timescale

Time is an integral feature of scientific theory and research; scientific investigations take time and often work to deadlines, and the different phases of an investigation have different timescales and focuses: the biologist testing the rate of growth of plants, the geologist concerned with the past and the physicist understanding general relativity. Topic 2.1.4 referred to the Cassini venture to Saturn (see page 79) and topic 2.2.3 to an experiment on plant growth (see page 108): time is an important element in both.

Investigating space

Topic 2.1.4 made reference to the costs and broad objectives of the Cassini venture to Saturn. In 1997 Cassini set off on a 3.5 billion km (2.2 billion mile) journey to Saturn; it took seven years. Its mission objectives were as follows.

- 26 April and 24 June 1998: Venus flybys
- 18 August 1999 at 1,171 km (727 miles): Earth flyby
- 30 December 2000 at 10 million km (6 million miles): Jupiter flyby
- Saturn arrival date: 30 June 2004 PDT (1 July 2004 UTC) (PDT = Pacific Daylight Time, UTC = Co-ordinated Universal Time = Greenwich Mean Time)
- Primary mission: four years
- Huygens probe Titan release date: 24 December 2004
- Huygens probe Titan descent date: 14 January 2005; Huygens' entry speed into Titan's atmosphere: about 20,000 kph (12,400 mph)

Time as a factor was important in this mission. The visits to the orbits of Venus and Jupiter and, ultimately, reaching Saturn required accurate calculations of planetary orbits and the velocities of both spacecraft and planets. These factors contributed to the accurate timing of the journey. Time is also a factor in sending the pictures – they take 87 minutes to reach the Earth.

'Two hours twenty-seven minutes after entering Titan's atmosphere, the probe landed near the moon's equator. Huygens survived the impact, and was able to communicate with the spacecraft for a few minutes after landing on the frozen surface of Titan. Huygens is now the furthest human-made object ever to land on a celestial body.'

NASA

Organic versus inorganic fertilisers

The experiment on which type of fertiliser is more beneficial to the growth of tomato plants required detailed preparation and patient recording of data over the growth period of the plants. For the experiment to be a success, all plants had the same time in which to grow. The collection of valid data at the end of the experiment required the plants to have matured sufficiently to bear fruit. Time is therefore an important element in the experimentation process and for the plants to grow.

TASK

1 Analyse these instructions and note where time becomes an important factor.

Plotting star trails as the Earth revolves

* Wait for a clear moonless night and avoid a place with too much light interference.
* You might want to include some foreground objects, such as trees or hills.
* Point a camera towards the Pole Star; record the time.
* Focus for infinity, set the exposure and open the diaphragm to full aperture for two hours.
* Close the shutter for two minutes without moving the camera, then open the shutter again for one minute and finally close it. Record the time.
* The developed film shows star trails as concentric arcs with the centre at the North Pole.

Figure 9: Star trails

2 Discuss the apparent paths of the Moon and the Sun across the sky.
3 Each of the following is the subject of an investigation you may have experienced as part of your GCSE Science course. Discuss the role of time in each investigation.

* Dark matt surfaces emit more radiation than light shiny surfaces.
* Test rods of different composition as conductors of heat.
* Test the products that are given off when hydrocarbons are burnt.
* How does the boiling point of oil compare with that of water?
* Measure the rates at which water infiltrates soil and moves down a slope.
* The effects of excessive alcohol consumption on health.

A scientist at work 'is completely free to adopt any course that his [or her] ingenuity is capable of suggesting. In short, science is what scientists do, and there are as many scientific methods as there are individual scientists'

Percy Bridgman

2.2.6 Evaluation and limitations of scientific methods

Evaluating an investigation

In an evaluation the researcher should assess the strengths and weaknesses of his/her work. It is as important to identify what went well and explain why, as it is to point out errors, misinterpretations or even poor planning. Such evaluations identify elements of study that should be revisited and how subsequent research can be improved. A full evaluation of a research project may combine elements of scientific methodology with more subjective factors such as motivation, appropriateness and thoroughness.

Figure 10 shows four sets of statements that could be used to evaluate the strengths and weaknesses of a science project. Notice that the lists contain assessment criteria as well as broad evaluations. The extent to which they would be used will depend on the topic and the researcher's choice of techniques.

Creative ability and originality
- Did the student research and use an accepted theory in order to develop the question or hypothesis?
- Was a question asked or a hypothesis stated?
- Was the question/hypothesis original?
- Is the approach to the work creative? Was the creativity needed for the study within the student's ability?

Scientific thought
- Is the scope of the study within the student's ability?
- Was the study well planned and did it show initiative and effective planning?
- Were goals and objectives well designed?
- Were literature and internet resources used/reviewed?
- Was a logical hypothesis developed?
- Do the data collected relate to the hypothesis?

Data collection and analysis
- Were all relevant data collected?
- Were controls identified?
- Were the dependent and independent variables identified?
- Did the student anticipate any problems encountered?
- Were the data collected in quantitative units?
- Was the experiment conducted more than once?
- Was the study stopped at a suitable point?
- Were the data fully analysed?

Skill
- Were the experiments designed with care and anticipation?
- Were data measurements precise and presented in a clear and relevant form?
- Was the study logically and manageably designed?
- Were problems overcome rather than avoided?
- Were a detailed set of recordings and notes kept by the student?
- Was the study the student's own work?

Figure 10

Evaluating scientific methods

What is the value of induction, deduction, classification and models to scientific investigations? A scientist *'is completely free to adopt any course that his or her ingenuity is capable of suggesting.'*

The framework offered by the hypothesis-testing model encourages the researcher to gather relevant data from which a level of agreement with the original theory and hypothesis is achieved. The great advantage of the scientific method is that it is not biased and a given researcher does not have to be believed; the experiment can be redone to determine whether the results are true or false.

Some people have questioned the place of induction in scientific research. By its very nature it is open-ended and exploratory, especially at the beginning. The physical sciences and the social sciences generally combine inductive and deductive approaches in their research.

There are some arguments that seem to point away from the apparent restrictions of the scientific method.

- The history of science is littered with stories of a flash of inspiration.
- How does science proceed to develop entirely new knowledge?
- Scientists not only test hypotheses in order to test theories, they explore the world.
- 'Trial and error' is an apt description of a lot of scientific work.
- The first nuclear explosion came as a surprise and accelerated thinking.
- Did the first person to see microorganisms in a pond have a theory saying that they should be there?

> **TASK**
>
> Refer back to topics 2.2.2 and 2.2.3. Consider the place of inductive and deductive methods in investigating: space exploration, the ecology of a woodland and a chemistry or physics laboratory experiment.

> **TASK**
>
> Discuss the relative roles of induction, deduction, modelling and the wonder of discovery in scientific research.

WHAT NEXT?

1 Find out more about classification by searching for
   - The Animal Diversity Web at the University of Michigan
   - Geological timescale sites
   - Web Elements: Periodic Table.

2 There had been theories of evolution before Darwin. Find out why his scientific method made the breakthrough for this way of explaining life on earth. Wikipedia is a good place to start.

EXAMINATION PRACTICE

1 Distinguish between inductive and deductive reasoning.
2 Outline *three* features of a good classification system.
3 Using an example for each, outline *three* ways in which time is an important element in scientific investigations.
4 Give *three* reasons why models are used in scientific investigations
5 Describe *one* classification system with which you are familiar and explain how this classification has

helped scientific understanding.
What problems might a scientist encounter in developing a classification system? [30 marks]
6 Using one example, explain and assess the role of experimental design in *either* the conduct of a scientific experiment *or* manufacturing an item for use by people. [30 marks]
7 A scientist at work 'is completely free to adopt any course that his or her ingenuity is capable of suggesting'. To what extent do you believe this to be true? Justify your answer. [30 marks]

2.3 Mathematical reasoning and its application

OVERVIEW

In this block of work we will look at

- the use and application of mathematics in everyday life
- numbers and algebra, including number patterns, special numbers and the use of formulae

- shape, space and measurement, including area, volume and directions
- manipulating numbers and symbols
- handling data and statistics, including data representation, charts, sampling, probability and the use of data to support or refute arguments
- informal logic puzzles.

QUESTIONS

1 If you were painting a wall, would you know how to work out how much paint you need?
2 What formulae would you use to convert litres to gallons, pounds to Euros, kilometres to miles?
3 How are surveys into the popularity of political parties carried out?
4 How do supermarkets assess the popularity of their products?
5 How might a biologist assess the biodiversity of an area of woodland?

2.3.1 The use and application of mathematics in everyday life

Maths is all around us: it's everywhere we go! Have you ever considered what might happen to a person in an average day?

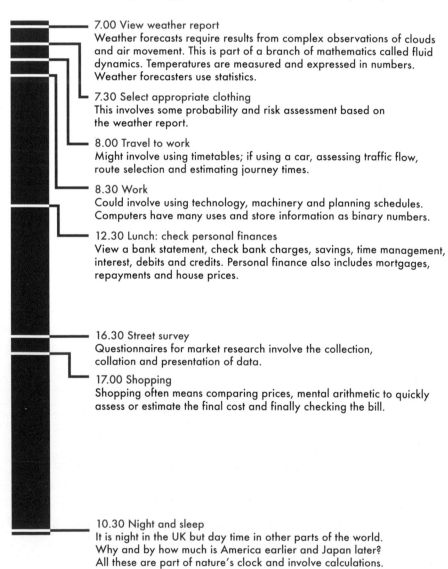

7.00 View weather report
Weather forecasts require results from complex observations of clouds and air movement. This is part of a branch of mathematics called fluid dynamics. Temperatures are measured and expressed in numbers. Weather forecasters use statistics.

7.30 Select appropriate clothing
This involves some probability and risk assessment based on the weather report.

8.00 Travel to work
Might involve using timetables; if using a car, assessing traffic flow, route selection and estimating journey times.

8.30 Work
Could involve using technology, machinery and planning schedules. Computers have many uses and store information as binary numbers.

12.30 Lunch: check personal finances
View a bank statement, check bank charges, savings, time management, interest, debits and credits. Personal finance also includes mortgages, repayments and house prices.

16.30 Street survey
Questionnaires for market research involve the collection, collation and presentation of data.

17.00 Shopping
Shopping often means comparing prices, mental arithmetic to quickly assess or estimate the final cost and finally checking the bill.

10.30 Night and sleep
It is night in the UK but day time in other parts of the world. Why and by how much is America earlier and Japan later? All these are part of nature's clock and involve calculations.

Figure 1

TASK

1 How are mathematical skills used in these situations?

a A footballer passing the ball precisely
b Baking a cake or cooking a meal
c A walker planning his/her route
d Reading and understanding an electricity bill
e Refurbishing a kitchen
f Planning a rail journey
g Playing a game of chess.

2 When doing calculations, at what stage do you use a calculator? Why?
3 List the ways in which you would find mathematics in modern languages, biology and physical education.
4 List six mathematical skills you might use in your daily travel between school/college and home.

For most people mathematics has become part of the daily routine. We use percentages, read timetables, pay bills, receive interest, earn salaries, pay tax and measure distances, areas and weights, etc. Counting the daily activities that involve number skills would produce a very big number! In reality it is not as daunting as it sounds. Most applications of mathematics involve straightforward calculations such as percentages, addition, subtraction, multiplication and division. The equations and formulae that some people find off-putting about maths are actually just a way of making complex calculations simpler.

The teaching of mathematics is partly concerned with relating mathematical skills to *real-life* situations, for example, how we might use mathematics in performing a particular task or in play or sport.

2.3.2 Numbers and algebra

Numbers are labels or symbols representing a quantity. We are used to numbers that are large or small, negative or positive and odd or even, but what about those that are square, prime, **perfect** or even amicable? The beauty of numbers lies in how we use them.

> *66 Number is the ruler of forms and ideas and the cause of gods and demons. 99*
>
> Pythagoras

TASK

Test what you know already about maths with these questions.

1 What do 6^3 and $\sqrt{169}$ mean?
2 Which is the greater, 6^2 or 4^3?
3 What does 45% mean?
4 Why is 47 a prime number?
5 Which of the following are square numbers: 125, 169, 1,000, 1,681 10,000?
6 Calculate $\frac{3}{5} \times \frac{7}{8}$.

7 40% of a number is 120. What is the number?
8 A group of three people wins £5,400 and splits the winnings in the ratio 2:4:6. How much does each winner get?
9 Express 65% as a fraction.

Special numbers

We use numbers all the time, but there are many different kinds of numbers and some of them have special uses. Let's have a look at a few of these and consider how they are used.

KEY TERMS

Natural numbers, such as 1, 2, 3, 4, 5, 6, etc., are the numbers we use to count. They are split into odd and even.

Integers are whole numbers as opposed to fractions and can be written as –1, –2, –3 or 0, 1, 2, 3.

A **perfect number** is a positive integer that is equal to the sum of its divisors. In simple terms, 6 is a perfect number because the divisors of 6 are 1, 2 and 3, and their sum is 6.

TASK

Why is 28 a perfect number? Try to think of another.

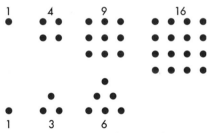

Figure 2: Square numbers and triangular numbers

KEY TERMS

A **factor** is a number that divides exactly into a larger number.

A **prime number** is a number that only has two factors, itself and 1.

Roman numerals are a little more cumbersome than Arabic numerals but it is still in common to see i, ii, iii, iv up to x. However, L (50), C (100), D (500) and M (1000) are less frequently used. CDXLVIII is 448. (Do you see why we switched systems?)

The Greeks used pebbles to form square numbers and triangular numbers. Square numbers are formed by multiplying a whole number by itself and triangular numbers can be formed geometrically. An interesting fact is if you add together any two triangular numbers, you will always make a square number.

The Greek mathematician Eratosthenes (276–194 BCE) is famous for his work with **prime numbers**. The following list has some examples.

Prime number	Factors
3	1 and 3
7	1 and 7
13	1 and 13

Pi (π) is a different kind of number because it involves the ratio of two numbers, i.e. the diameter and circumference of a circle. Although an approximation of π is often written as a fraction ($^{22}/_{7}$), π is actually an infinite string of decimals (3.1415926535897932384 and so on) that cannot be expressed as a fraction. π is usually shortened to 3.142.

Some number patterns

Numbers can be grouped in many ways and understanding patterns of numbers helps us to explain and predict things. Here are some examples of where a pattern occurs in a set of numbers.

- Every fourth year is a leap year.
- The next number in the sequence 10, 100, 1,000 is 10,000.
- A Fibonacci sequence contains a logical and frequently used pattern; here are the first 20 numbers: 0, 1, 1, 2, 3, 5, 8, 13, 21, 34, 55, 89, 144, 233, 377, 610, 987, 1,597, 2,584, 4,181…

Sudoku and Kakuro are logic-based number-placement puzzles. Using the constraints or rules of the puzzle, predictions are made in order to complete a grid.

TASK

Here are two curious patterns. Why do they work?

a prime numbers	sums	reversed
7 + 11 + 13 =	31	13
17 + 19 + 23 =	59	95
29 + 31 + 37 =	97	79
41 + 43 + 47 =	131	131
53 + 59 + 61 =	173	371
67 + 71 + 73 =	211	112
79 + 83 + 89 =	251	152
TOTAL	953	953

b		
81	$= (8+1)^2$	$= 9^2$
512	$= (5+1+2)^3$	$= 8^3$
4,913	$= (4+9+1+3)^3$	$= 17^3$
17,576	$= (1+7+5+7+6)^3$	$= 26^3$
234,256	$= (2+3+4+2+5+6)^4$	$= 22^4$
1,679,616	$= (1+6+7+9+6+1+6)^4$	$= 36^4$

What number methods do we use?

There are many different ways of dealing with numbers. One of the most common ways to make dealing with numbers easier is rounding off.

Rounding off is used when we need to approximate or simplify long complicated numbers, e.g. age to the nearest year, weight to the nearest kilogram, stars to the nearest light year. Rounding off can be combined with using decimal places, and significant figures.

Decimal places (dp) are counted to the right of the decimal point and sometimes you need to round them off to a more manageable size.

- If the number following the decimal place that you want to round off to is less than 5, the remaining digits stay the same: so 44.562314 to 3 dp is 44.562 (rounding down)
- If the number is 5 or more, add 1 to your final digit: so 44.56275 to 3 dp is 44.563 (rounding up)

We can also round numbers off to a required number of significant figures (sf). The rules are the same as with decimal places, with one exception; you may have to add a 0 to ensure the correct number is given.

Simple rules apply to numbers of significant figures.

- 236.567 to four sf is 236.6
- 236.567 to three sf is 237
- 236.567 to two sf is 240 (use zero)

Scientists often deal in very small or very large numbers. It becomes rather tedious to write out lots and lots of zeros and it is difficult to work with them. For example, the distance from the Earth to Jupiter is 783,000,000 km and the distance to our nearest star is 408,500,000,000,000 km. **Standard form** is a way of making this easier. In standard form the distance from Earth to Jupiter is 7.83×10^8 and the distance to our nearest star is 4.085×10^{14}.

KEY TERMS

A number in standard form can be written as $a \times 10^n$ where a is a number between 1 and 10 and n is an integer (n can be positive or negative).

TASK

1 Put the following into standard form: 105,065, 0,0145, 0.000034.
2 Put these back into ordinary numbers: 2×10^5, 6.5×10^{-2}, 1×10^7

Algebra

Equations are like scales: the sides must balance. In algebra

- we can work out what a letter represents by manipulating the equation: e.g. in $a - 50 = 150$, we think 'what number when you take 50 from it would give 150?', and work out that $a = 200$.
- we can add or subtract numbers from each side of an equation to make it easier to solve – remembering that what you do to one side of an equation, you must do to the other.
  So $b + 5 - 13 = 25 - 13$ is easier just as $b + 5 = 25$.
- a number next to a letter means multiplies, so $2x$ means two lots of x.
- brackets like this $(x - 5)$ mean treat the things inside as one thing. So $2(x + 3) = 10$ means two lots of '$x + 3$' equals 10. If x was 2, would this equation be right? How about $4(5 - y) = 20$? Use that 4 to divide each side and you get $5 - y = 5$, so $y = 0$.
- a factor is a smaller number that divides exactly into a larger number, and factorising means taking out a common factor from an equation. So to factorise $2n + 6$, the number 2 is a common factor: $2n + 6 = 2(n + 3)$.

Sometimes an equation on its own doesn't have enough information to be solvable. But adding another equation then gives you the key to solving both. These are called **simultaneous equations**: you use them at the same time to find the only correct answer for both. For example:

$x + y = 20$. Here x and y could be any number of numbers: no solution possible.

$2x = 10$. This gives us a key to solving the first equation: if $x = 5$ then to solve the first equation y must be 15.

Quadratic equations are more complicated and may need factorising before a solution can be found. What would be the answer to the quadratic equation $x^2 - 4x = 0$? Factorising would give $x(x - 4) = 0$ so x would be either 0 or, if the term $(x - 4)$ was itself 0, x would be 4.

How about $x^2 - 10x - 24 = 0$?

$-24 = -12 \times 2$ and $-10 = -12 + 2$ so:

$(x - 12)(x + 2) = 0$

$x = 12$ and $x = -2$.

What if the quadratic equation cannot be solved by factorising? In this situation we would need to use a different method.

To solve the equation $ax^2 + bx + c = 0$ we can use the formula

$$x = \frac{-b \pm \sqrt{(b^2 - 4ac)}}{2a}$$

TASK

Now think back to GCSE maths. How good are you at solving simultaneous equations?

Solve these equations for x and y.

$5x - 3y = 21$
$2x + 5y = -4$

TASK

What happens to the value of x when the balance in the equation is changed and the 0 is replaced with different number,
e.g. $2x^2 + 5x - 12 = 21$?

TASK

Now try these.

1 $4x^2 + 3x - 5 = 0$
2 $3w^2 - w - 8 = 0$
3 $12 + 6n - 2n^2 = 0$
4 Now solve $2x(3x + 5) = 3$ to two significant figures and then three decimal places.

There are three main types of exam questions in this part of the OCR General Studies specification.

- short questions often involving calculations
- brief descriptions and analyses of data presented in a variety of forms
- more discursive essays that might review the place of mathematics in everyday life.

Questions involving numeracy can take the form of short structured questions or longer essays. Shorter questions often involve calculations, number sequences and algebra; essay topics involve the use and application of numbers.

Short answer questions should be straightforward but students often make the simplest of errors and come up with the wrong answer. Some tips for dealing with short answer questions:

- read the question and make certain you understand what you are to do with the data, i.e. follow instructions
- if the question requires a number of stages, present them in order and neatly; remember you need to be able to follow your own work and the examiner needs to mark it
- full marks are often awarded for a correct answer without workings but you will get nothing if the answer is wrong
- if using a calculator, take care with rounding up or down, decimal places and significant numbers.

You will not have much time to think, plan and write essays. So spend a couple of minutes on a plan: a brief list or spider diagram. In the Examination Practice below, questions 5 and 6 are on the same theme but have different approaches. In which ways are they different? Try one.

WHAT NEXT?

It is worthwhile revising these topics and skills from the GCSE maths you have studied or look on some websites such as BBC Bitesize.

1 The number 28 is said to be a perfect number because its factors (1, 2, 4, 7 and 14) add up to 28. Demonstrate that only one number below 10 is a perfect number. Show how you reached your answer.
2 a Put the following numbers into standard form: 453,010 and 0.0867.
  b Put the following into ordinary form: 4.9×10^{-3} and 5.2×10^{4}.
3 The general term for a sequence of numbers is given as $n(n + 4)$.
  a What are the first five numbers in the sequence?
  b Calculate the 45th number.
4 Two groups of people bought tickets for entry into a park. The first group of four adults and five children paid a total of £48.50 and the second group of two adults and four children paid £30. Find the charges for adult and child tickets.
5 Using examples, describe the application of mathematical techniques needed in everyday life. [30 marks]
6 'Why study maths; we are never going to need it?'. Using examples, examine the validity of this statement. [30 marks]

2.3.3 Shape, space and measurement

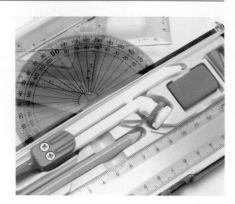

Figure 3: What do all three of these pictures have in common?

The answer is **geometry**.

Geometry is one of the most ancient branches of mathematics. It was made into a workable format by Euclid (300 BCE). Geometry is central to mathematics and we make full use of it through measurement, construction, formulae and our understanding of shapes, areas and volumes. The properties of squares, cubes rectangles, circles, spheres and prisms are shown in Figure 4.

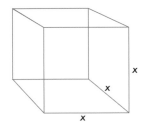

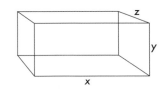

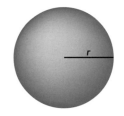

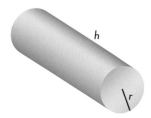

A cube has six square faces.
Each face area = x^2
Surface area = $6x^2$
Volume = x^3

A rectangular prism has six rectangular faces.
Surface area
  = $2xy + 2zy + 2xz$
Volume = xyz

A sphere has a circular cross-profile.
Maximum circumference
  = $2\pi r$
Surface area = $4\pi r^2$
Volume = $\frac{4}{3}\pi r^3$

A cylinder is a prism with a circular cross-section.
Surface area
  = $2\pi rh + 2\pi r^2$
Volume = $\pi r^2 h$

Figure 4: The properties of plane and three-dimensional shapes

TASK

1 For any pyramid, volume = ⅓ base area × perpendicular height. A cone can be considered as a pyramid but with a circular base. Using your own dimensions, work out the volume of a cone and a pyramid.
2 Saturn has a diameter of 1.2×10^5 km. What is its surface area and volume?
3 Calculate the size of the cylindrical container you would need to hold six tennis balls, each of 8 cm diameter.

Angles and directions

Geometry also has applications in planning journeys. Whether we are walking, cycling or driving it is useful to be able to use a map to plot directions and distances. We are concerned with the relative locations of where we are and where we are going. We cannot always rely on having satellite navigation systems to guide us! Route planning involves a number of important skills

- you might use a compass; it measures in degrees and provides bearings
- as maps are drawn to scale, conversions are necessary
- calculated distances need to be converted into time
- you need to know at what speed you walk, cycle or drive
- how do you select a route: shortest distance or shortest time?

TASK

1 Select a route of about 30 miles (50 km) across open country; mountainous areas are ideal. You will need a start, a finish and an overnight camp or hostel. Your route-planning equipment includes an Ordnance Survey map of 1:50,000 or 1:25,000 scale, a compass, a ruler and a route sheet.
Walking at an average speed of 3 miles per hour (5 km per hour), with about ten stages, plan your route. You could draw out a table like this one to help you plan.

Stage	Places and route	Grid references	Direction in degrees from north/bearing	Distance in km or miles	Time allowed	Departure time	Expected time of arrival
1							
2							
3							

2 Plan a car journey between Worcester and Oxford. You have two alternative routes: one cross-country and one using motorways. Use a road atlas to plan both routes, noting directions, distances and average speeds of each stage. Then, using an internet site (e.g. RAC or AA), see how well yours compare with the professionals' routes.
3 Using your school or college grounds, design a 5 mile (8 km) orienteering course.

2.3.4 Handling data and statistics

Figure 5: Laboratory experiments and field trips both involve collecting data

KEY TERMS

Quantitative data have numerical values and can include quantities, dimensions and distances, and use units such as metres, percentages and joules. This type of information can be split into discrete or continuous data. A word of warning though: it is possible to put continuous data into classes so that they become discrete.

Qualitative data are used to measure qualities such as colour, brightness and aesthetic factors that do not have a numerical value. A qualitative investigation might look at *why* and *how* as compared to *what*, *where* and *when* (for example: shopping habits, planning applications and social phenomena).

Students performing laboratory experiments or measuring the flow of water in a stream are demonstrating two ways of collecting data. The results of such work can be seen in GCSE projects and field study reports. Scientific journals, newspapers and magazines publish data in the forms of graphs, statistics and illustrations for public use.

Types of data

Data refers to quantities, observations, conditions, facts or other premises from which results may be found. In most cases scientific, geographical or social data should be clearly defined, precisely collected and accurately recorded so that they can be presented to a wide audience. There are two basic types of data: **quantitative** and **qualitative**.

Discrete or discontinuous data can only take specific values and there are no intermediate values between classes or counts. Bar graphs or pie charts may be used to represent such information.

Continuous data include all values within a given range. The values are continuous and line graphs are a simple way of representing them.

TASK

1 Discuss whether discrete or continuous data would be used in each of the following: monthly car sales, temperature and rainfall statistics, the height and weight of people, biodiversity, the relationship between smoking and lung cancer, gravity.
2 Were there any examples of where it was difficult to decide upon whether your information was discrete or continuous? If so, why?
3 Using three different subjects (e.g. a modern language, biology and business studies) discuss how (a) discrete and (b) continuous data might be used.

Quantitative information would be used to depict trends in illnesses, for example, whereas qualitative information would be used to highlight the causes.

Collecting data

An early task in research is the collection of data. The choice of an appropriate technique that will yield valid data is vital and needs careful consideration. Researchers generally obtain their data from primary and/or secondary sources. The testing of a hypothesis (see page 108), or research into a scientific phenomenon or social issue, often requires **primary data**. Laboratory research achieves precision through the use of equipment and experimentation. Physicists, biologists and chemists use theories and hypotheses as bases for their experiments and the research process yields results in the form of data.

Although data collection is often an interesting stage in any investigation, the researcher must always consider

- the relevance of the data
- accuracy
- data recording methods
- collation or simplification and final presentation.

Constraints such as time and cost might mean that the researcher selects a small part of the whole. This selection is sampling. As the sample should be representative of the whole it is important that it is unbiased. Statistical tests are often applied to data collected in this way in order to achieve a level of confidence in the results.

Secondary data can be easier and cheaper to collect and sources such as the internet, statistical records, government records and texts are frequently used. However, care must be taken with secondary data and researchers should question how the information was collected and its authenticity.

Displaying data

Displaying information in a visual form is valid if it gives us a clear understanding of the data and provides new information. Illustrative methods such as pictograms, bar charts, pie charts for discrete sets of data and line graphs for continuous data can be hand-drawn or computer-generated. Each of these could involve the following stages.

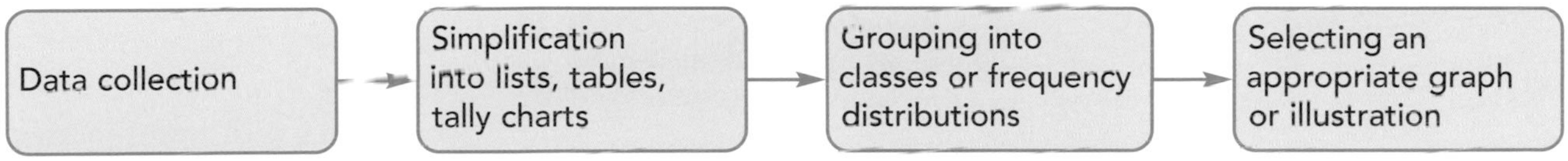

| Data collection | → | Simplification into lists, tables, tally charts | → | Grouping into classes or frequency distributions | → | Selecting an appropriate graph or illustration |

Figure 6: The stages of displaying data

The importance of accuracy and clarity in this progression becomes obvious when, for instance, we view rail or air timetables, medical reports and even weather data.

Correlation is the strength of a relationship between two or more variables.

Scatter diagrams (or scatter plots) are used to find the strength of a relationship or **correlation** between two variables. Where a link is suggested it is possible to draw a line of best fit. These graphs can indicate a negative correlation, a positive correlation or no correlation; the closer the plots approach the line of best fit, the stronger the correlation.

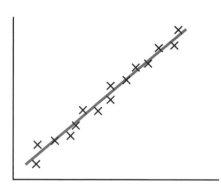
a A strong positive correlation

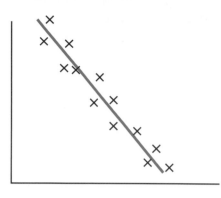
b A strong negative correlation

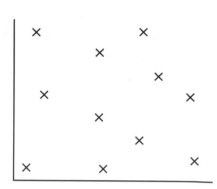
c No correlation

Figure 7: Scatter diagrams indicating correlation

Statistics

Mortgage provider	Current rate	Overall cost for comparison	Booking fee
Choose Us	5.99%	6.2%	6.2%
Company 2	6.54%	7.1%	7.1%
Company 3	6.69%	7.1%	7.1%
Company 4	6.99%	7.3%	7.3%

Table 1: Comparing the cost of a mortgage

There are **3** kinds of lies

lies, damn lies, & statistics

We're looking for someone who can make all three work for us.

Figure 8: A job advert

You could argue that Table 1 and Figure 8 are linked. There are hundreds of mortgage providers. The three competitors (2, 3 and 4) may have been selected by the first company for this comparison table, but what about the unmentioned companies with lower rates?

TASK

In small groups, carry out the following investigation, then report back to the whole class.

- Make a list of companies you think try to attract customers using accurate statistics but providing an incomplete picture.
- What methods do they use?
- How effective is this technique?

2 Science, mathematics and technology

Statistics are a useful way of representing data and are commonly used in subjects like science, sociology, economics and geography. We see statistical information in newspapers and textbooks, on television and billboards, and as soon as words like average, range and distribution are used, we might well be interpreting statistical data. Finding averages and the spread of a set of data are useful ways of clarifying statistics.

Averages fall into three types: mean, median and mode. These terms are frequently confused. They are each ways of describing a number that is somewhere in the middle of a set of values. Table 2 illustrates the types.

Average measure	Numbers set A 1, 3, 4, 4, 5, 6, 8, 9, 12, 15, 15	Numbers set B 1, 3, 4, 4, 5, 6, 8, 9, 12, 15
The **mean**: add up the figures then divide by the number of figures in the set	Adding up the numbers 1+3+4+4+5+6+8+9+12+15+15 = 82 There are 11 numbers in the set so divide by 11 82 ÷ 11 = 7.45 (to 2dp) the mean is **7.45**	Adding up the numbers 1+3+4+4+5+6+8+9+12+15 = 67 There are 10 numbers in the set so divide by 10 67 ÷10 = 6.7 the mean is **6.7**
The **median** is the middle number in a set of figures when they are placed in rank order	The numbers are in rank order: 1, 3, 4, 4, 5, <u>6</u>, 8, 9, 12, 15, 15 The middle number is 6	The numbers are in rank order: 1, 3, 4, 4, <u>5</u>, <u>6</u>, 8, 9, 12, 15 Here we have two numbers in the middle: 5 and 6 The median is the mean of these two numbers: i.e. (5+6) ÷ 2 = 5.5, the median is 5.5
The **mode** is the most common or popular number in a set	1, 3, <u>4</u>, <u>4</u>, 5, 6, 8, 9, 12, <u>15</u>, <u>15</u> The numbers 4 and 15 each occur twice so they are the modal values. The set is bimodal	1, 3, <u>4</u>, <u>4</u>, 5, 6, 8, 9, 12, 15 4 is the most frequent number and is the mode

Table 2

The **mean** (or arithmetic mean) is most frequently used. Since it uses every number in the set it is said to be representative of all numbers. Median and mode pose some problems.

- The **median** might be closer to the bottom or the top values in the data. In the example above, 6 and 5.5 are closer to the bottom of the range of values.
- The table shows that, although the **mode** is the most common number in a set, it might not be representative of all numbers if it occurs towards the top or bottom of the range. This number is frequently used when stating earnings or sales and can be misleading.

The **range** is sometimes useful to show the spread of the set of numbers. It is found by subtracting the lowest value from the highest value. The range for 1, 3, 4, 4, 5, 6, 8, 9, 12, 15, 15 will be 15 – 1 = 14. A more sophisticated measurement of the spread of the data is to find the **standard deviation** (SD). A high SD indicates a wide spread whilst a low SD shows that the data cluster around the mean.

TASK

Try using the standard deviation (σ) function on a scientific calculator with a set of numbers.

2 Science, mathematics and technology

There are many other statistical tests that are appropriate to different types of investigation. Correlation determines if there is a causal relationship between two variables. The Chi squared test relates expected frequencies to observed frequencies. Biology, sociology and geography textbooks contain numerous applications of statistical tests.

Probability

Probability measures the likelihood of an event occurring. Determining this usually involves the collection of data.

Here are some examples of where we use probability.

- How probable is it that next summer will be warmer than usual?
- Is it likely that 100 m athletes will ever break the 9.0 seconds barrier?
- How confident can we be that global warming is not just a product of natural processes?
- What is the likelihood that there is life in other solar systems?

We can also use probability to determine

- the chance of drawing an ace or king from a pack of cards
- the probability of a twelve-sided spinner stopping at 6
- the probability that the next sidelight bulb to blow on a car will be at the rear.

In each case we might like to test our calculation against empirical investigation which involves experimentation and collecting and using data.

2.3.5 Informal logic puzzles

Have you ever been confronted with a mind-boggling problem when suddenly light dawns and you scream 'eureka: that's logical'? (Archimedes might have!) The word *logic* comes from the Greek word *logos*, sometimes translated as *reason*, *rule* or *ratio*. In a modern sense we might define logic as the study of correct reasoning.

We apply **informal logic** when we try to assess, analyse and improve the ordinary problems and issues we come across every day. Personal exchanges, political debate, the media and our home and work routines all raise problems and issues that need careful analysis.

A clear thinker
- gathers information from all senses.
- raises vital questions.
- comes to well-reasoned conclusions and solutions.
- thinks with an open mind.

Figure 9: What makes a clear thinker?

2 Science, mathematics and technology

Is this a correct piece of logic? Think about it, particularly the word 'therefore'.

- If Tom is a philosopher, then Tom is poor.
- Tom is a philosopher.
- Therefore Tom is poor.

Can you think of situations where such thinking might occur?

These are quite simple. However, many problems we come across every day are more complex and surprisingly like some of the puzzles to be found in books and on the internet.

Puzzle time

When tackling the following four problems

- read the questions and clues carefully
- don't miss out any words
- find relationships between important elements
- work logically through each stage and be prepared to return to an earlier position.

> **TASK**
>
> Discuss these.
> Do people make judgements such as these?
>
> 1 If A = B, does it then follow that, if B = C, then A = C?
> 2 If a dog has four legs, and a cat has four legs, does it then follow that a cat is a dog? The logic here is flawed, but why?

TASK

1 The Tower of Hanoi Puzzle dates from 1883.
   - Move all discs onto the third peg.
   - You can only move one disc at a time.
   - Each move involves taking the upper disc from one peg and placing onto another peg.
   - A bigger disc cannot go on a smaller disc.
   - You need to transfer the tower from one peg to the other in as few moves as possible.

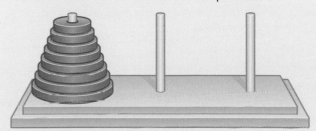

Figure 10: The Tower of Hanoi puzzle

   a Describe how the Tower of Hanoi problem is clearly defined.
   b How might engineers and scientists use models like this to solve problems?

2 Jack has three boxes of building bricks: one box with yellow bricks, one box with red bricks, and one box with yellow and red bricks. The boxes have labels that describe the contents, but none of these labels is on the right box.

   How can Jack, by taking only one brick from one box, determine what each box contains?

3 A man has a fox, a chicken and some corn. He must cross a river with the two animals and the corn. There is a small rowing boat, in which he can take one thing with him at a time. If the fox and the chicken are left alone, the fox will eat the chicken. If the chicken and the corn are left alone, the chicken will eat the corn.

How can the man get the fox, the chicken and the corn, safe and dry across the river?

The objective is to get the three items safe and dry across a river, but when solving this problem many people cheat. Is it possible to bypass the rules?

4 The River Pregel flows through the city of Konigsberg now Kaliningrad in Germany. Seven bridges link two islands in the river to the mainland. On a Sunday, Konigsberg citizens tried to stroll around the city with the objective of walking over each bridge once without crossing it a second time. The map is below: have a go.

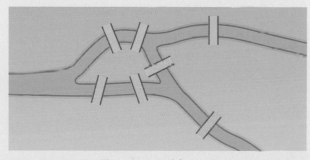

Figure 11: The seven bridges of the River Pregel

Frustrated? So was a Swiss mathematician called Euler (1707–83). The citizens did not solve it. Why?

You might like to do some internet research on Euler's theorem.

WHAT NEXT?

It is worthwhile revising these topics and skills from the GCSE maths you have studied, or look on some websites such as BBC Bitesize.

You might also like to try some problems and puzzles. The following internet sites have plenty.

Brainteasers: http://puzzles.about.com/od/brainteasers
The Ultimate Puzzle Site: www.puzzle.dse.nl/index_us.html
www.edcollins.com/logic
www.businessballs.com/puzzles.htm
www.puzzles.com

EXAMINATION TALK

Remember, with short questions involving calculations, lay your work out neatly in stages with the answer clearly stated. If you go straight for the answer without workings, make certain you have the correct answer.

A good example of how your knowledge of averages could be tested is the following.

> The average income of a group is given £25,000, £30,000 and £35,000. Show how it is possible that all of these figures can be correct. Explain any terms you use.

The first question in Examination Practice (page 131) shows how a set of data can be used to assess the use of graphs and charts and develop some calculations. Remember

- to study the data before you start
- to note which column of the table shows mass and which shows diameter
- to read the questions which follow carefully
- that under examination conditions people make mistakes: take your time.

An essay assessing the use of statistics in everyday life might take the form of question 2.

1 Table 3 gives information about the eight planets in our solar system. The planets are given in order of distance from the Sun.

Planet	Diameter (km)	Mass (kg)
1 Mercury	4,878	0.33×10^{24}
2 Venus	12,104	4.87×10^{24}
3 Earth	12,756	5.98×10^{24}
4 Mars	6,787	0.64×10^{24}
5 Jupiter	142,800	1898×10^{24}
6 Saturn	120,000	568×10^{24}
7 Uranus	51,118	86.8×10^{24}
8 Neptune	49,528	4.87×10^{24}

Table 3

a (i) Which planet has the largest diameter? [1 mark]
  (ii) Which planet has the smallest mass? [1 mark]
b These three charts show three ways of presenting data from Table 3.

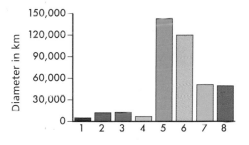
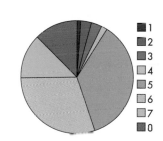
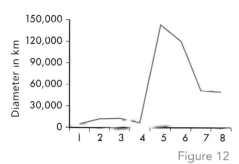

Figure 12

  (i) Why is the bar chart an appropriate way to illustrate the data? [2 marks]
  (ii) Why is the pie chart not an appropriate way to illustrate the data? [2 marks]
  (iii) Why is the line graph not an appropriate way to illustrate the data? [2 marks]
c Calculate:
  (i) The radius of Mercury in metres. You can use standard form. [2 marks]
  (ii) The volume of Mercury in m³. The volume of a sphere is $\frac{4}{3} \pi r^3$ [3 marks]
  (iii) Which planets have their mass given in standard form? [1 mark]
  (iv) Suggest why the other figures are not given in standard form. [3 marks]
2 Outline ways in which statistics are useful and powerful, but can also mislead.

3.1 Examination and appreciation of ideologies and values in society

> **OVERVIEW**
>
> In this block of work we will look at
>
> - some of the dominant political ideologies of our time
>
> - some social, economic and political issues which arise from differences in values in society
> - how values in society are developed, transmitted and affect daily life.

Figure 1: A child is taken to Holy Cross School through the demonstrators who are held back by the army

> **If we'd been born where they were born, and taught what they were taught, then we would believe what they believe.**

Anne Tanney, headteacher at the Holy Cross School, Belfast, adopted this motto for her school in 2004. Her pupils, some as young as five, had to walk to school each day through a noisy and frightening demonstration staged by those politically opposed to having a Roman Catholic School in a Protestant area. Apart from expressing a remarkable degree of tolerance, these words express an important truth about why we believe what we believe.

QUESTIONS

1 Is the fact that someone is prepared to die for an ideology any indication of its validity?
2 Are ideologies as much accidents of birth as results of conviction or conversion?
3 What causes our values to change or develop?
4 Does self-interest play a stronger role in determining our ideologies than idealism?
5 Left-wing politicians talk about the world as they wish it to be, but right wingers look at the world as it actually is. Is this a fair comment?
6 Socialism, like Christianity, is an excellent idea. The problem is that it has never really been tried. Would it work if it were?
7 How far should society accommodate the values of other cultures?
8 How far are your own values affected by those of your family?
9 Ideology, for most people, is an 'intellectual luxury'. Is this true?
10 What role does ideology play in your own life?

3.1.1 Political ideologies

Defining an **ideology** is difficult, and often involves complex language, which seems to be designed to defy understanding. Ideologies also develop and change as the society which they inhabit evolves.

The brief descriptions below of some well-known ideologies aim to provide a basis for further study and discussion.

Anarchism holds that established forms of government are validated mainly by the threat of force. Anarchist society is based on shared ownership, with laws arrived at by voluntary agreement. Change in anarchist society can only happen as the result of individuals in the society rethinking their attitudes and beliefs. Some anarchists believe that the use of violence to bring about change is justified. Although anarchism can work in a small community, it is hard to see how it could effectively govern a complex industrialised society.

Fascism is an ideology in which the state controls every aspect of national life. Fascist governments tend to be extremely nationalist, and in practice have usually been totalitarian. The glorification of the state often centres on a charismatic leader, such as Adolf Hitler (Germany), Benito Mussolini (Italy) and Francisco Franco (Spain).

Liberalism originally stood for freedom from state control, promoting individual human rights, civil liberties and the right of every citizen to own private property. In modern politics it is seen as the party of the centre.

Conservatism originally emphasised respect for tradition and minimal government intervention in economic activity, and opposed radical social change as being disruptive. Modern conservatism continues to advocate the free market, but recognises the need for some control of private enterprise. It still embodies a strong respect for conventions and traditions.

Socialism began as a movement which sought to abolish capitalism and private enterprise. In a socialist society, the state owns and controls the means of producing and distributing goods, and operates state systems of medicine and education. Karl Marx saw Socialism as a stage on the road to the extreme of Communism, where private property would be abolished. Modern Socialism (called in the UK 'New Labour') has abandoned nationalisation as a principle, advocating a mixture of public and private provision in all areas. The welfare state is still a central element of New Labour policy.

Feminism states that as women are equal to men, society should treat them as such – in terms of status, power, employment and reward. Its 19th-century origins concentrated on women acquiring the rights to vote and to own property. After the Second World War (and partly because of it) feminists began to apply their principles to

KEY TERMS

Ideology is defined in different ways according to whether the word is being used politically, socially or individually. Politically, ideology means a set of political, economic and social views or ideas, particularly concerned with the form and role of government. Socially, it means a system of values, beliefs or ideas shared by a social group, often taken for granted as being self-evidently true. Individually, ideology can describe a philosophical stance adopted by an individual, which influences how that individual treats others and expects to be treated.

INTEGRATING KNOWLEDGE

Look back at AS topic 1.1.2 (pages 12 and 13). What ideologies lie behind the main UK political parties?

relationships, family matters, education and careers. This has led to major alterations in attitudes towards domestic violence, the rearing of children and the financial structures of family life. Feminism is primarily a social ideology, attracting support from all social classes.

Pacifism is primarily an individual ideology rejecting violence as a means of resolving conflict. Pacifists will not participate actively in wars of any kind, or in violent revolutions. During the Second World War pacifists were often accused of double standards – they stood to benefit from a war in which they refused to fight. In response, some agreed to do work which supported the war but which did not involve armed service. As a result, some pacifists undertook duties just as hazardous as combat, for example in battlefield ambulance units.

When defining ideologies it is easy to give the impression that all those who follow them believe the same things. Such an impression would be false. All political parties contain factions which may be in bitter dispute with one another. As Winston Churchill remarked, *'When you rise to address the House of Commons, the opposition is in front of you, but your enemies are behind you'*.

TASK

Seven ideologies are listed above. Select one of these ideologies and, in groups, trace what you think would be the social consequences of its adoption. Present your findings to the rest of the class.

3.1.2 Social, economic and political issues

The rights of animals

Figure 2: Fox hunt

On 10 December 1948, the United Nations General Assembly ratified the Universal Declaration of Human Rights. This stated that human beings had the right to be treated as individuals and could not be defined solely as subjects of a state. Individuals have inherent value, and they must be enabled to live by the principles and priorities they choose, so long as these do not infringe the rights of others.

Using the Universal Declaration of Human Rights document as a model, a group of animal rights activists – Uncaged – has produced a similar declaration on behalf of animals. This is based on their belief that, although humankind differs in many respects from the rest of the animal kingdom, the theory of evolution teaches us that the similarities far outweigh the differences. DNA mapping has shown that we are genetically almost identical to our closest primate relatives. Human beings therefore have no right to dominate and exploit other species.

The Universal Declaration of Animal Rights

Inasmuch as there is ample evidence that many animal species are capable of feeling, we condemn totally the infliction of suffering upon our fellow creatures and the curtailment of their behavioural and other needs save where this is necessary for their own individual benefit.

We do not accept that a difference in species alone (any more than a difference in race) can justify wanton exploitation or oppression in the name of science or sport, or for use as food, for commercial profit or for other human ends.

We believe in the evolutionary and moral kinship of all animals and declare our belief that all sentient creatures have rights to life, liberty and natural enjoyment.

We therefore call for the protection of these rights.

If this declaration were to be ratified and pass into law, it is instructive to list the consequences which could possibly follow, depending upon what legal interpretations were eventually placed on the phrase 'wanton exploitation or oppression' in the declaration.

- The end of all scientific research based on animal testing, dissection or vivisection.
- The end of sports such as angling, hare-coursing, beagling, horse-racing, greyhound-racing, pigeon-fancying, show-jumping.
- The end of the selective breeding of pedigree dogs and other animals.
- The collapse of the farming of beef, mutton, pork, venison, poultry and salmon.
- The end of dairy farming and egg production.
- The destruction of the commercial fishing industry.
- The imposition of a vegan diet on society.

Each of these consequences would have far-reaching effects: on medicine and scientific development, on the economy and on the population at large.

It would also be possible to claim that the ratification of the Declaration of Animal Rights could infringe the Declaration of Human Rights.

> **INTEGRATING KNOWLEDGE**
>
> AS topic 1.1.2 (page 14) considered pressure groups. As a pressure group, how might Uncaged seek to get their ideas across to voters?

Ideologies in conflict: green energy and the environment

The issue: peak oil

It is estimated that a thousand billion barrels of the world's supply of oil have already been extracted and refined, and that a similar amount remains, in either known or 'yet-to-find' fields.

> **INTEGRATING KNOWLEDGE**
>
> AS 2.1.3 has more on energy: pages 74–76 give you more information on the issues of renewable and non-renewable energy.

Colin Campbell, a British petroleum geologist, believes that the peak oil moment could arrive in 2008. At this point, oil production will begin to fall, and competition for the remaining stocks will begin to intensify. The initial decline in production will be up to 3 per cent a year, but the consequences will be incalculable. The cost of everything – travel, electricity, agriculture and trade – will rise, and plastic will become a luxury. As one American analyst said, once peak oil is a reality, 'you can kiss your lifestyle goodbye'.

Apart from minimising oil consumption – which will probably not happen until we are faced with no alternative – we should lose no time in seeking alternative energy sources. Most European countries now have a Green Party, and one of their main preoccupations is the provision of green energy.

In the UK several wind farm projects have already started with Green Party support. In 2007, 152 farms were supplying enough energy to power all the households in Bristol, Manchester and Edinburgh combined.

Wind energy is good news. Or is it?

Figure 3

The Thames Estuary wind farm proposal

The Government has approved a giant wind farm project in the Thames Estuary, which will occupy 90 square miles (233 km^2) of water, with a total of 341 wind turbines. A second project will see a further 100 turbines off Margate.

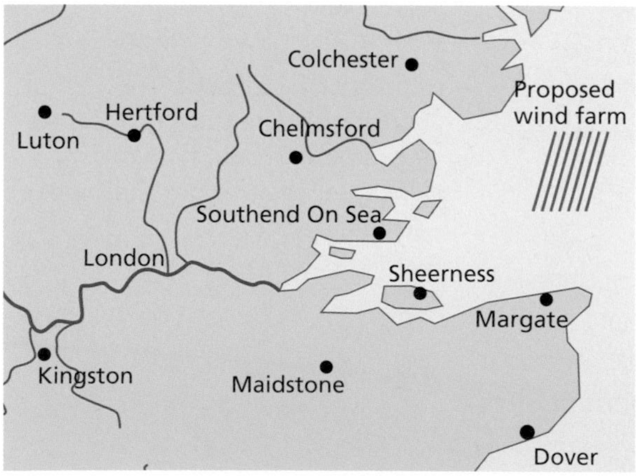

United Kingdom Independence Party MEP Jeffrey Titford raised the following concerns in a UKIP newsletter.

> The Chamber of Shipping…is anxious about the turbines interfering with radar and about the environmental risk from a collision involving an oil tanker. Guidelines about the minimum distance between wind farms and shipping lanes have, apparently, been ignored, jeopardising the safety of those using the estuary. More than 100 ships a day would pass close by.
>
> Greenpeace has welcomed the decision – but have they given even a minute's thought to the impact on the marine environment of drilling 341 holes in the seabed and filling them with concrete and metal? What about the hundreds of miles of cable that will have to be laid on the seabed to link all these metal monstrosities to land? How about the energy that goes into manufacturing turbines, which takes years to achieve payback?
>
> Local fishermen are up in arms and they are right to be concerned as there will be significant disruption to fish shoals and spawning areas leading to serious reductions in catch rates. There will be long term changes to the water flow because of the disruption of the seabed profile and disturbance of organisms that live on or near the bottom substrate, all of which affect the availability of food for fish and shellfish.
>
> Then there is the effect on migrating birds – I could go on. It is high time that organisations like Greenpeace, which claim to be so dedicated to the protection of the environment, threw off their rose tinted spectacles regarding wind technology.
>
> I am as interested in preserving the environment as anybody but I prefer a realistic approach, rather than wholesale environmental vandalism in pursuit of a green myth.

INTEGRATING KNOWLEDGE

Look back at AS 1.1.3 Voting issues (pages 17–19). What issues does UKIP campaign on? How might these affect the views of this MEP?

TASK

Organise a debate on a question involving ideologies in conflict. Topics might include these.

- Should socialists send their children to private schools?
- Are 'green' principles an ideology or a fashion statement?
- Should those who promote animal rights eat meat?

3.1.3 The influence of ideologies and values on everyday life

Our beliefs and **values** affect the way in which we try to live. This, crucially, is not something we do on our own. We form part of many communities. Some of these are 'compulsory', such as families, schools or workplaces. We can choose whether we belong to others such as clubs, societies, churches, political parties and social circles. Most such communities have rules, some formal, others not. Such rules usually hinge on the way people treat one another and, crucially, how they would expect to be treated.

KEY TERMS

Values arise from ideologies and affect the way in which people live from day to day. Many proverbs – *do as you would be done by, shy bairns get nowt* – exemplify values, the ideologies of the everyday.

Below is part of the Professional Code of Conduct for members of the National Union of Teachers. What are the values that lie behind it?

> The following is a list of actions which the NUT sees as being unprofessional.
>
> a) For any teacher to take an appointment from which another member of the Union has been unjustly dismissed.
>
> b) For any teacher to make a report on the work or conduct of another teacher without at the time acquainting the teacher concerned with the nature of it.
>
> c) In any case of dispute between members of the NUT settled by arbitration, for any member not to abide by the decision.
>
> d) For any teacher to censure other teachers or to criticise their work in the hearing of the pupils or other persons not directly involved in the running of the school.
>
> e) For any teacher to seek to compel another teacher to perform outside the ordinary school hours any task which is not essentially connected with the ordinary work and organisation of the school.
>
> f) For any teacher to impose upon another teacher, out of the ordinary school hours, an excessive and unreasonable amount of work of any kind.
>
> g) For any teacher to discriminate, to harass or be guilty of discriminatory or offensive remarks by reference to the race, nationality, colour, ethnic origin, disability, gender or sexual orientation of others including, in particular, colleagues and pupils.

The interesting thing about this professional code is how closely it derives from the traditional values which used to be thought of as 'schoolboy honour'.

It could be summed up in the saying 'Do as you would be done by'.

a says it is wrong to kick someone when they are down.
b says that telling tales is wrong.
c says that everyone should be treated in the same way.
d says that loyalty is more important than personal feelings.
e says that bosses should not bully their subordinates.
f says that employees have a right to a private life.
g says that everyone deserves to be respectfully treated.

TASK

What are the values which the rules of your school or college seek to instil in its students?

Our values have a direct effect on how we treat others. Our ideologies tend to affect the larger decisions we take about how we live our lives. Religious or political principles affect what we may see as our duty to society at large. The difference between ideologies and values is, for the most part, a question of scale.

3 Domain exploration: applying synoptic skills

The emphasis in testing this part of the specification is less on what you know than on how you can use what you know to make a case or develop a line of thought. In the examination you will be presented with tasks testing your critical and thinking skills and also your ability to interpret and evaluate opinion.

If you are studying politics or sociology then you may have acquired detailed knowledge of various ideologies. You must use this knowledge with care. Use it only where it helps you to focus your answer and clinch your points with relevant illustrations. Do not give in to the temptation to write down everything you can think of in connection to the topic in the hope that some of it will be relevant.

WHAT NEXT?

There are hundreds of websites where you can research all of the ideologies mentioned in this topic block (and more). When you look at these websites you should do so critically. Official party websites aim to recruit support; others aim less to promote their own ideologies than to attack those of others. Always try to keep a clear distinction between information and propaganda. This particularly applies to online encyclopaedias such as Wikipedia, which are not always objective.

The following websites may prove helpful.

www.conservatives.com	official website of the Conservative Party
www.labour.org.uk	official website of the Labour Party
www.libdems.org.uk	official website of the Liberal Democrat Party
www.greenparty.org.uk	official website of the Green Party
www.communist-party.org.uk	official website of the Communist Party
www.ukip.org	official website of the United Kingdom Independence Party
www.bnp.org.uk	official website of the British National Party
www.anarchism.net	books, articles, forum and a Q & A section
www.thefword.org.uk	a British feminist site which includes news and opinion

If you wish to research a particular ideology then use a search engine and key words (e.g. *animal rights*).

Use these questions in both study and revision. To save time you may prefer to make a detailed plan of your answer rather than write it out in full.

1 What influences – family, peers, community – have helped to form your beliefs and values? Evaluate the relative importance of these influences.
2 Is ideology a framework or a strait-jacket? Illustrate your answer with reference to at least three different ideologies.
3 Over the next 30 years your values will probably change. What changes do you think are likely? How will they arise? Why?

3.2 The nature of objectivity in social science

OVERVIEW

In this block of work we will look at

- how social science looks objectively at society
- how social scientists collect information and use it

- different outlooks on social science as illustrated in the work of seven key workers in the field.

Figure 1: Hogarth's *Gin Lane*: 18th-century social science?

QUESTIONS

1 How scientific can social science be?
2 'The only possible conclusion the social sciences can draw is: some do, some don't.' (Ernest Rutherford) To what extent is this true?
3 Laboratory science has many practical outcomes. What practical use can be made of social science?
4 'Religion hinges upon faith, politics hinges upon who can tell the most convincing lies or maybe just shout the loudest, but science hinges upon whether its conclusions resemble what actually happens.' (Ian Stewart) How far does this statement apply to social science?
5 'As long as there are entrenched social and political distinctions between sexes, races or classes, there will be forms of science whose main function is to rationalise and legitimise these distinctions.' (Elizabeth Fee) Is the function of social science simply to describe?

6 'Until politics are a branch of science we shall do well to regard political and social reforms as experiments rather than short cuts to the millennium.' (JBS Haldane) How valid is this critique of social science?
7 '75 per cent of all statistics are invented, including this one.' Are people right to be suspicious of statistics and statisticians?
8 Is society too diverse to be analysed scientifically?
9 'To understand the true quality of people, you must look into their minds, and examine their pursuits and aversions.' (Emperor Marcus Aurelius) To what extent is this the basis of social science?
10 'He was a sociologist; he had got into an intellectual muddle early on in life and never managed to get out.' (Iris Murdoch) This is an entertaining remark – but is it fair?

3.2.1 Introduction

It is said, with a great deal more wit than truth, that **social science** consists of the elucidation of the painfully obvious. Those who find the ideas of social scientists unpalatable or challenging are particularly liable to say this. The term social science is itself imprecise, including as it does elements of human geography, political theory, sociology, philosophy, economics and theology.

Few would pretend, however, that the phrase 'social science' is not at least partly a contradiction in terms. Society is vastly complex, and seems to defy the orderly classification and measurement involved in scientific method. Individual circumstances provide many exceptions to any rule that may be proposed about the way society works and progresses – if, that is, we can agree on what progress means. To some, the abolition of capital punishment in our legal system was a progressive change; to others, the beginning of social disintegration.

Sociology and science have the collection of **empirical evidence** in common. Once facts, data, statistics, narratives and opinions are collected they can be examined and collated, and conclusions proposed from them. It is here that sociological and scientific methods diverge. A scientific law is based on a controlled experiment yielding the same result as often as it is repeated. The nature of a sociological hypothesis depends, in part, on the theory of society held by the social scientist putting it forward.

KEY TERMS

Social science can be defined in many different ways, but its basis is the study of the social lives of groups and individuals, and of society and the relationships between individuals within it. It is by its nature multidisciplinary.

KEY TERMS

Empirical evidence is that which is based on observation and experience, and which may be verified (or disproved) by further observation and experiment.

KEY TERMS

Objectivity means the ability to consider things without being dependent on personal opinion, or being affected by one's personal prejudices.

The nature of **objectivity** in social science is thus a matter partly of interpretation. It is also a kind of informed and exemplified generalisation, which may take several forms.

An empirical relationship between two phenomena may suggest both correlation and social effect. The collapse of the British coal industry in the 1980s, for instance, produced a surge in couples referring themselves for counselling to Relate. People with self-esteem damaged by redundancy may become more prone to introspection. Evaluating their personal relationships and finding them wanting could be a significant element in such a process.

A social scientist may draw conclusions about why certain societies evolve. Many sociologists would see economic chaos, national demoralisation and a charismatic leader offering simplistic solutions which scapegoated a social minority as important factors in the rise of National Socialism in 1930s Germany.

Changes in one social institution may be related to changes in another. The decline in Christian church-going, and hence in the traditional observance of Sunday, has transformed the British weekend out of all recognition in the past 50 years, with far-reaching effects on the economy, the family, leisure and entertainment.

Other generalisations involve theories of societal development, such as the evolutionary model proposed by the philosopher Auguste Comte. More complex are the theories proposed by Adam Smith about the economic development of society – theories that are still consulted today. Finally, sociologists such as Emile Durkheim seek to make patterns involving systems, structures and ethics binding individuals to society.

In thinking about society, the interpretation of evidence is as important as the evidence itself. In looking at this interpretation we need to know the context in which the social scientist involved applied his or her own developed values to the evidence.

3.2.2 Research methods

Researchers collect information from two kinds of source.

Primary sources are those consulted by the researcher, via observation, interview, laboratory-based experiments or participant observation.

Secondary sources consist of information already gathered by someone else. They may include government reports, previously published research, documentaries (films, radio and TV) and journalism. Such sources must be evaluated as to their reliability and viewpoint.

Novels, poetry and drama can also be useful as 'unwitting testimony' in social science research, as may diaries, journals or autobiographies. These may provide valuable comparisons with official sources.

INTEGRATING KNOWLEDGE

AS 2.3.4 investigates sources of data in more depth.

3 Domain exploration: applying synoptic skills

Research methods involve dealing directly with people, who will bring their own values and interests to what they tell the researcher, who must also be aware of his or her own involvement and viewpoint.

Structured interviews ask a large number of people the same set of questions. This may produce quantifiable data. It is essential that structured interviews consist of questions which do not lead the interviewee or demonstrate the questioner's views. If you show someone a photograph of a politician and ask them 'Would you buy a used car from this man?' you have told them what answer you expect or hope to get. A fairer question would be 'What is your first impression of this man?'.

Conducting unstructured interviews needs a skilled technique, so that a probing exploration feels like conversation. Direct questioning may well cause an interviewee to clam up if the topic is a difficult one, but equally a more open style may encourage the interviewee to respond in a way which shows them in a good light. Asking someone directly if they have ever been unfaithful to a partner is unlikely to get an honest response (and in some ways such a question does not deserve one). An interview dealing with the more general topic of trust and honesty in relationships could encourage greater openness.

Interviews need to cover a range of age, social class, occupation and outlook if they are to produce worthwhile data, and the sample of interviewees needs to be appropriate.

Using a questionnaire raises problems similar to a structured interview, and offers the same opportunities for respondents to reply in a way that does them credit. Questionnaire design needs to combine closed questions (which need to be answered yes or no) with open questions (where there is a choice of response) in a way which can produce reliable data.

During the 1998 World Cup, three social scientists lived for three weeks with groups of English and Scottish football fans, observing and recording their behaviour, whilst a fourth colleague recorded media coverage in the UK. Such participant observation can often produce vivid and authentic data, but can also place the observer in a difficult position. If they are living a role authentically there may come a point where they have to do something criminal or unethical to sustain the role or risk being unmasked.

Statistics provide data on many social issues. Computers give access to an objective scientific data bank which forms the basis of much research as well as enabling the reality testing of its conclusions.

INTEGRATING KNOWLEDGE

Look back at page 44 to see some of the key influences on people (Figure 3). How might these influences affect research?

TASK

Choose a topic which is local and fairly small scale, and form groups to research it, each using a different method – questionnaire, structured interview, unstructured interview and statistical data. If possible, record sample interviews.

Present the conclusions arrived at by each group (perhaps as a poster), and evaluate the similarities and differences between them. Try to account for these. Were there flaws in the questionnaire design? Did the structured interview give hints to the interviewees about the answers you expected? Did the unstructured interview lack focus? Were the statistics collected methodically and recorded accurately?

Possible topics for research include an evaluation of students' use of and attitudes to the cafeteria in your school or college, or methods of transport to and from school, or the provision of common room or study facilities.

3.2.3 Different viewpoints within the social sciences

Whatever the method of research (in reality, a mixture of approaches will be used), the results will be interpreted in the light of the theoretical standpoint of the social scientist. One will use a discourse of class struggle and power relationships; another may account for social phenomena in the light of bureaucratic control. In a series of lectures delivered in 2001, the anthropologist and historian Alan McFarlane identified seven major figures who dominate social scientific schools of thought.

Figure 2: Baron de Montesquieu

KEY TERMS

A **paradigm** serves as a model (see page 110) or an especially clear and typical example of a phenomenon.

Baron de Montesquieu (1689–1755) recognised that society consists of discrete institutions influencing and interacting with one another – a scientific perception. He described three classes: monarchy, aristocracy and common people, sharing two kinds of power. Sovereign power dictated events; administrative power made them happen. His revolutionary proposal was for the separation of powers – legislative, executive and judicial – between the three classes such that each would have a power over the other. Montesquieu's social **paradigm** aimed to eliminate theocracy (the power of the church) and also the last vestiges of feudalism. His ideas underpin the American Constitution still in operation today.

Adam Smith (1723–1790) felt that social institutions resulted incidentally from individual human action rather than by design. His declaration that *every man is first and principally recommended to his own care; and every man is certainly, in every respect, fitter and abler to take care of himself than of any other person* is an affirmation of individualism which finds a strong echo in Margaret Thatcher's insistence in 1987 that *As we know, there is no such thing as society. There are individual men and women, and there are families. And no government can do anything except through people, and people must look to themselves first.* In *The Wealth of Nations*, Smith's advocacy of the deregulation of commerce laid the foundations of the *laissez faire* free trade which dominated the 19th century.

Alexis de Tocqueville (1805–1859) also believed strongly in individual liberty, but saw that, even in a democratic society, there was potential for individuals or institutions to accrue to themselves an unhealthy amount of power, initially by economic means. His view of society was that successful democracy depended on people enjoying equality. However, if democracy produced the centralisation of power, and weakened local democratic institutions in the process, then democracy could become a context for despotism. Social scientists concerned with the state of democratic government in the modern UK will find much to consider in the writings of de Tocqueville.

Karl Marx (1818–1883) maintained that workers should enjoy the fruits of their labours. He saw the capitalist economic system as a means of preventing this. He made a simple division of society into two classes – workers, who owned nothing, and their owners, who did no work. He called this situation alienation, which would last until the capitalist system was overthrown, workers would take control of what they produced, and class division would become obsolete. In terms of social science, Marx's ideas see class struggle as both the motive force of history and the central process of society. Despite the collapse of European communism (which was based on Marxism) and the adoption of a free market economy in China, social scientists still see the Marxist critique of society as a valuable one.

Figure 3: Karl Marx

Emile Durkheim (1858–1917) was a social scientist to whom methodology was as important as social theory. He too felt that workers were alienated from society – though he saw technology and mechanisation, and the consequent loss of individual craftsmanship, as agents of this. Whilst recognising the enormous increase in prosperity brought about by capitalism, he also saw it as an agent of greed and acquisitiveness which could destabilise society. He also coined the term *anomie* to describe social instability or personal disconnectedness resulting from a breakdown of social standards caused by the loss of ideals or social purpose. It is not surprising then that he saw religious belief and a sound education system as being the most effective agents of social progress.

Figure 4: Emile Durkheim

Max Weber (1864–1920) was the son of a liberal politician and a Calvinist, and his work owed much to these influences. Calvinist Christianity, like Puritanism, instils hard work, thrift and self-discipline in its followers. This is a strong element in Weber's most important work, *The Protestant Ethic and the Spirit of Capitalism*, which controversially equates worldly success with eternal salvation. His work on class, law, power, urbanisation and the arts in society showed a strong theoretical sense, and he did much to turn sociology into an academic discipline. Perhaps his greatest legacy to social science was the understanding that until we can discover what motivates people we cannot begin to understand what they do.

Ernest Gellner (1925–1995) was a **polymath** among social scientists. His interests included the nature of modernity, nationalism, the relevance of philosophy to modern life, the rise of international Islam and industrialism. An independent thinker, he was equally scornful of right- and left-wing orthodoxies, but was able to empathise with those who found personal security in political (as well as religious) belief. He had little sympathy for the notion that ideas could change the world, and even less for psychoanalysis. His work on Islam has gained posthumous relevance in the light of the events of 11 September 2001.

KEY TERMS

A **polymath** is someone who is learned and skilled in several branches of academic study. The best social scientists tend to be polymaths.

EXAMINATION TALK

Questions will test skills as much as they ask for information. You may well be presented with a small set of data (which is unlikely to be mainly statistical) and asked to write a commentary on it. In this answer you will draw conclusions, evaluate their validity and offer a comment as to how the research could be developed further.

The components of social science are varied, and the questions posed will reflect this.

WHAT NEXT?

The width of this topic block makes it unlikely that you will have time to research very far beyond the outline given. There are a number of excellent school websites giving a social science overview, and one of these is included below.

www.hewett.norfolk.sch.uk   the website of the Hewett School Norfolk which has an excellent section called *Sociology at Hewitt*

www.polity.co.uk   this clear introduction to Social Theory online has an useful chapter *Introducing Social Theories*

www.answerbag.co.uk   this has a comprehensive section giving basic information on many of the disciplines that make up social science.

EXAMINATION PRACTICE

These two questions explore the two sides of social science which have been outlined in this topic block. The first requires you to describe how you would set about conducting a small-scale survey, and assess the reliability of the conclusions you might obtain. The second presents you with a range of information such as might be obtained in a survey and asks you to draw a range of conclusions from it.

1 You have been asked to conduct an investigation into the use of your local library by the neighbourhood, which is a middle-class suburb. The library's facilities include books, computers with internet access, the rental of CDs and DVDs and study cubicles.
   Outline the methods you might use to do this, including examples of the kind of information you would seek to obtain by
   a questionnaire
   b structured interview
   c unstructured interview
   d statistical research.
2 You have been given the following information about the regular congregation of a suburban church in a north-eastern Anglican parish.
   • The population of the parish is 6,500.
   • A total of 311 people attend the church each week.
   • The congregation includes 207 women and 104 men.
   • The age groups of the congregation break down as follows:

0–10	23	31–40	51	61–70	54
11–20	6	41–50	76	71–80	17
21–30	19	51–60	61	81–90	6

In the 21–60 age groups the following occupations are represented:

University lecturing	11
School teaching	28
Doctors and surgeons	6
Nurses and paramedics	14
Accountancy	7
Civil service	23
Self-employed	11
Business-owner	16
Retail assistant	9
999 services	8
Homemakers	48
Retired	9
Unemployed	17

Using the information above, write a profile of the parish. Distinguish between facts you have drawn from the above and ideas that you have deduced. What do these facts and ideas suggest about the long-term future of this parish?

3.3 The relationship between law, society and ethics

OVERVIEW

In this block of work we will look at

- the origins of our legal code
- the creation of a law and the criminalisation of smokers
- ethical dilemmas – their causes
- some ethical dilemmas outlined.

God

1: Do not worship any other gods
2: Do not make any idols
3: Do not misuse the name of God
4: Keep the Sabbath holy

Man

5: Honour your father & mother
6: Do not murder
7: Do not commit adultery
8: Do not steal
9: Do not lie
10: Do not covet

Figure 1: The Ten Commandments

In the western world, the Ten Commandments are often cited as being the basis of our legal code. In fact

- only **two** of them refer to **laws** – killing and theft are illegal
- **four** of them refer to **ethics** – families, relationships, honesty, friendship
- **four** of them refer to **religious belief** – belief, faith and observance

Similarly, the seven deadly sins – **pride**, **envy**, **anger**, **avarice**, **despair**, **gluttony** and **lust** – have caused humanity endless trouble down the years but none of them is actually illegal. Some of them may motivate people to break laws, however, for example, envying someone their iPod is not a good reason for stealing it, but may none the less lead to such a crime being committed.

It is in the areas where law and ethics overlap and interlock that some of the most difficult social issues emerge. It is this area which this topic explores.

QUESTIONS

1. Is everyone equal under the law? What factors might militate against equality?
2. Do the police have too much power?
3. Is the jury system outdated?
4. Is everyone presumed innocent until proven guilty?
5. Is ethical disagreement with a law sufficient reason for breaking it?
6. Should there be a compulsory DNA databank?
7. Would identity cards affect the crime rate?
8. Is the adversarial legal system the best one?
9. Can more than one legal system operate in one country?
10. Is the law sometimes an ass?

3.3.1 Crime, law enforcement and the criminal justice system: a case study

The relationship between **law**, **ethics**, society and law enforcement is complex. It is very rare for a law to attract universal support. For example, on 1 July 2007 a new crime entered the criminal justice system.

It became illegal to smoke in public places in England, a law passed in the Commons by 384 votes to 184. England thus joined the rest of the UK as a smoke-free zone. Despite the large parliamentary majority, there is still fierce controversy over the ban.

Those who supported the law tended to do so on medical, social and personal grounds, maintaining that

- passive smoking is dangerous: the British Medical Association estimates that it causes 1,000 deaths each year
- passive smoking is unpleasant: before the ban, nearly three-quarters of the population had to inhale other people's exhaled tobacco smoke
- most people supported a ban: a 2004 BBC opinion poll showed that 73 per cent of those surveyed wanted a total ban
- a ban would encourage smokers to quit: 15 per cent of smokers said that they would give up if their habit was banned: this could prevent up to 13,000 more deaths a year
- voluntary bans have had only limited success – bars, pubs, clubs and many restaurants still allowed smoking.

Opponents of the ban saw it partly as a question of individual freedom and interference in personal choice, arguing that

- a ban restricts personal liberty: another BBC poll showed that 64 per cent of people felt the decision to smoke or not should be purely personal
- the link between passive smoking and ill health remains unproven: FOREST (a pressure group – Freedom Of Right to Enjoy Smoking Tobacco) says that there is no clear causative link between passive smoking and illness
- restrictions would have been a better way forward: a Populus poll conducted in May 2004 showed that people preferred to see smoking restricted rather than banned altogether
- bans are bad for business: bars, restaurants, casinos and night clubs will lose significant income; for example, it was estimated that up to a quarter of public houses in Wales would close
- self-regulation would have been workable: pubs and restaurants would have introduced their own bans in order to accommodate their customers' preferences.

One or two anomalies arose as the new law was introduced. When Keith Richards and Ronnie Wood of the Rolling Stones lit cigarettes on stage during a gig they were officially warned that a recurrence would cost them £50. If the plot of a play required actors to smoke in their workplace (the stage), then the local council would have to decide whether or not to allow it. In Stoke-on-Trent, the ban was not enforced for a fortnight simply because no one knew whose legal responsibility enforcement was.

The smoking ban also illustrated a 'law' which is not on the statute book. This is the law of unintended consequences, where legislation leads to unforeseen outcomes. In the case of the smoking ban, these included

- a realisation that pubs smell: non-smokers generally have a better sense of smell than smokers, and as the tobacco fug cleared, they began to smell other things: stale beer, stale sweat, inefficiently cleaned toilets
- air pollution: as is their right, smokers can now gather in pub gardens or restaurant terraces, and on a still day prevent their non-smoking companions from enjoying the fresh air – which is also a right conferred on them by the smoking ban.

Much more importantly, this new law has led to speculation that the government may seek to regulate other areas of our lives for our own good. If a smoking ban is introduced, why not ration alcohol, ban the sale of fish and chips, cream cakes, or the full English breakfast? These ideas may seem fanciful, but it is possible to make a sound case on health grounds for introducing them.

Enforcing the ban

Enforcement of this law is not a matter for the police. Officials of the Chartered Institute of Environmental Health said

> 'It is our expectation that the legislation will be largely self-enforcing, with managers of premises, responsible persons and members of the public individually and collectively willing to challenge and confront persons smoking in contravention of the law.'

Enforcement of the ban will be carried out, in practice, by environmental health officers. Smoking in a smoke-free place could lead to a fine of up to £200, with a fixed penalty notice option of £50. Failure by the responsible person to prevent smoking in a smoke-free place will lead to a fine of £2,500 with no option for a fixed penalty notice.

INTEGRATING KNOWLEDGE

What impact might this sort of health legislation have on public funding on the NHS? Look back at AS 1.2.3 for more on the NHS and its issues (pages 28–31).

TASK

What changes would you make in the system of law enforcement of the smoking ban to make It more effective?

3.3.2 The law and important ethical and social dilemmas

The law aims to create order and balance in society. Its basic principle is utilitarian, aimed at creating the greatest good for the greatest number.

It applies to society as though it were homogeneous – composed of individuals with similar aims, goals, ethics and principles. In fact our society has always been heterogeneous and, since the Second World War, has become more and more diverse.

INTEGRATING KNOWLEDGE

You will find more on tensions within society in AS 1.3.3.

Individuals and groups in society have their own values. These arise from sources which are often at odds with one another, leading to tensions and dilemmas which can express themselves in conflict.

Religious belief

Religious teachings often influence human relationships, affecting attitudes to sexuality, marriage, divorce and the upbringing of children. The Civil Partnerships Act of 2006 made it legal for homosexual couples to undergo a ceremony having the same legal status as a heterosexual civil marriage. However, when a Church of England vicar and his partner exchanged their vows legally, their action caused problems for the Church. Officially, Anglicans tolerate homosexual clergy so long as they are celibate. Anglican doctrine is that sexual relationships should take place only within heterosexual marriage. The tension between legal rights and Christian ethics is not easy to resolve.

Political conviction

Political principles often affect matters of social equality of opportunity and of treatment. If you are a socialist, you are expected to use state education and medicine. You also want the best education for your children and the best (and quickest) medical treatment for your family. Local state provision may not be able to meet your children's needs so you can pay for a private school. If your wife urgently needs surgery, but the NHS waiting list is five months long, you may pay £4,000 so that she can have her operation next week. The law is clear that you are free to use your money to buy these privileges. Political principle says one thing, common sense says another.

Social class

Some legal issues still tend to be seen as class-based. The 2004 fox-hunting ban was a case in point. Arguments were advanced on both sides, concerned with the effects – positive and negative – on rural economies, farming, biodiversity, and with the ethical principles of field sports. However, the most emotive arguments were class-based, as summed up in this anecdote. At a hunt meeting, a protester said to a hunter 'We're going to make what you do illegal.' The hunter looked down from his horse and said, 'People like you obey the law.

People like us make the law.' Similarly, those who opposed the law pointed out that modern hunts include many ordinary people who simply enjoy riding. Pastimes perceived as 'working class' – hunting rabbits with ferrets, competitive angling – also involve inflicting pain on animals. Class division was an underpinning issue, which generated much heat over the problem, but on the whole shed little light.

Family values

In 1969, the age of majority in the UK was lowered from 21 to 18 years. Reaching the age of majority allows an individual full control over all aspects of life. This is an area where conflicts and dilemmas can often occur. Parents have the legal right to refuse financial support to children in further or higher education. Would this decision be ethical? Parents could use their financial clout to ensure that their children studied a subject they approved – but should they? There is also licensed privilege, which accrues at various ages. For example, in England, Wales and Scotland an individual may consent to heterosexual or homosexual sex at the age of 16 (17 in Northern Ireland). In this area of a teenager's life, parents would expect their views to be listened to and respected, if not obeyed. But once their children reach 16, those views can legally be ignored. In patriarchal communities, such dilemmas can be agonising for entire families, and can lead to crimes like 'honour killings' and forced marriages.

Some legal and ethical problems: look at the facts, debate the issues

Abortion

- A woman has the legal right to an abortion from the age of 16.
- The operation may be performed up to the 24th week of pregnancy.
- Religious believers see this as destroying a life which began at conception.
- Advances in neonatal care mean that a 24-week foetus could be viable, though such a child could well be severely disabled.

Religious symbols: do we need a *laïcité* law?

- British Airways suspended a woman from work for wearing a Christian crucifix.
- Muslims who work for BA are allowed to wear hijab and al-amira.
- A teaching assistant lost her job for wearing her niqab in class.
- A Sikh is exempt from wearing a crash helmet when motorcycling.
- Some say Islamic pressure groups use dress issues to make trouble.

Travellers: free spirits or social parasites?

- There are 250,000 travellers and Gypsies living in the UK.
- There are many more travellers than places for them to stay.
- Many assume that travellers are scroungers living on the state. In fact many are self-employed or do seasonal work.
- They have the same right to their lifestyle as others do to theirs.

KEY TERMS

The principle of laïcité separates religious and governmental authority, so that neither can influence, or interfere with, the other. In France, a law passed in 2004 forbade the wearing in state schools of clothing or jewellery that clearly indicates a student's religious affiliation. Although the law applies equally to all religions, it was seen by many French Muslims as an attack on their religious observance.

The British National Party: an exception to freedom of speech?

- The British National Party is a legitimate political party.
- It fields legitimate candidates in local and national elections.
- The Association of Chief Police Officers (ACPO) has banned police officers from BNP membership.
- The National Association of Schoolmasters Union of Women Teachers has sought to expel teachers who are active in the party.
- The BNP advocates racist policies and thus breaks the law: racism is an offence.

Cannabis: time for legalisation?

- Cannabis supply involves a turnover of £3.5 billion annually.
- Cannabis does not cause violent behaviour or psychosis.
- It can be of therapeutic use for some medical conditions.
- Fatal cannabis overdose is practically impossible.
- Cannabis and hard drugs are linked, but only because it is illegal.

DNA: new forensic science and double jeopardy

- Until March 2005 no one could be tried twice for the same offence. The law forbade this as 'double jeopardy'.
- A new law allows re-trial if 'new and compelling' testimony such as DNA-based evidence is produced.
- For now re-trial will be permitted only in cases involving serious crime such as murder, rape, Class A drug offences and war crimes.
- Supporters of the change say that it will convict guilty people who got away with their crimes through lack of evidence; opponents say that it could lead to persecution of certain defendants, as well as allowing prosecutors a routine second chance when cases fail.
- Others are concerned that the new law will also allow hearsay evidence to be credited.

TASK

Make a group case study of one of the following

- the pros and cons of euthanasia
- the conflict between law and religious belief.

3.3.3 Opposition to the law and how it is expressed

The most direct opposition to the law is that expressed by the criminals who break it. However, individuals and groups in society, for reasons of conviction and conscience, oppose laws and work to bring about change and improvement.

If a law is felt to be anti-social or unfair then its opponents can campaign to have it first rescinded and then replaced.

An example of such a law was Section 28 of the Local Government Act 1988 which prohibited local authorities from 'promoting' homosexuality, as well as declaring homosexual relationships to be bogus imitations of heterosexual marriage. Its supporters said that its purpose was to prevent the spread of gay propaganda in the guise of sex education.

In practice, Section 28 caused confusion and difficulty. Teachers were unclear about how to respond honestly to pupils' questions about sexuality. Was shielding students from homophobic bullying promoting homosexuality? Local authorities were unsure as to what facilities they could provide to their gay, lesbian and bisexual ratepayers without 'promoting' their lifestyle.

The repeal of Section 28 had been supported by a coalition of children's organisations, teachers, school governors, local authorities, trade unions, health experts and lesbian, gay and bisexual groups. How was it done?

Opposing and changing a law: the process

The first task is to catch the public's attention, probably by holding a demonstration: a march, a rally, or a campaign of civil disobedience. Road haulage companies, for example, when demonstrating against rises in diesel fuel prices, drove large convoys through cities, or three abreast, slowly, on motorways. They were not breaking the law, but caused such congestion and inconvenience that their cause made headline news for days on end.

Public interest must be sustained and support gained. This can be done in a number of ways.

- Further demonstrations dramatising a particular aspect of the law.
- Petitions, both on paper in shops, workplaces, and recreational facilities, and online.
- Letter-writing campaigns to local and national press.
- Participation in radio and television discussions, especially phone-in programmes.
- Recruiting high-profile celebrity support: one of the anti-Section 28 campaigners was the actor Sir Ian McKellen.

These activities can all be organised and coordinated by a pressure group, a small band of activists able to maintain the momentum of a campaign.

Crucially, political support must be obtained if opposition to a law is to be effective: laws can only be made in parliament. A campaign consisting of noisy demonstrations will have nuisance value only. The riots of 1990 demonstrated opposition to Margaret Thatcher's Poll Tax in a shockingly violent way. However, sustained civil and political campaign, leading to a 15-point Labour lead in opinion polls, convinced her that the law needed changing.

Some pressure groups are temporary, dissolving when their aim is achieved. However, a feature of modern activism is the permanent campaigning group. The independent organisation **Liberty**, for example, campaigns on a variety of issues, including free speech, privacy and the rights of young people and the elderly.

TASK

Choose an area of UK society where you think a change in the law could be helpful. This might be a change in the age for voting, the legalisation of something currently illegal, or the extension of a law already in force.

Draft a law which would work, critically examine any drawbacks you identify, and make provision for any exceptions you might need to make.

KEY TERMS

Liberty was founded in 1934 as the National Council for Civil Liberties. It is a non-political campaigning organisation promoting the values of individual human dignity, equal treatment and fairness. Recently it has concentrated on human rights law.

3 Domain exploration: applying synoptic skills

EXAMINATION TALK

This is an area of the specification where students often fail to distinguish between their right to hold an opinion and their ability to support it so that it can be taken seriously. The law and ethics are areas which attract huge amounts of media coverage, much of it biased in one way or another, and like all secondary sources, this coverage needs to be read critically.

It is a good idea to read a newspaper with which you are not in political sympathy. If you are a Socialist then you should read the *Daily Mail*; if a Tory, then look at *The Guardian*. Doing this will subject you to journalism which goes against the grain of your own thinking and help you to subject it to reality testing.

This is also an area where urban myth – for example about racism, political correctness and government bureaucracy – is particularly unhelpful. If you cite examples from real life, you should be able to vouch for their authenticity. Don't rely on the FOAF ('friend of a friend') 'Chinese whispers' that pass for reporting in some newspapers.

WHAT NEXT?

Internet research in this area is probably best done on a case-study basis, so your first resort should be a search engine. Googling the names of those involved in significant legal/criminal cases will produce many hits. If you wanted to research the story of (say) the late Dr Harold Shipman, then the following sources would help to provide a fairly full picture.

www.murderuk.com	a factual archive of studies of murder in the UK
news.bbc.co.uk	will offer both news and opinion
www.people.co.uk	will provide vivid and sensational coverage
www.guardian.co.uk	may examine the case from sociological/criminological angle
www.thetimes.co.uk	often produces both balanced leading articles and thoughtful criminal/legal analysis

EXAMINATION PRACTICE

These questions are typical of this specification area in that they invite you to narrate, discuss, compare and evaluate. Before planning an attempt to answer any of them, re-read the examination talk above.

1 Give examples of how personal beliefs and principles can affect an individual's attitude to the law. You should illustrate your answer by reference to three areas of belief and/or principle.
2 'Stealing is wrong. However, if you steal the ammunition from a gun you suspect may be about to be used to commit a crime, is it still wrong?' What answers would you give to this question? Refer to the legal and ethical issues involved.
3 'Men are not hanged for stealing horses, but that horses may not be stolen' (Lord Halifax, 1633–1695). Evaluate this statement on the purposes of law enforcement.

3.4 Religious belief and experience

OVERVIEW

In this block of work we will look at

- some key definitions and ideas related to the religious impulse in humanity

- the key tenets of six major world religions
- the social outcomes of religious belief
- alternatives to religious belief.

Here is an extract from a review by Stephen Tomkins of Richard Dawkins' *The God Delusion* on the website 'Ship of Fools'.

ONE AND A HALF CHEERS FOR RICHARD DAWKINS

Richard Dawkins is right. His deicidal bestseller *The God Delusion* attacks the absurdities and cruelties, the contradictions and superstitions, the rip offs and fantasies of religion across the world and throughout history. I couldn't agree more. It's enough to make you wish Abraham hadn't been in when God called round.

The problem is, like other fundamentalists, Dawkins won't stop talking when he's finished talking sense. Rather than surveying the countless varieties of religion, weighing up their mixed record, and arguing that on balance we'd be better off without it, he is only willing to see the dark side, and writes off the whole thing, dismissing evidence that makes a monochrome worldview uncomfortable.

He sees the moral failures, but not the moral breakthroughs. He lists the atrocities and ignores the triumphs. He cuts through the supposed proofs of God's existence like a particularly moist sponge cake, but shows no conception at all of why people actually believe – other than that they're a bunch of morons who don't know any better.

QUESTIONS

1 Why has religion been involved in so many conflicts and wars?
2 Where was God in Auschwitz?
3 If God is all-powerful, why doesn't he prevent natural disasters?
4 Very few young people attend church regularly. Why do you suppose this is?
5 Is religion a way of bullying people into good behaviour?
6 Why do some religions treat women as second-class citizens?
7 Is fundamentalist religion always dangerous?
8 'If God did not exist it would be necessary to invent him.' (Voltaire) Is this true?
9 Should religious leaders be allowed to influence governments?
10 Are faith schools a mechanism for indoctrinating the young?

3.4.1 Introduction

Key distinctions: truth, belief or knowledge?

The fact that **religion** deals with aspects of human experience which cannot often be analysed logically means that we need to be careful about the words we use when discussing it. It is far from easy to distinguish between truth, belief and knowledge in this area.

A Christian who believes the Bible to be the literal word of God will accept the accounts of the miracles of Christ as documentary evidence for their truth. Such a person will see their **faith** as a simple acknowledgement of a fundamental *truth*.

KEY TERMS

Religion is a belief in a supernatural being or beings a set of beliefs and customs generated by a religion.

Faith is belief in an idea or proposition which cannot be proved.

INTEGRATING KNOWLEDGE

Look back at AS 1.4.1 for more on the nature of belief.

On the other hand, those who take a more sceptical approach may see their *belief* as an opinion formed on the balance of probabilities. Such people may read their scriptures critically, and perhaps acknowledge that their belief is more metaphorical than literal.

Likewise, there are those who base their faith on an intellectual appreciation of the facts or truths they see embodied in their religion. For these people faith can be said to be based on *knowledge*, at least so far as they are concerned.

Why religion?

The religious impulse in humankind seems to have developed alongside our socialisation. Few cultures lack a creation story, and rites of passage – birth, marriage, death – are often marked with religious ceremonies. Many religions teach that life on Earth is a journey that does not end with physical death, and that what happens to us after we die depends on how well or badly we have lived.

TASK

Pascal's Wager states that it is a better bet to believe that God exists than not to believe. This is because you have everything to gain if God does exist, and little to lose if he doesn't. What do you see as the advantages and disadvantages of a religious belief?

The existence of God can be neither proved nor disproved. If we could prove that God existed, there would be no need for faith. If we step out of a fourth floor window, what happens to us next does not depend on whether or not we believe in the law of gravity. However, whether God made man or vice versa, the six major world religions have had an immense influence on the societies to which they minister. Art, music, literature, education, medicine, the law, politics, all of these would have been radically different had they developed in a godless society.

3.4.2 Which religion?

There are many world religions, some, like Scientology, comparatively recent. The six religions described below (in order of their age) are generally accepted as being the most important and influential. You need to remember that within each religion there is much diversity of belief and custom. This affects how believers live out their faith in their daily lives.

Figure 1: World religious leaders

In thinking about and exploring this topic, a good starting point would be to assess how much these religions have in common, and where the major differences between them lie. More important than that, however, is the way in which religious beliefs can impinge on family, societal and political life.

Judaism

Fourteen million Jews now practise Judaism, and date its foundation to 2000 BCE. They believe that God created the universe and continues to govern it. God gave the Jews 600 *mitzvot* (commandments) which are written in the *Torah*, the holy book. Of these the first group – The Ten Commandments – are familiar to many people besides Jews. They set out rules for religious observance, family life, fidelity within marriage, and social life which still form the basis of many moral and legal codes. The range of the full 600 *mitzvot* is enormous, dealing in detail with matters of dress, diet and the correct observance of *Shabbat* (the Sabbath, which lasts from sunset on Friday until sunset on Saturday).

Judaism is not a matter of simply observing rules, but involves using them to underpin and develop a moral code. Core Jewish beliefs are now enshrined in *The Thirteen Principles*, formulated in the 12th century. The first of these says *I believe with perfect faith that the Creator, blessed be His Name, is the Creator and Guide of everything that has been created; He alone has made, does make, and will make all things.*

This asserts both the centrality of God and his absolute power over the universe he made.

Hinduism

There are one billion practising Hindus, most of whom live on the Indian subcontinent. The core of their belief is that there is a universal, eternal soul called Brahman, who created and is present in everything. The characteristics of Brahman can be seen in different gods (Hinduism is polytheistic) such as Ram, Shiva, Lakshmi and Hanuman, who govern different aspects of life. Hindus believe in reincarnation, and that the cycle of birth, death and rebirth enables the soul to pass through many successive lives. The quality and status of the next incarnation always depends on how the previous life was lived.

The moral responsibilities and duties of a Hindu vary according to their circumstances – age, gender, education, profession and social caste. However, all are required to respect all living things, to be truthful, honest and non-violent. Like Muslims, Hindus see their religion not as one aspect of their lives, but as a set of values governing all moral, social and political conduct.

Buddhism

Three hundred and fifty million Buddhists follow the teachings of Siddhartha Gautama (the Buddha), dating from 500 BCE. Buddhism is a non-theistic religion aiming to lead its followers into enlightenment, peace and truth. This progress is enabled by acceptance of the Four Noble Truths, which state that

- all life is suffering, whether this is caused by birth, ageing, illness, death or deprivation
- all suffering is caused by desire
- the cessation of desire leads to the cessation of suffering
- the cessation of suffering may be achieved by following the Noble Eightfold Path, which consists of a life lived according to these principles
  - right speech: speaking truthfully but offering no hurt to others
  - right actions: acting wholesomely and avoiding harm to others
  - right livelihood: earning a living in a way which does not injure others
  - right effort: striving always to improve
  - right mindfulness: seeing things clearly and without prejudice
  - right concentration: meditating without internal or external distraction
  - right thoughts: considering the rights, needs and wishes of others
  - right understanding: seeing reality as it is, not being deceived by appearances.

Christianity

Two point one billion Christians now follow the teachings of Jesus Christ, a Jewish prophet whom they believe to be the Son of God. Christ was executed in about 30 CE, and his resurrection from the dead (celebrated at Easter) is the central event of the Christian year. Although Christ himself seems to have seen his teachings as an extension of Judaism, the Nicene **Creed** makes it clear that Christians see Christ as the Messiah foretold in the Old Testament, for whom Jews are still waiting.

Christianity is the dominant religion in Western Europe and the Americas, and comprises many different groups and denominations.

> **KEY TERMS**
>
> A **creed** is a summary of the central and essential elements of a religion.

I believe in God, the Father almighty, creator of heaven and earth. I believe in Jesus Christ, God's only Son, our Lord, who was conceived by the Holy Spirit, born of the Virgin Mary, suffered under Pontius Pilate, was crucified, died, and was buried; he descended to the dead. On the third day he rose again; he ascended into heaven, he is seated at the right hand of the Father, and he will come again to judge the living and the dead. I believe in the Holy Spirit, the holy catholic church, the communion of saints, the forgiveness of sins, the resurrection of the body, and the life everlasting.

The Nicene Creed

Islam

Around 1.4 billion Muslims follow the path of submission to the will of Allah – which is what the word Islam means. Muslims believe in absolute adherence to their holy book, the *Qur'an*, which is the revelation given to the prophet Muhammad by Allah in the 7th century.

The five Pillars of Islam embody its five core beliefs and practices. These are as follows

Shahadah: an acknowledgement that Allah is the true god and that Muhammad is his prophet

Salah: a requirement to pray five times a day, facing Mecca (Makkah in Arabic) while doing so

Zakat: the giving of alms to the poor and needy, based on a proportion of one's income

Sawm: fasting during the month of Ramadan, during which one should abstain from food, drink and sexual intercourse from dawn until dusk

Hajj: the requirement to make a pilgrimage to the holy city of Mecca at least once during one's lifetime.

Additional tenets are derived from these Pillars: that life is sacred, that men and women are equal, and that humankind must show respect for Allah's creation, the world in which we live.

Islam is unusual in that as well as dealing with spiritual matters it also has a complete legal code – Sharia Law – which extends its influence into all areas of a believer's life.

> **TASK**
>
> Investigate how these central tenets of Islam translate into daily life for Muslims.

Sikhism

Six million Sikhs now follow the teachings of Shree Guru Nanak, who founded the religion in the 16th century. It is a syncretic faith – Nanak sought to bring together the best aspects of two other faiths, Islam and Hinduism. Its central tenet is that God is one, eternal and present in everything – leading to the belief that all human beings are worthy of equal respect. This belief in equality means that there are no priests in Sikhism, since no one should enjoy better access to God than anyone else. A symbol of this can be seen in the *gurdwara*, where Sikhs worship: all people are equal, so all sit on the floor.

Conscientious Sikhs meditate daily, both singly and in groups, believing that this brings them closer to God. This introspective habit of worship is balanced by much practical concern for the needs of others, especially those who are vulnerable in any way.

> **TASK**
>
> 1 What are the benefits and drawbacks of organised religion, as opposed to a personal faith lived out in daily life without reference to fellow believers?
> 2 In a group, take a topical aspect of daily life – women's rights, sexuality, education, family relationships – and research each religion's stance on it. Report back to the group and discuss similarities and differences in your findings.

Belief and practice

Religious belief does not operate in a vacuum, but affects the way people think and behave in their family, social and political lives. In exploring the impact of religion on daily life, it is interesting to research how different beliefs influence customs and practices in the following areas

- family life, marriage, divorce
- the status and rights of women – dress codes, behaviour, work
- the status and rights of children – corporal punishment, education
- law, justice, crime and punishment
- relationships with members of other faiths
- sex – outside marriage, within marriage
- contraception
- homosexuality
- alcohol, drugs, tobacco
- diet
- war and peace
- tensions between religious belief and the law of the land
- prejudice, discrimination, equality and human rights
- conflict between generations within families
- religious observance and the world of work.

3.4.3 Alternatives to religion

Many people see no need for a supernatural element in their lives. Such people may be *atheist* (believing that there is no god) or *agnostic* (believing that the only honest position is to say that no one can know for sure either way). Both would probably agree to be called *humanists*. Humanists affirm the dignity and value of all people, and see humankind's rationalism as the tool which can be used to solve social and political problems. Like Voltaire, they believe that humankind created God in its own image in order to meet psychological needs which could not fulfilled in any other way.

Other people find that a fervent loyalty to their country, *nationalism*, can take the place of religious belief. Such nationalism tends to invest a nation and its people with special qualities and powers, and can lead to such statements of belief as 'my country, right or wrong'. In modern times nationalism is perhaps most noticeable during international sporting events, when the enthusiasm of crowds of supporters takes on an almost religious fervour.

At a more individual level, *materialists* believe that all the needs of humankind are purely physical and material, and can be satisfied at that level. People who believe this tend to see humankind as a part of the animal kingdom, albeit one which is highly developed, with an intricate and sophisticated set of appetites.

Equally indivdual but perhaps less physical are *hedonists*, who measure all their experiences in the light of how much pleasure and how much pain they generate. Their ideal is to maximise the pleasure and minimise the pain, a notion partly derived from John Stuart Mill's philosophy of utilitarianism, which directs that all actions, whether personal or political, should aim at achieving the greatest good for the greatest number.

TASK

1 What problems may develop in societies where more than one faith is practised?
2 Organise a debate on the topic 'Religion is the opium of the masses' (Karl Marx).

EXAMINATION TALK

Thinking and writing about areas of life where you hold strong beliefs – no matter what kind – presents a problem. An answer which simply states your beliefs without evaluating the reasons why you hold them is not an essay but a sermon, and will be judged as such. Examiners set questions in this area very carefully, to enable the writing of answers which are considered and objective.

It is more than usually important, therefore, to read the question thoroughly to make sure that you know what you are being asked to do, and to write your answer as objectively as you can. At the same time examiners cannot expect you to leave your personal convictions outside the examination room.

It is for this reason that an acknowledgement of your own beliefs is useful provided it is placed in context. The statement that 'contraception is against the will of God' is an opinion that an examiner will expect you to justify. However, if you write 'As a practising Catholic I accept the church's teaching that artificial methods of contraception are contrary to the will of God' you have placed your belief in a context which gives a reason for it and which the examiner can accept. If the grounds for your belief hold water theologically then you will have supported your argument.

Remember that examiners have their own convictions, and that part of their professionalism is to set these aside as they mark your work as objectively as possible. Objectivity on your part will work in your favour.

WHAT NEXT?

Internet research into any of the religious beliefs and their alternatives dealt with in this topic block can begin by putting a keyword – Islam, hedonism, agnosticism, etc – into a search engine. The same caveat applies to these websites as to the political ones – you need to evaluate the information on offer according to the purposes of the writers.

EXAMINATION PRACTICE

Examination questions on this area of the specification tend to concentrate on the social and ethical outcomes of religious belief (or lack of it) and thus invite analysis by the candidate which is less theological than practical. From time to time open-ended questions are asked, of which question 2 below is an example.

1 'When people cease to believe in God, it's not that they believe in nothing, but that they will believe in anything.' (GK Chesterton) What evidence for this view do you see in society at large?
2 Is god a delusion?
3 On the whole, does the existence of religious belief and religious believers help society or hinder it?

3.5 Media and communications 2

OVERVIEW

In this block of work we will look at

- the moral basis of the mass media
- their professional codes of practice
- the internet and cyber journalism
- the influence of the media on public opinion
- how the press and broadcast media exert their influence.

WHO'S LORD JONES?

I DON'T KNOW. BUT HE'S DEAD NOW.

DAILY NEWS

LORD JONES DEAD

Figure 1

'It is the one great weakness of journalism as a picture of our modern existence, that it must be a picture made up entirely of exceptions. We announce on flaring posters that a man has fallen off a scaffolding. We do not announce on flaring posters that a man has not fallen off a scaffolding. Yet this latter fact is fundamentally more exciting. Busy editors cannot be expected to put on their posters, 'Mr. Wilkinson Still Safe,' or 'Mr. Jones, of Worthing, Not Dead Yet.' They cannot describe all the things that are not stolen, or all the marriages that are not judiciously dissolved. Hence the complex picture they give of life is of necessity fallacious; they can only represent what is unusual.'

A quotation from *The Ball and the Cross*, by GK Chesterton

QUESTIONS

1 'Only bad news makes a good story.' Is this a true reflection of how news is selected and printed?
2 Journalism is far less important than journalists think it is. Do we really need news?
3 Is the circulation of a newspaper an indicator of its quality, and, if so, in what way?
4 Is television a truthful medium?
5 What governs the selection of broadcast news, the importance of the story or the quality of the film?
6 Is the influence of the media on the public a positive or a negative one?
7 Should there be a law on press intrusion into privacy?
8 Is the growth of 'infotainment' broadcasting a danger to good journalism?
9 What is the point of 24-hour television news coverage?
10 Will the print media survive the 21st century?

3 Domain exploration: applying synoptic skills

3.5.1 Moral activities

Journalism, said Philip Graham, publisher of the *Washington Post*, is the first rough draft of history. The playwright Arthur Miller described a good newspaper as 'a nation talking to itself'. The award-winning journalist Nicholas Tomalin, on the other hand, said that 'the only qualities essential for real success in journalism are ratlike cunning, a plausible manner and a little literary ability'. Whatever we may believe, we all consume news journalism in one form or another – through newsprint, radio, television and the internet. Because what we read, hear and see affects how we think and act, it is important to know what values and ethics lie behind the news **media**.

Trainee news-reporters used to be taught to get their story into the first paragraph, answering six basic questions: Who? What? When? Where? Why? How? This discipline emphasises the importance of facts, and the necessity to respect them. More than that, a journalist is expected to respect and work to a professional and ethical code.

The code emphasises

- the obligation to tell the truth – and the importance of using original sources of information, referring to more than one source if the material is controversial
- loyalty towards and respect for the audience – you should not report what you think people want, or ought to want, to know
- independence – the reporter should not try to please the editor or the management, political parties, or the people the story is about
- the importance of balance – between objectivity and scepticism, and between **reporting** as many aspects of a story as possible
- where the story involves conflict, the importance of reporting all sides – biased reporting disrespects the story and those who read it
- if confidentiality is promised to a source, then this must be respected – but journalists should not promise this if doing so would make them accessories after the fact of a crime
- favours – either in cash or in kind – should not be accepted from the subject of a story, and even the appearance of doing so should be avoided
- if the journalist has a interest in the story, then it should be declared, and, if possible, the story passed on to someone who can be objective about it.

Respecting the code?

There are no special controls on printed or broadcast journalism in this country other than those imposed by civil and criminal law – notably the laws of libel, slander and defamation.

INTEGRATING KNOWLEDGE

This topic area builds on your AS studies – link it with topic block 1.5, pages 56–61.

KEY TERMS

Media represent the way in which society communicates with itself. Modern media consist of the press, television, radio and, increasingly, the internet.

KEY TERMS

Reporting the news means covering the facts and events of a story in an objective way.

The Press Complaints Commission seeks to impose an editorial Code of Practice on printed journalism, although it has no powers to punish those who breach it. It rules on the following points additional to the professional journalists' code

- the opportunity for reply
- respect for privacy
- harassment
- intrusion into shock or grief
- the interests of children
- the protection of children in sex cases
- entry into hospitals
- the reporting of crime
- the use of clandestine devices, subterfuge and entrapment
- the protection of victims of sexual assault
- discrimination
- financial journalism
- the protection of confidential sources
- payment for information relating to criminal trials
- payments to criminals.

The internet and cyber-journalism

Although 25 million newspapers are still sold in the UK each week, there is a growing community which reads its news online. The sources used by this community include online editions of national, local and weekly papers and websites sponsored by the major news organisations – BBC, ITN, Sky, CNN and Fox News. There is also a new phenomenon – the citizen journalist. Many of these are bloggers who write commentaries on their daily lives, but others offer grassroots views on important news stories, or comment on them from a specialist viewpoint.

Some see blogging and cyber-journalism as a positive development, giving the citizen journalist a say in a news media dominated by a small number of large organisations. The conspiracy theories about the destruction of the World Trade Center in 2001 may or may not be true – but their circulation initially was down to citizen-journalists prepared to risk their credibility.

Others see blogs as a dangerous opportunity for troublemakers. In May 2005, the magazine *Newsweek* printed a story claiming that an interrogator had flushed a Holy Qur'an down a prison toilet to humiliate a Muslim terror suspect. The story, later proved to be untrue, was sourced from an anonymous weblog. Among the repercussions were riots in Pakistan which led to 15 deaths. Needless loss of life is a high price to pay for irresponsible journalism.

3.5.2 Influence on public opinion

The press

Apart from news, written and broadcast media also offer opinion and analysis. Journalists such as Kate Adie, Peter Hitchens, Richard Littlejohn, Andrew Marr, Matthew Parris, Melanie Phillips and John Simpson are as well known for their opinions as they are for their news journalism. What matters, though, is that their contributions should always be identified as opinion.

For example, if you opened a 1950s copy of *The Times* to the centrefold, you knew that everything on the left was news, and that everything on the right was opinion. Four unsigned leading articles giving the paper's views on major issues of the day were the most prominent features.

It is now rare for news media to distinguish fact from opinion. Most British newspapers align themselves with one of the main political parties, and present the news in ways which demonstrate this. During General Elections, not only will editorial and feature articles seek to influence readers' voting, but also news reports will be slanted in the same direction.

Newspapers also seek to influence their readers in other areas. For example, the British Royal family is one of the strongest long-running stories in all the news media, and the sharply polarised views of the public on what they do and what they stand for reflect similarly bi-partisan press coverage.

How the press exerts its influence – some examples

Editorial

> Who breaks a butterfly on a wheel?

Times, July 1967

In 1967, Rolling Stones Mick Jagger and Keith Richards were sentenced to six months' imprisonment for possessing cannabis. These sentences were overturned on appeal, but many felt that Jagger and Richards were being punished partly for being young and disrespectful of authority. *Times* editor William Rees-Mogg wrote a powerful editorial defending them, beginning with these words.

Headline

> MURDERERS
> The Mail accuses these young men of killing. If we are wrong, let them sue us

Daily Mail, 14 February 1997

Frustrated by a fruitless police investigation which charged no one with the racially motivated murder of Stephen Lawrence, the *Daily Mail* appointed itself policeman, jury and judge. None of the five men named complained.

> **&#6;&#6;** I still believe that if your aim is to change the world, journalism is a more immediate short-term weapon. **		**

Tom Stoppard, playwright

Language

> 'Spin is the pornography of politics. It perverts. It is deceit licensed by the Government. Statistics massaged. Expenditure announced and re-announced. The record reassessed. Blame attributed. Innocence proclaimed. Black declared white: all in a day's work.'

'The Erosion of Parliamentary Democracy', October 2003

This extract from a pamphlet by John Major punches home three key concepts – pornography, perversion and deceit – to reinforce the idea that New Labour is not only wrong, but indecent. That it then goes on to use a favourite spin-doctor's device – verbless sentences which say nothing – may be consciously ironic.

Figure 2

Photographs

This famous photograph of the late Diana, Princess of Wales at the Taj Mahal in India featured in many newspapers. The juxtaposition of this monument to undying love and the lone, alienated Princess implied a great deal which could probably not have been said in print at the time about her relationship with her husband and his family.

Figure 3

Cartoons

This cartoon from the later years of the premiership of Tony Blair parodies one of the best-known trademarks in the world – the dog listening to His Master's Voice on the horned gramophone. The original fox-terrier is replaced by a poodle with Blair's head, and his master on this occasion is George W Bush.

3 Domain exploration: applying synoptic skills

How the broadcast media exert their influence

The nature of broadcast media makes them relatively easy to manipulate. Most programmes are pre-recorded, and even in live broadcasts such as news bulletins, many of the filmed inserts and sound-bites are pre-recorded.

What is recorded can be edited.

Editing

Editing can improve a recording, removing hesitations and mistakes. It can also be used to alter the focus of what is said. In television, the editing process can be used deliberately to distort, as the following newspaper report makes clear.

> 'I'm not changing anything. I've had enough of dressing like this, thank you very much' is going into the quotation dictionaries, because it was said by the Queen. Clever editing of a trailer for a documentary *A Year with the Queen* made it look as though the Queen had lost her cool, and walked out in the middle of a photo shoot. In fact, she made the remark while walking to the photo shoot with her attendant. The BBC later apologised for distorting reality.

The Times, 13 July 2007

The selection of images

The images used to accompany a news story can be made to offer a comment on the story.

In 1993, the politician John Redwood, then Conservative Secretary for Wales, was filmed at a meeting in Cardiff which opened with the singing of the Welsh National Anthem *Hen Wlad fy Nhadau*. Knowing neither the words nor the tune, but aware of the camera trained on him, he attempted to mime. This (essentially trivial) mistake made him look foolish, even shifty.

Fourteen years on, BBC News ran that piece of film to accompany Mr Redwood announcing new Conservative policies. Although an apology was later issued, the clip of film dominated the news item, implying that nothing that this man had to say could be taken seriously. It is difficult to know whether this sabotage was deliberate or accidental. However, few can now remember what it was that Mr Redwood actually announced.

Scheduling

The demography of television and radio audiences changes throughout the broadcasting day. This is something to which broadcasting schedulers pay close attention.

Morning television tends to be family viewing as viewers breakfast and get ready for work, whilst programmes such as Radio Four's *Today* are like a morning newspaper for people too preoccupied to read.

Daytime broadcasting has to cater for the young, the elderly, parents and small children, shift workers and the housebound. Family viewing resumes in the evenings, and continues up to the watershed hour of 9.00 pm, after which programmes with strong adult content can be broadcast.

A scheduler responds not only to the demands of the various audiences, but also to the agenda of those in charge of output. A programme may be 'buried' on a less watched channel, broadcast very late at night or scheduled against very strong programming on another channel in order to ensure that it does not reach a large audience.

Other scheduling tactics include

- *junctioning*, where a scheduler deliberately chooses to start a programme just before a rival's begins, or carry it over to finish just before the beginning of the programme starting on another channel
- *hammocking*, where a weaker programme is sandwiched between two stronger offerings in the hope that people will not reach for the remote control
- broadcasting *trails* for subsequent programmes during advertising breaks or previewing them as a news item to publicise forthcoming transmission.

Why do such tactics matter?

Many **commentators** say that modern audiences are media-savvy and know that what they read, see and hear puts across a point of view along with the facts.

This may be true, but if readers, listeners and viewers need impartiality, should they be fobbed off with spin? And should they be allowed to think that they are in charge of their choices about viewing when in fact they are being constantly manipulated?

> ### KEY TERMS
>
> Columnists and commentators treat the news less objectively, often speculating about the story behind the story.

TASK

Compare the coverage of BBC Radio Four's 6 pm news bulletin with that of the 6 pm BBC1 television news broadcast on same day.

Begin by watching and listening to each broadcast and, at the end, list as many of the stories as you can remember. Account for any differences you notice.

Then compare the running order, the allocation of time, the use of live inserts and editorial comment.

EXAMINATION TALK

In the area of journalism and the media, it is relatively straightforward to prepare yourself for the examination. Read as wide a range of newspapers as you can find the time for, find Radio Four on your radio and listen to its news coverage, and watch and compare BBC, ITV and Sky news bulletins.

However, remember that you are not being examined on current affairs, so don't get too interested in the content of what you are reading, listening to and watching. You will be asked more about the media than their message – at least their overt one. Jeremy Paxman, it is said, begins each interview with a politician by asking himself the question 'Why is this lying bastard lying to me?'. It is probable that this quotation (like so many quotations from journalists) owes more to good phrasemaking than to the truth, but the scepticism underlying it is not a bad starting point for you when considering this complex phenomenon.

WHAT NEXT?

Internet research in this topic area is, like that in the law and ethics, perhaps best undertaken on a case-study basis.

The major television news broadcasters – BBC, ITV, Sky – all have websites which are regularly updated, and all of the national daily and Sunday newspapers likewise maintain websites where their cyber-editions can be viewed.

Some of the newspaper websites charge for access to their archives, but generally speaking access to today's edition is free of charge, although sometimes marred by far too many pop-ups.

www.thebigproject.co.uk has excellent access to news media in the UK and abroad.

EXAMINATION PRACTICE

1 'The purpose of the BBC is to enrich people's lives with programmes and services that inform, educate and entertain.'
   To what extent do the televised media in this country fulfil this ideal?
2 'The job of the newspaper is to comfort the afflicted and afflict the comfortable.' (Finlay Peter Dunne)
   In your view, is this a reasonable definition of the function of the press?
3 'I deplore the putrid state into which the newspapers have passed and the malignity, the vulgarity and the mendacious spirit of those who write them.' (Thomas Jefferson)
   This critique of the media of the day was made in the 18th century. Evaluate it in the light of the current state of the media.

3.6 Understanding and appreciation of the changing nature and importance of culture

OVERVIEW

In this block of work we will look at

• varieties of culture, including western, popular and high culture

• the culture and values of a minority group – the Amish of Lancaster County, Pennsylvania, USA.

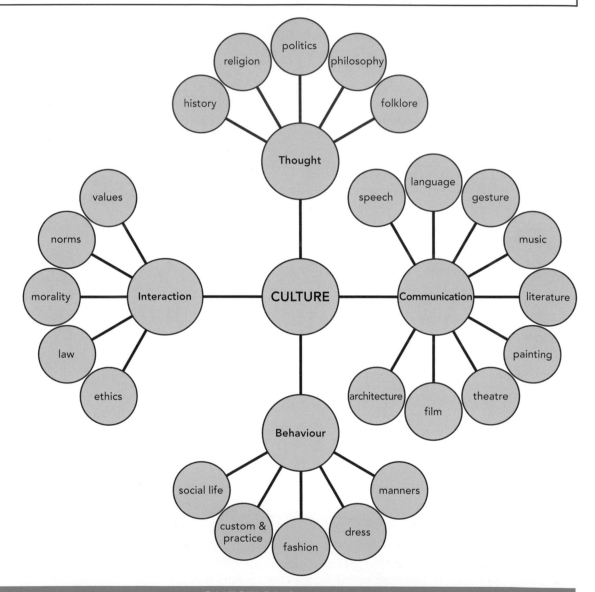

Figure 1

1 What are the cultural values you have received, either explicitly or implicitly, from
  a your family
  b your social class
  c your race
  d your peers
  e your education
  f your religious heritage (or absence of it)
  g your sex and sexual orientation
  h the media?

2 Is one kind of culture (e.g. classical music) inherently better than another?

3 Is the process of acculturation automatically an improvement?

4 Do you think that your cultural values will change? If so, how?

5 Can widely differing cultures learn to co-exist?

3 Domain exploration: applying synoptic skills

3.6.1 Varieties of culture: western, popular and high

What we mean by the word **culture** is to some extent what we can agree it to mean. However, of five definitions found on **www.webdictionary.co.uk**, three are concerned with growing or cultivating things: plants, animals or bacteria. The other two refer to social definitions, the taste in art or manners favoured by a social group, and the state of a particular society at a particular time and place. The cultivation image implies a modification of nature, and this applies to society as much as it does to horticulture. Wild animals empty their bladders and bowels wherever and whenever they wish. So, initially, do infant human beings. The process involved in training them not to is part of their initiation into a complex matrix of speech, behaviour, interactive social codes, norms, moralities and values, which is a key aspect of what we mean by culture.

Culture is about much more than norms of behaviour. Social cultures in the western world have been shaped by many influences, of which the three most powerful were the Christian church, the invention of printing, and the industrial revolution.

The Church

We owe much of our legal codes, ethical norms and social values to the Church. The first teachers, doctors, scientists, philosophers and scholars were either priests or monks, and the academic dress worn by university graduates reminds us of this. Tensions between church and state have fuelled social development, sometimes inadvertently. When Henry VIII dissolved the monasteries in 1536, huge tracts of land passed into private ownership, altering irrevocably the balance of economic power in England. The traditions of scholarship, medicine and science built up by monasticism were secularised, and this was the beginning of civic responsibility for schools and hospitals.

Printing

The invention of printing meant that knowledge and ideas could be circulated beyond national boundaries, and shared. Language is the currency of intelligence, and the written word not only preserves ideas but also stimulates their development. In a world without printing, artistic culture – music, poetry, drama, storytelling – remains the possession of a privileged and educated few. If political ideas cannot be widely circulated and disputed, they cannot develop into movements capable of shaping the destiny of whole nations. A world without printing will remain, in many significant senses, a tribal one.

The industrial revolution

The industrial revolution had effects on western culture which are still visible in modern society. Increased food supply, manufacture of goods, the growth of towns and cities, the doubling of the

---

KEY TERMS

Culture is defined as the integrated pattern of human knowledge, belief and behaviour that depends on human capacity for learning and transmitting knowledge to succeeding generations; and the customary beliefs, social forms and material traits of a racial, religious or social group.

TASK

Twenty-four aspects of culture are outlined in the diagram on page 170. Choose one of these and prepare a brief (five-minute) presentation on it to give to the rest of the group.

population in a century – all of these were huge and visible effects. The response to the cholera epidemic of 1830 pointed also to a growing sense of society as a series of independent but overlapping subcultures. Science identified the cause of the epidemic – bad sanitation; and civil engineering provided the remedy – better water supply and sewage disposal. However, it was a new sense of civic responsibility which provided the motive.

The division of society into three classes – working, middle and upper – is a cultural phenomenon with its roots in the industrial revolution. This is reflected in other cultural areas such as speech and language. The notion of **accent** and **dialect** as class indicators still survives in modern Britain.

If the way we speak is a cultural signifier, then so are behaviour, dress, fashion and social life. Fifty years ago deference towards authority figures – teachers, doctors and the police – was automatic. Perhaps modern manners – neither good nor bad, but the same manners for everyone – show a healthier respect. However, statements about ourselves are no longer confined to our conversation and etiquette. Clothes, jewellery and make-up classify us, as do the foods we eat, the way we drink our beer and where we drink it. The socialising habits of young people in particular have become a prominent part of urban culture. Moreover, these habits tend to cut across social classes to a remarkable extent. The groups of young people who throng town and city centres each weekend could be factory workers or civil servants or schoolteachers on a night out.

The industrial revolution also accelerated and deepened the split between high and popular culture. **High culture** had long been the preserve of those who could afford to pay for it. The first patrons of classical western painting, music, drama and architecture were Archbishops of the Catholic Church. Secular patronage of the arts later became a measure of aristocratic prestige and accomplishment – a nobleman who did not employ a court composer and orchestra was a rarity. The opportunity to appreciate high culture had thus been limited to the upper classes.

The industrial revolution, and social upheavals which followed in its wake, began to change this. Redistributed wealth and expensive education created a large upper-middle class with a taste for the arts and the money to pay for them. These people formed audiences for the Liverpool Philharmonic Orchestra (founded in 1840) and the Manchester Hallé Orchestra (founded in 1857).

Before the industrial revolution, **popular culture** – folk song, folk dance and traditional folk theatre – was purely oral. Few folk songs were written down until late Victorian times. Migration to the fast-growing cities was accompanied firstly by a dilution of folk culture and then its assimilation into the traditions of music hall and variety

KEY TERMS

Accents give variety and colour to the way people speak, identifying people's origins. **Dialect** refers to vocabulary and habits of sentence construction. If someone tells you he's 'bostin fettle' you will know that he's from the Midlands and feeling good.

TASK

List some dialect words from your area and check their meanings in other localities – you can do this by finding dialect dictionaries online. What might account for the variations in meaning?

KEY TERMS

High culture was traditionally that of the ruling classes – serious literature, poetry, classical music, painting and sculpture. It is now more widespread and is thought by some to be improving and constructive.

Popular culture has its origins in folk culture, but is now thought of as being entertainment of which there is widespread acceptance and approval.

theatre. Folk song had dramatised and celebrated rural life; music hall provided an escape from repetitive drudgery in the factory and at home. The development of the popular press, with its emphasis on personalities and sensationalism, also played a role in defining popular culture, a process accelerated and intensified much later by radio, film and television.

Figure 2: Music hall

The industrialisation – and commercialisation – of popular culture completed its separation from high culture. Popular culture is immediate: its central aims are entertainment, escapism and making money. High culture can and does achieve all of these, but the synergy involved in creating a work of art – the process whereby the whole is greater than the sum of the parts – means that whilst its appeal may be less immediate, it works on its audience at a different, probably deeper level.

TASK

1 In the light of your specialised knowledge of youth culture, work in groups to define and describe current trends and movements among young people. Your presentation could take the form of a poster detailing preferred music, dress, appearance, language, norms of behaviour and socialisation.
2 The British Isles has historically consisted of four cultures – English, Scottish, Welsh and Northern Irish. What differences – actual and stereotypical – exist between them? Report your findings to the rest of the group.
3 Organise a debate on this motion. 'Popular culture is a commercial product, and represents nothing significant about the societies it seeks to entertain.'

3.6.2 The culture and values of a minority group

On 3 October 2006, Carl Roberts, a 32-year-old truck driver, shot dead five young girls in their Amish schoolroom in Lancaster County, Pennsylvania, USA. He wounded six others before killing himself. This incident made world-wide headlines, but not only because of its peculiar dreadfulness. The response to Carl Roberts and his actions by the families of the dead and maimed Amish children astonished and touched the world.

The grandfather of one child said 'We must not think evil of this man'. Another said 'I don't think there's anybody here that wants to do anything but forgive, and not only reach out to those who have suffered a loss in that way but to reach out to the family of the man who committed these acts.'

The Amish also offered practical comfort to Carl Roberts's family. Amish neighbours, including fathers who had lost daughters in the shooting, visited them and offered support and forgiveness for Roberts within hours of his death. A charitable fund to support the Roberts family was also set up by the Amish community.

The basis of this forgiveness was the religious belief of the Amish – descendants of a Christian sect who fled to Switzerland during the Reformation and eventually settled in Pennsylvania in 1730 as part of William Penn's experiment in religious tolerance in the young American nation.

The Amish of Lancaster County are a tourist attraction, partly because of their appearance and strict adherence to horse-powered transport. Because of the inward looking nature of their community they have also preserved a culture which gives an insight into life in 17th-century Europe.

Amish live by a set of rules known as *Ordnung* (= order), which dictates not only personal appearance but also the design of their horse-drawn buggies and the way they farm their land. Each community is self-contained, and there is some variation in *Ordnung* as a result. Some Amish will use motor cars, although they are not allowed to own one. Others will not allow electric lights of any kind.

The most visible part of Amish culture is that of dress and grooming. Clothes are made in plain fabrics in dark colours and from purely functional designs. There are often no collars, cuffs or lapels on an Amish suit, and clothes are worn un-ironed. Amish women usually wear a long-sleeved, full-skirted dress under a cape, and an apron. Amish men remain clean-shaven until they marry, when they are required to grow a beard, although moustaches are forbidden. Women never cut their hair, which is worn braided under a small white cap.

Figure 3: An Amish couple with their child

3 Domain exploration: applying synoptic skills

The significance of all this is humility, separation from the world and simplicity. Simplicity and separation also underpin their attitude to technology. Electricity and the devices that use it – radio, television, motor cars, computers – are seen as temptations to acquisitiveness and envy. More importantly, they are seen as interferences with family and community life. Electricity may be acceptable if it is naturally generated, e.g. by a windmill, and horse-drawn buggies have electric lights for safety reasons. Similarly, Amish will use a telephone for emergencies, but usually it will be shared by a whole community, kept in a wooden box in a field.

Children are educated in Amish private schools, but not beyond Year 8. They are exempted from Federal law by their religious principles. Schooling emphasises basic literacy and numeracy, along with Amish culture and values. Education is also part of home life, with farming and domestic skills playing a large role in Amish upbringing.

The family is the foundation stone of Amish culture, and reflects a patriarchal model long abandoned by the rest of America. The father is head of the household, and leads the other males in farming. The wife's role is purely domestic; she defers to her husband's decisions about family life. German is spoken at home, although English is learned at school and used to speak with non-Amish people. The preservation of this way of life is possible largely because Amish are allowed to marry only other Amish. Intermarriage would lead to the shunning (*meidung*) of the culprit – expulsion from the community and the cutting off of all communication, even that with family. Divorce is forbidden and separation extremely rare.

Amish are self-reliant, looking to their community for support in times of difficulty. They accept no welfare payments or government grants, and their pacifism exempts them from military service.

Amish worship is held in members' homes, led by a bishop, two ministers and a deacon – all male. Worship is simple, reflecting Amish belief that what binds generations together is tradition. This is nowhere better exemplified than in their rites of passage.

Their belief in adult baptism is what divorced them from the Lutheran Reformation 400 years ago. The commitment of Amish teenagers to this is tested by the custom of *rumspringa* – running around. During this period they are encouraged to sample life in the outside world, although still ultimately subject to their parents. They may start smoking, dress 'English', date other Amish on *rumspringa*, and experiment with alcohol. *Rumspringa* ends when the teenager requests baptism into the church or decides to leave altogether. Most request baptism and return to the austere way of life which nurtured them.

1 Use the internet to find examples of minority cultures inhabiting societies that do not accept their values. These minorities may be religious, ethnic or social. What problems may be caused by their existence?

2 Britain's transformation into a multicultural society involves learning about, and accepting, the norms and values of other cultures. Which aspects of British life may be enriched by this process, and which may be endangered?

An Amish wedding has at its centre the couple – although the bride wears blue rather than white. Weddings take place in the autumn, and involve no rings, flowers, photographs or reception. The ceremony takes place in the bride's home and is followed by a huge feast, after which the newly weds spend their wedding night there, before getting up early the next day to help with the clearing up.

Amish funerals are similarly simple. The service is held in the deceased's home. The coffin is a plain wooden box, and is often buried in an unmarked grave. Since ostentation plays no part in an Amish life, death is no reason to do things differently.

A critique of Amish culture could cite its attitude to women, its fundamentalism and illiberalism. However, a society in which the average wedding costs £20,000 (and the subsequent marriage has only a 50 per cent chance of surviving) should perhaps be slow to point its finger.

EXAMINATION TALK

Questions about culture are often couched in personal terms, asking you to describe yourself as a representative of the cultures – family, social, peer and age – to which you belong. It is common for candidates to see these as easy questions which can be answered by simplistic autobiography. This is a major mistake. The fact that you know all about yourself does not mean that a description will suffice. By all means write about your personal cultural norms, beliefs and values – but do so *analytically*, describing and judging yourself as objectively as possible. In other words, write such an answer as a small-scale case study with yourself as the subject. It may even help you to write your answer plan in the third person, as though you were writing about someone else.

WHAT NEXT?

This topic block approaches the notion of culture with such a wide perspective that it ought to be possible for you to follow your own interests within it, applying your other subject specialisms to it if this is appropriate. Internet research would then consist of websites in your preferred topic area.

A more general overview of various aspects of culture can be found at **www.religioustolerance.org** – an interesting website about Goth culture.
www.quehuong.org.vn is a website dealing with aspects of village culture in Vietnam.
www.culturefund.eu is a website about cultural trends and activities in EU countries.

EXAMINATION PRACTICE

1 What aspects of British culture would you wish to preserve, and which would you try to change? Illustrate your answer and give reasons for your choices.

2 Can minority cultures such as travellers and gypsies survive in modern Britain? What difficulties might be involved in preserving their culture?

3 What relationships can be seen to exist between social class and culture? Are such relationships real or imaginary?

3.7 Aesthetic evaluation

OVERVIEW

In this block of work we will look at

- the appeal and effect of art
- the message of art, with reference to literature, music, painting and architecture

- how we respond to art, with more examples from sculpture and novels.

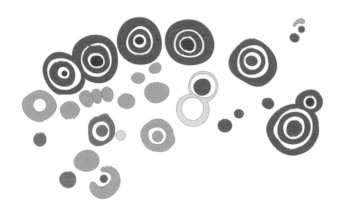

Figure 1

Look at the illustration above.

What could it be?

- A flying saucer park?
- A wallpaper design?
- A blood sample under the microscope?
- A sketch of the surface of the moon?

What is it?

It is one of over 1,000 rock carvings to be found throughout Northumberland. They have been dated to the Neolithic and Early Bronze Age between 4000 BCE and 1500 BCE.

Why the carvings were made and what they mean remains a mystery. The rock is on a hilltop, a natural outcrop, far too big to have been moved there. Traces of ten ancient burial mounds were found on another hilltop half a mile away, which suggests that this may have been on a prehistoric hill-route.

Most of the carvings so far discovered have the circular and cup-and-ring designs in common, but they cannot have been the work of the same person. Using the tools available at the time, making a carving like this one would have been a very long job. The panel measures nine feet by four, and has eight different motifs in it – arcs, semi-circles, concentric circles and cup-and-ring markings among them.

The carving suggests time, effort, thought, purpose, technique, design – and (certainly) meaning. It was made in an era when daily life was a struggle for survival. That it was made at all suggests that the creative instinct in humanity is as strong as the other instincts – food, shelter, sex – and that art is historically as much a part of the human experience as mathematics, technology and science.

QUESTIONS

1 Are the arts necessary?
2 'Music, of all the arts, has the greatest influence over the passions.' (Napoleon Bonaparte) Do you consider this to be true?
3 'Music expresses that which cannot be said and on which it is impossible to be silent.' (Victor Hugo) What does this mean?
4 'Architecture is frozen music.' (Goethe) Is it possible to describe one art only in terms of another?
5 'Critics are like eunuchs in a harem; they know how it's done, they've seen it done every day, but they're unable to do it themselves.' (Brendan Behan) Is this a fair summation of the value of critics?
6 'Literature adds to reality, it does not simply describe it. It enriches the necessary competencies that daily life requires and provides; and in this respect, it irrigates the deserts that our lives have already become.' (CS Lewis) Is this a realistic summary of what literature means to you?
7 'Drama lies in extreme exaggeration of the feelings, an exaggeration that dislocates flat everyday reality.' (Eugene Ionesco) Does art have to exaggerate to make its point?
8 'Poetry is just the evidence of life. If your life is burning well, poetry is just the ash.' (Leonard Cohen) Is poetry therefore the most personal of all the arts?
9 'You don't take a photograph, you make it.' (Ansel Adams) Can a photograph be a work of art in the same way that a painting can?
10 'Where the spirit does not work with the hand there is no art.' (Leonardo da Vinci) What is the relationship between craftsmanship and artistry?

3.7.1 The appeal and effect of art

INTEGRATING KNOWLEDGE

Look back at AS 1.6.1 on page 62 for more on this topic.

One purpose of art is to communicate, and the process begins with the questions which a work of art invokes from its audience.

When we read a novel or a poem, or watch a play or a film, we ask ourselves 'what is it about?' Looking at a picture or a sculpture we ask ourselves 'why has the artist seen the subject in that way?' Our response to architecture often begins with the question 'what is this building for?' Our response to music may be 'how does this music make me feel?' or 'what is the composer hoping to make me feel?'

3 Domain exploration: applying synoptic skills

That we ask these questions, and that each of them points in a different direction, shows how varied the appeal and effect of art is. As long as civilisations have left traces behind them, part of those traces has been artistic.

The oldest of these traces is sculpture. *The Venus of Tan-Tan*, perhaps the oldest representation of a female figure, was found in Moroccan sediments half a million years old. *The Willendorf Venus* – perhaps an element in a fertility cult – was carved 22,000 years ago. A religious element is also seen in carved relief work in Egyptian temples, as well as in the most famous monument of all, the *Sphinx*.

Preservation of the earliest drawings and paintings has depended on a favourable environment. The best prehistoric examples are 16,000-year-old paintings discovered in caves at Lascaux in France. No one knows why these detailed and colourful paintings of bulls, horses and antelopes were made, but a star map also found in the caves suggests a mixture of scientific and religious purpose.

Drama and poetry survived by oral transmission long before the development of writing 6,000 years ago. In this way folklore and religious traditions were preserved. Greek drama, which flourished in the millenium BCE, reflects a more complex society. The theme of Aristophanes' *Lysistrata* – women withholding sex from their men to stop them fighting wars – reflects a sophisticated view of how the world works as well as offering a wry comment on marriage.

Figure 2: Cave painting, Lascaux, France

Music is at least as old as drama – musical instruments have been found on archaeological sites dating back 4,000 years. It was not until 1200 CE that a reliable method of writing music down could be preserved. Since then music has become the most varied of all art forms, and probably the only one to which nearly everyone responds in some way.

The youngest art form – film – is less than a century old, but is probably the most widespread and the most popular of all. It is also, like photography, the one which bears the closest apparent resemblance to reality. Because of this, film and photography have become powerful tools in advertising and propaganda. The camera not only *does* lie, but it also has to – whether it is selling a lifestyle or telling the story of an alien invasion. (See the photos of George W Bush on page 59 and Princess Diana on page 166.)

Art also plays a role in everyday life. The character and flavour of the towns and cities we live in is a function of their architecture, a very public form of art. As well as symbolising power or wealth, buildings can tell the story of how a society has developed. What does the architecture of Cambridge tell us about the relationship between the mediaeval church and academic scholarship? How did a village consisting of a Norman castle, a Norman church and a row of cottages work?

INTEGRATING KNOWLEDGE

What do you see as the role of art? You will have thought about this at AS: look back at topic 1.6.3 (page 64) to make a link with your AS studies.

Also on the everyday scale is fashion, which many people see as an art form, not least those who see clothes as a branch of semiotics – the philosophy of signs and symbols. In the past, clothes, jewellery and hair-styles often symbolised rank and office. In modern times what we wear often says something about who we think we are. The basis of fashion is design, which has also become very important in many areas of everyday life. The houses we live in and the cars we drive reflect the age in which we live by their marriage of form, function and material.

Despite their variety and scope, all the arts have things in common. They incorporate design, technique, form and function and, above all, they communicate. They do so in such a way that the whole work of art somehow becomes greater than the sum of its parts – a phenomenon called **synergy** – which is why what we call great art does not wear out.

KEY TERMS

The principle of synergy explains why we continue to be moved or excited by a work of art long after we become familiar with it, and despite knowing precisely how it works.

TASK

1 Compile your own personal list of 'Desert Island Discs' – eight pieces of music which would last you the rest of your life. The reasons for your choices are as important as the music you choose. Write a short essay listing the pieces and the reasons why you chose them. When you have done this, see if you can draw any conclusions about what music means to you.
2 The 'Desert Island Discs' idea could be applied to other art forms – favourite novels, poems, paintings or buildings. The important element is to try to hone your critical faculties by giving reasons for your choices which are as much about the work of art as they are about you.

Bury College
Millennium LRC

3.7.2 The message of art

What do the arts have to say to us? Written and spoken forms of art are at least explicit. From a play, a novel or a film we expect a story, from poetry the evocation of an emotion, a place or a person. However, is the 'story' the whole story?

Plays, novels and films work on several levels, which is why our response to them is so complex. Arthur Miller's *The Crucible* tells the story of the Salem witch trials in 17th-century Massachusetts. It is a story of lying accusations of witchcraft, and confessions extorted by threat and torture. It is also about the infamous House Un-American Activities Committee led by Senator Joseph McCarthy, before which Miller appeared. This committee was dedicated to weeding out supposed communist infiltrators in US government, a product of Cold War paranoia. Miller testified before the Committee, but refused to incriminate other people. *The Crucible*'s hero, John Proctor, took the same line and was hanged for it.

Casablanca, a film which regularly appears in 'top ten' lists of greatest films, is a tightly plotted melodrama based on the eternal triangle theme, set against the background of the Second World War. In terms of its characters – Rick Blaine, Louis Renault, Victor Laszlo and Ilsa Lund – the story focuses on notions of honour, duty and self-sacrifice. Its underlying themes can be seen as an essay on the implications and consequences of neutrality in war. When the film was being made, America was not involved in the Second World War. By the time it was released in 1942, the USA, like Rick Blaine and Louis Renault, had opted for involvement.

This kind of analysis can readily be applied to art forms relying on words, action and pictures. However, when we look at less explicit forms of art the problem is different. What do music, paintings and buildings 'mean'?

Beethoven: *Symphony no 3 in E flat major*, Opus 55, 'Bonaparte'

Had Napoleon Bonaparte not crowned himself Emperor of France in 1804, this is how we would know the *Eroica* symphony. Beethoven's admiration for Napoleon – he compared him to the consuls of Ancient Rome – underlay this music and the original title page shows the dedication to him.

Beethoven's bitter disappointment in what he saw as Napoleon's betrayal of his ideals can still be seen on the title page of the symphony's manuscript. The name 'Bonaparte' is crossed out so violently as to have torn the page.

What can this story tell us about the music? We can assume that Beethoven attempted to celebrate the concepts underlying Napoleon's presumed political vision – nobility, unselfishness, idealism, democracy. These ideas may be useful as a guide, but no more than that – it is impossible to make a piece of music sound explicitly like *Magna Carta*.

Rather, we may hear Beethoven's own idealism in this music, which is monumental in scale and emotionally powerful. In the second movement's funeral march we may hear also the bitter regret underpinning Beethoven's alternative title – '*A heroic symphony, in memory of a great man*'.

Some people would say that such a historical context says little that is helpful to the listener, who should experience the music for what it may be worth to him or her emotionally. There is much to be said for this point of view. Music is both explicit and abstract, and that is why our reaction to it is primarily a sensual one. It was another composer, Ralph Vaughan Williams, who said 'Music has no use – and that is its greatest glory'.

Picasso: *Guernica* (1937)

On 26 April 1937, bombers of the Luftwaffe 'Condor' legion, supporting General Franco's Nationalist armies, bombed the Basque town of Guernica. At least 300 people were killed, and many more were injured.

Picasso began the painting – commissioned for the 1937 World's Fair – a week later. In his own words

> 'In the panel on which I am working, which I shall call *Guernica*, and in all my recent works of art, I clearly express my abhorrence of the military caste which has sunk Spain in an ocean of pain and death.'

The painting, which measures 23 feet by 11 feet (7 m × 3.3 m), is black and white, and presents brutal images of death and suffering. There is no explicit reference to war in the picture, which is a domestic interior. A bull grieves over a dead child held in a woman's arms; a horse, speared through by a javelin, falls, in its death agony, on top of a dismembered soldier; terrified women look on, helplessly.

Guernica remains a powerful and iconic image of the cruelty of war. Picasso refused to allow its return to Spain until the establishment of a republic there. It was not until 1978, five years after Picasso's death and three after Franco's, that this happened.

Durham Cathedral

Durham Cathedral and Castle face each other across the Palace Green, symbols of ecclesiastical and temporal power. The cathedral was founded in 1093 and took 40 years to build. Its Norman design and craftsmanship have remained largely unaltered in 1,000 years. It is strategically positioned on a hill surrounded by a loop of the River Wear, the banks of which form a precipitous gorge. From its roof, on a clear day, you can see over 20 miles (32 km) in all directions.

English history is told in this building. The Reformation saw its monastic foundation surrendered to Henry VIII and many of its treasures destroyed or confiscated. In 1650 it was closed and used by Cromwell as a prison for 3,000 Scots prisoners of the Civil War, and the damage done by his soldiers to the statues can still be seen. In 1832, the Bishop founded the University of Durham, the third oldest in England.

However, the building is more than its history. It represents an astonishing achievement (as well as devotion) on the part of its builders, as well as a religious tradition reaching back 1,000 years. You do not, however, need to believe in God to find in its atmosphere a flavour of the eternal.

3.7.3 How we respond to art

With art, as with people, first impressions mean a lot. Consider these opening sentences from famous novels.

'It is a truth universally acknowledged, that a single man in possession of a good fortune must be in want of a wife.'

Pride and Prejudice, Jane Austen

'Hale knew, before he had been in Brighton three hours, that they meant to murder him.'

Brighton Rock, Graham Greene

'It was a bright cold day in April, and the clocks were striking thirteen.'

Nineteen Eighty Four, George Orwell

Each of these openings has something in common – a challenge to the reader.

Do all wealthy single men need a wife? Who says so? Who are these people who acknowledge this universal truth? And who is Jane Austen to make such an all-embracing claim?

Who is Hale? What is he doing in Brighton? Who are 'they'? And why are they going to murder him? Graham Greene's opening grips the attention like good journalism.

And what sort of a world is it where clocks strike thirteen?

Having engaged the reader's attention, then it is the author's task to sustain it. Similar criteria apply to theatre and film. The opening scene of *Hamlet* and the battle sequence which opens the film *Saving Private Ryan* are supremely effective beginnings, but they need contrast and a change of pace in order to sustain an audience's interest.

The importance of the initial response applies also to musical and visual art. Whether or not our interest is sustained depends on the ingenuity and craftsmanship of the composer or painter.

Then, having listened to the music, read the novel or watched the film or play, how do we respond?

Consider these four responses to Leonard Bernstein's *West Side Story*.

A

'It was great – I was hooked from the start, and there wasn't a dull moment in it. And the ending was so sad.'

B

'I can't see how you could improve on this. Marvellous dancing, so many different types of music, a really strong plot – well, it would be, seeing that it's borrowed from Shakespeare. The song lyrics were good as well. I was in tears at the end, but there were some really funny moments along the way. Ten out of ten!'

C

'Four great talents on top form doesn't always guarantee a result, but in *West Side Story* it works beautifully. Bernstein is a really versatile composer – jazz, rock, latin, ballad, music-hall – he can handle them all wonderfully. In Stephen Sondheim he has the kind of lyric-writer a composer dreams about – original, witty and inventive, with his own sense of rhythm, and Arthur Laurents' dialogue gives a real flavour of how these kids talk. Put these together with Jerome Robbins' inventive and athletic dance sequences, and you have a masterpiece.'

D

'While critics speculated about the comic-tragic darkness of the musical, audiences were captivated. The story appealed to society's undercurrent of rebellion from authority that surfaced in 1950s films like *Rebel without a Cause*. *West Side Story* took this one step farther by combining the classic and the hip. Robbins' energetic choreography and Bernstein's grand score accentuated the satiric, hard-edged lyrics of Sondheim, and playwright Arthur Laurents' capture of the angry voice of urban youth. The musical also made points in its description of troubled youth and the devastating effects of poverty and racism. Juvenile delinquency is seen as an ailment of society: 'No one wants a fella with a social disease!' One writer summed up the reasons for the show's popularity in these terms: 'On the cusp of the 1960s, American society, still recovering from the enormous upheaval of World War II, was seeking stability and control.' Extracted from a review in *Time* magazine, 6 October 1957

3 Domain exploration: applying synoptic skills

Each of these responses is authentic, but it is worth looking at what they actually say.

A is completely subjective: the personal reaction is the sole criterion. **B** knows that musical theatre is about collaboration between music, lyrics, story and dance, and recognises that good theatre contains contrasts of mood and tone. **C** evaluates and comments on the individual contributions of each collaborator. It is possible that this writer is a fan of musical theatre and may know other work by Bernstein, Sondheim, Laurents and Robbins. **D** takes a broader view, placing the work in its social as well as its theatrical context, and linking it with the **zeitgeist**. Someone writing a history of musical theatre in 100 years' time would certainly refer to critic D, and possibly use critic C as the starting point for further commentary.

Analysis depends on knowledge as well as taste, and an informed response to art takes notice of both. Being able to relate a work of art to its genre and period helps to develop taste, as does some technical knowledge of the creative processes involved in making it.

If art has a functional aspect, then it must fulfil that function as well as appealing to the senses. A new concert hall may be a beautiful building – but it must have good acoustics, and be soundproof, warm and comfortable. Portrait paintings need to be realist in style. An abstract portrait may satisfy the artist, but we need to be able to recognise the subject.

Civic art is the means whereby towns and cities enhance their individuality in an age where commerce tends to make all high streets and city centres look the same. As well as providing colour and interest, works of civic art often pick up and illustrate local references as well as national preoccupations. The bronze bull at the new Bull Ring Centre in Birmingham, the statue of Alison Lapper in Trafalgar Square, and the statues of Jackie Milburn and Alan Shearer which will soon welcome visitors to St James's Park, Newcastle, are all examples of how art can enhance an urban landscape.

KEY TERMS

Zeitgeist is German for 'spirit of the time'. In arts criticism it refers to the prevailing intellectual trends and moral development of an historical period. Thus 'the permissive society' of the 1960s suggests a period when – in the arts and in everyday life – rules were seen as things to be challenged and broken.

TASK

Split the class into small groups, and go to see a play, a film, an opera, an art exhibition, a cathedral or a concert. If possible, choose an art form you have not experienced before. Before you go, research some background information about what you are going to see or hear.

As soon as you can afterwards, compile a group review of the experience, giving your personal reactions as well as the reasons for them. Compare these reviews with any newspaper or website reviews published by professional critics. What can you learn from the comparison?

TASK

Compile a short biography of an important fashion designer, photographer, painter, sculptor, playwright, director, poet, composer or architect who is still alive or who was born in the 20th century. Concentrate on the artist's motives, preoccupations and major themes. Produce a small poster for display. Suggestions include

Artists:	Banksy, Jacob Epstein, Antony Gormley, David Hockney, Rachael Whiteread
Playwrights:	Samuel Beckett, Alan Bennett, John Osborne, Harold Pinter, Tom Stoppard
Poets:	Ted Hughes, Philip Larkin, Benjamin Zephaniah
Composers:	Benjamin Britten, James MacMillan, Michael Nyman
Architects:	David Chipperfield, Richard Rogers, Basil Spence

EXAMINATION TALK

'Writing about music,' said Frank Zappa, 'is like dancing about architecture.' The pungency of this observation perhaps distracts attention from its accuracy. Good art can only say what it says in the medium chosen by the artist. A composer who makes a verbal explanation of his music seems to acknowledge that his music does not of itself fully speak his mind. In answering questions on aesthetics, an ounce of fact is worth a ton of fine writing.

Generally speaking, questions on this area will allow you to write about the art-form of your choice. (Choose a piece of music, a poem or a building which moves you and analyse why this is so.) Examination preparation should include exploring the background of (say) your favourite writers, listing their themes and preoccupations, identifying writers whose influence is evident, placing the work in context and finally assessing their importance.

Resist the temptation to gush, or be anecdotal, or concentrate on the artist rather than the art. Doing the latter would let you in for Frank Zappa's (wholly merited) condemnation of pop music journalism: 'Rock journalism consists of people who can't write interviewing people who can't talk for the benefit of people who can't read.'

WHAT NEXT?

These websites are recommended.

www.artswebsites.co.uk – an overview of artistic activities and facilities in the UK.
www.bbc.co.uk/arts – news and views on all kinds of art in the UK and beyond.
www.artscouncil.org.uk – information on the support offered by the state for the arts.

This is also an area where research in local arts centres – theatres, concert halls, galleries and libraries – can be useful.

To understand more about the nature of criticism, read reviews in the press of, for example, TV programmes you have watched. Try to analyse the differences between informed opinion and gut reaction.

EXAMINATION PRACTICE

1 'I don't know anything about music, but I know what I like.' Evaluate this viewpoint, and assess how valuable criticism of music produced from it might be.
2 'Art produces ugly things which frequently become more beautiful with time. Fashion, on the other hand, produces beautiful things which always become ugly with time.' (Jean Cocteau) If this statement is true, what conclusions may be drawn from it?
3 Choose a piece of art – sculpture, painting, literature, music, theatre – which seems to you to be a masterpiece. What features of your chosen masterpiece might a critic use to develop a case to suggest that it might not be one?
4 Use the research you carried out for your poster presentation (on page 185) as the basis for an essay on the artist of your choice, using the same emphases of preoccupations, motives and themes.

3.8 The nature of scientific objectivity and the question of progress

---

OVERVIEW

In this block of work we will look at

- how progress in scientific techniques influences functions of society
- how scientific discoveries are made and progress achieved

- what society demands and needs of science and scientists
- how science and society influence what people believe
- brief biographies of two important scientists.

The fictional detective Sherlock Holmes was modelled by Sir Arthur Conan Doyle on his teacher, Dr Joseph Bell. In diagnosing illness, Bell insisted on meticulous observation, scientific testing, and the drawing of conclusions by rigorous deduction.

The most famous scientific detective was fictional. However, the scientific methods which Holmes practised – observation, igniting a suspicion, gathering clues and fashioning proof – were authentic.

What has changed is the contents of the scientist's toolbox. Holmes's imaginary laboratory (which probably looked a bit like Figure 1a) is cluttered with reagent bottles and apparatus; the modern Holmes clinches his investigation using possibly the most powerful tool of all, the computer (Figure 1b).

Figure 1a: a 19th-century chemist in his laboratory

Figure 1b: a researcher in a modern laboratory

QUESTIONS

1 Is scientific progress always achieved methodically?
2 'Science proceeds along a zig-zag path toward what we hope will be ultimate truth, a path that began with humanity's earliest attempts to fathom the cosmos and whose end we cannot predict.' (Brian Greene) Will science one day understand everything?
3 'One can not impede scientific progress.' (Mahmoud Ahmadinejad) Why then might people try to do this?
4 'How wonderful that we have met with a paradox. Now we have some hope of making progress.' (Niels Bohr, atomic physicist) What is a paradox, and why would it be valuable to a scientist?
5 Should scientists try to respond to the needs of society, or give it what they think people ought to want?
6 What social needs do you think are currently not being met by scientific progress?
7 Why do people capable of believing in God disbelieve in science?
8 Are scientific intelligence and religious belief incompatible?
9 Can a political ideology be founded on scientific principles?
10 Which modern scientists do you think will be remembered for as long as Isaac Newton? Why?

3.8.1 Influence of developing scientific techniques on progress

In 1905 Mr and Mrs Thomas Farrow were murdered, for the contents of the cash-box, at the Chapman Oil & Colour Stores in Deptford. Two brothers, Alfred and Albert Stratton, were seen near the crime scene at the relevant time. They owned burglar's masks, and, after reading about the crime, had altered their appearance. They were spending more money than usual, and had tried to persuade a friend to give them an alibi.

This circumstantial evidence would not have secured a conviction, especially for murder. However, a thumbprint, left by Alfred Stratton on the cash-box, did. This scientific evidence sent the Stratton brothers to the gallows – the first time a death sentence had been passed on evidence using the new technique of fingerprinting.

The central principle of forensic science is that 'every contact leaves a trace'. The individuality of some of those traces has been recognised for centuries. The first systematic work on fingerprinting was done in India, partly because of the custom of Indian merchants sealing contracts using their thumbprint as a signature.

Fingerprints have been accepted as evidence in law since 1905. Initially, reliable prints could only be taken from non-absorbent surfaces – paint, metal, glass, polished wood. However, it is now possible to take prints from absorbent surfaces like paper and cardboard. The modern fingerprint officer has methods specific to different surfaces, as well as different light sources – infrared or ultraviolet – to read the evidence. Comparisons are made using digitised images on a computer, saving thousands of hours.

Crucially, fingerprints are now only one of the contact traces used by forensic scientists to locate an individual at a crime scene. The genetic fingerprint carried by everyone in their DNA can be read from minute quantities of bodily fluids – sweat, blood, saliva, mucus, semen – or from body parts such as skin and hair.

However, despite the technical progress which enables these advances, the basic objective scientific principles remain. Observation, the gathering of evidence, and logical deduction remain of paramount importance. Disproof of ideas is also progress – the disproof of an untruth is as important as the proof of a truth. As Sherlock Holmes remarked, whenever you have eliminated the impossible, whatever remains, however improbable, must be true.

INTEGRATING KNOWLEDGE

Link what you study here back to AS: topic block 2.2 covered understanding scientific methods, principles, criteria and their applications.

TASK

In groups, research a criminal trial where forensic evidence was especially important to the outcome of the case. Prepare a summary of how the evidence was obtained, evaluated and used.

3.8.2 How science progresses

Penicillin was discovered in 1929 by Alexander Fleming, and the story of how he did it is a classic of scientific history.

He was conducting experiments on a strain of *Staphylococcus* – the bacterium responsible for pneumonia, wound infections, septicaemia and food poisoning. One Friday afternoon, the technician locking up the laboratory forgot to close the windows. When Fleming returned on the Monday he found that a spore, which must have entered the lab through the open window, had formed a mould in his Petri dish and had destroyed the culture of *Staphylococcus* he had prepared. Penicillin had been discovered.

This anecdote illustrates the role played by chance in scientific discovery – or does it? A closer look tells a more complicated story.

Fleming's research was concerned with wound infections – an important area, since post-operative septicaemia was still a common hazard of even simple surgery. He identified the mould attacking his staphylococci as *Penicillium notatum*, and derived the name penicillin for its anti-bacterial agent. Penicillin was, however, very unstable, and Fleming was unable to purify it to a concentration in which it would be clinically useful. He made a crude penicillin ointment which controlled eye infections, but nothing more.

In 1934, Ernst Chain and Howard Florey began research at Cambridge University into naturally occurring anti-bacterial substances. *Penicillium notatum* is one of the group of moulds which form on stale bread, so it was natural for them to pick up Fleming's findings. Using the new technique of freeze-drying, they produced a penicillin concentrate a million times more powerful than Fleming's. By 1939, they had successfully tested penicillin on mice, and by 1942 human tests proved penicillin to be a revolutionary advance in the treatment of bacterial infection.

At this stage penicillin was still a laboratory substance, not a marketable drug. A research team at Peoria, Illinois, headed by Dr Robert Coghill, refined methods of growing the mould *Penicillium notatum* in bulk, then of extracting penicillin from it, and finally of refining it to the required potency. Only then, 15 years after Alexander Fleming's laboratory accident, could penicillin be marketed.

Sixty years later, antibiotic drugs – targeted to specific bacteria following years of research and development – are a major tool of modern medicine.

However, who should take the credit? Fleming, Chain and Florey were jointly awarded the Nobel Prize for Medicine in 1945 for their pioneering work. Between their original concept and the final product stood an army of scientists pooling their expertise towards their common goal.

Figure 2a: Alexander Fleming

Figure 2b: Ernst Chain

Figure 2c: Howard Florey

3 Domain exploration: applying synoptic skills

The historian Thomas Carlyle defined genius as an infinite capacity for taking pains. Thomas Edison more prosaically said that it consisted of one per cent inspiration and 99 per cent perspiration. Both of these observations apply to scientific progress.

Some scientific developments have been accidental to an extent. Wilhelm Roentgen was researching into cathode radiation when he discovered another form of radiation. It still bears the name he gave it – the X-ray. Other scientific developments have occurred as spin-offs from other research. Edison was refining his telephone and telegraph inventions when he first recorded the human voice. Because the reproduction was so poor he suspended that research to do further work on electric light, and returned to it only when Alexander Graham Bell threatened to market a refined phonograph before Edison did.

However, scientific progress mainly results from unspectacular and meticulous research. Archimedes' curtailed bath, Newton's apple and James Watt's singing kettle make pleasant anecdotes, but poor scientific history.

TASK

Choose a scientific discovery which has changed society and trace its development. What effects and influences has it had on science and society?

3.8.3 The influence of social demands, needs and beliefs on science

Social demands

In 1901, new-born children in the United Kingdom had an average life expectancy of 47 years. Men died on average at the age of 45, women at the age of 49, a pattern which was reflected in most of Western Europe. There was a high rate of infant mortality – 14 per cent of children died perinatally (from about three months before to one month after birth) – and life was shortened by people's vulnerability to common illnesses such as influenza, food poisoning and septicaemia. The influenza pandemic of 1918 killed 238,000 British citizens, the greatest loss of life through illness since a cholera epidemic in 1849.

In 1999, British children were born with an average life expectancy of 77.5 years. On average, boys born in 1999 will die in 2074, girls in 2079. This is partly down to vastly improved medical care – the infant mortality rate is now 0.58 per cent – as well as better diet, safety legislation and the decline of dangerous occupations such as coal-mining and fishing.

With increased life expectancy, however, comes a greater expectation of what life should be like.

TASK

Medical science has played a large role in the extension of active life. Organise a debate on the advantages and disadvantages of this.

In terms of age, 50 is the new 30, and 70 the new 50. People not only expect to live longer, but also to remain in good physical, mental and sexual health. There is therefore a huge and growing demand for scientists to develop if not the elixir of life, then at least several lesser versions of it.

Obesity, for example, is a growing problem – the British Heart Foundation estimates that 28,000 deaths are caused by it each year. The best treatment for obesity has been known for over 2,000 years, as the Latin proverb *optima medicina temperantia est* (moderation is the best medicine) suggests.

However, the social demand for a slimming 'treatment' has led to anti-obesity drugs becoming available on prescription. Though they were originally intended for morbidly obese patients whose lives were endangered by their weight, there is now a flourishing commercial trade in these drugs. They are marketed to those who expect science to solve all their problems – even those brought about, as in this case, by their own self-indulgence.

Social needs

'Civilization as we know it is coming to an end soon. This is not the proclamation of a doomsday cult, apocalypse bible prophecy sect, or conspiracy theory society. Rather, it is the scientific conclusion of the best-paid, most widely-respected geologists, physicists, bankers, and investors in the world. These are rational, professional, conservative individuals who are absolutely terrified by a phenomenon known as Global Peak Oil.

Oil will not just 'run out' because all oil production follows a bell curve. This is true whether we're talking about an individual field, a country, or on the planet as a whole.

Oil is increasingly plentiful on the upslope of the bell curve, increasingly scarce and expensive on the down slope. The peak of the curve coincides with the point at which the endowment of oil has been 50 per cent depleted. Once the peak is passed, oil production begins to go down while cost begins to go up.

In practical and considerably oversimplified terms, this means that if 2005 was the year of global peak oil, world-wide oil production in the year 2030 will be the same as it was in 1980. However, the world's population in 2030 will be both much larger (approximately double its current figure of 6.5 billion) and much more industrialized (oil-dependent) than it was in 1980. Consequently, world-wide demand for oil will outpace world-wide production of oil by a significant margin. As a result, the price will skyrocket, oil dependant economies will crumble, and resource wars will explode.'

www.lifeaftertheoilcrash.net

Global peak oil (see page 136) will cause enormous economic and political difficulties. However, the practical solution will have to come from a dedicated cooperative scientific effort to solve the problem – which is society's need for abundant cheap energy.

In the past, similarly focused efforts have been mounted by dedicated teams of scientists. The Manhattan Project of 1942 and the 1969 NASA Moon landings were two examples. Devising ways to meet society's demand for cheap energy needs the same cooperative scientific focus, and above all the same level of financial investment.

Figure 3: Moon landing

Social beliefs

Society has an ambivalent relationship with science. We think that science can achieve anything, including solving problems we have inflicted on ourselves. At the same time, science A-level entries are falling off, university science departments are closing for lack of students, and the popular understanding of science is haphazard.

For example, it is accepted by most people that global warming is currently happening at a rate which could have serious consequences by the end of this century. Some scientists claim that it is a phenomenon that is a result of human activity; others that it is a current phase in the global climatic cycle. Still others maintain that it is a combination, with natural processes accelerated to an irreversible point by human contribution. What is clear is that global warming is a problem, and an urgent one.

So what do lay people think about it? Look at this extract from a discussion on a Sky News website.

> **Question:** The weather has been completely different in the last two years, is it global warming?

And here is a selection of the answers.

A
'Yes, it is global warming, because as the ice caps are melting the water is rising, and the ice caps keep the world cold and because they are melting it is getting hotter. At this current moment in November it is hot and we are in winter.'

B
'The Ice caps are not melting!!! Antarctica gets to −80°C in the winter and a balmy −30°C in the summer (four months of the year). This means that the global temperature would have to increase by these amounts for any melting to occur. A 5°C global increase would then make it −75°C and −25°C. Hardly melting temperature is it?'

C
'Sorry to burst bubbles, but this is a perfectly normal phase for the planet. All this planet-warming rubbish that the world population is swallowing is done for one simple reason. Keep taxes high and people's minds off other more important issues, the issues the politicians don't want you thinking about.'

A society that knows so little about the world it inhabits has problems (other than global warming) that it cannot begin to understand.

INTEGRATING KNOWLEDGE

AS 2.1.2 studies the science of global warming and greenhouse gases (page 69). Do you consider that current social and political debates over global are informed enough by real understanding?

3 Domain exploration: applying synoptic skills

3.8.4 The influence of science and society on beliefs

When Charles Darwin published his *Origin of Species* in 1859, 'Darwin's bulldog', the scientist Thomas Huxley, warned him that believers in **creationism** would attack the notion that men and apes shared a common ancestor. Sure enough, at a British Association meeting in June 1860, Bishop Samuel Wilberforce asked Huxley scornfully, 'Is it on your grandfather's or your grandmother's side that you claim descent from a monkey?'

However, as this extract from a paper presented to the British Academy in 2003 shows, the relationship between science, society and belief is a complex and subtle one. Questions such as Bishop Wilberforce's often generate unexpected answers.

> 'Huxley succeeded in attracting wide publicity for Darwin's thought, but at the cost of arousing needless antagonisms, and distorting the whole tenor of subsequent discussion. His set-to marks the beginning of the rift between the Two Cultures, with the withdrawal of professional scientists into an intellectual ghetto, and the banishment of science from the mainstream of national life. Biology has suffered from not being able to engage with the humanities.
>
> One example is racism. Wilberforce was a leading anti-racist, and one of his worries about Darwinism was that it could be used to justify the enslavement of negroes. Modern opinion is anti-racist too, so much so that for many racial research is a no-go area. If a scientist were to maintain as a scientific truth that black men were on average less intelligent than white men, he would be excoriated. Wilberforce could allow that evolution could be true, or that there are significant differences between the races, and still maintain that we are not just animals, and that all men, whatever the colour of their skin, are children of God. But a science that claims both to be autonomous and to give us the complete truth cannot do this. Faced with this dilemma, some people will accept the science and deny the moral status of mankind: others, however, will sense the immoral implications of Darwinism, and, on that account, reject it out of hand.
>
> Huxley thought he was fighting for science, but by being so confrontational, he stimulated an anti-science counter-attack. He did not realise it, but Huxley helped to create creationism.'

Recently there has been controversy over the theory of **intelligent design**, which says that life is too complex to have evolved by a natural process, and must have been designed by an intelligence of some sort. Whatever your personal beliefs, it is a notion worth considering. However, should this be done in science lessons, or as part of the religious studies syllabus?

KEY TERMS

Creationism is the belief that the creation stories in the *Book of Genesis* are literally true.

INTEGRATING KNOWLEDGE

Evolution continues to be a battleground of beliefs. Outline some different ways in which scientific, religious and social beliefs interact on this topic.

KEY TERMS

The theory of **intelligent design** represents an attempted compromise between creationism and Darwinism. It is not a new idea, being based on William Paley's *Evidences* of 1802, which asked the question 'If we found a watch, would we argue that it came into being by chance?'

TASK

TASK

In groups, choose one of the following propositions about science and belief, and discuss it. Present a brief summary of your conclusions to the rest of the class. (It might be a useful starting point to look up the people who made these propositions.)

'When religion was strong and science weak, men mistook magic for medicine; now, when science is strong and religion weak, men mistake medicine for magic.' *Thomas Szasz*

'Science makes major contributions to minor needs. Religion, however small its successes, is at least at work on the things that matter most.' *Oliver Wendell Holmes*

'It is idle to pretend, as many do, that there is no contradiction between religion and science. Science contradicts religion as surely as Judaism contradicts Islam – they are absolutely and irresolvably conflicting views. Unless, that is, science is obliged to change its fundamental nature.' *Brian Appleyard*

3.8.5 The biographies of important scientists

Michael Faraday (1791–1867) Electricity is so much a part of modern life that few of us think much about what it is or where it comes from. People knew about electricity before Faraday, but he worked out how to use it as a source of power.

Faraday was born in London to a poor family and had only a very basic education but he went to the public lectures of the famous scientist Humphrey Davy and was inspired by them. He became Davy's assistant and learned to be an excellent experimental scientist: working things out through careful testing and experiments. Interestingly, his maths was never that good – he was practical rather than theoretical.

Although Davy gave him his big break in science, he also seems to have grown jealous of Faraday and stopped his early work on electromagnetism and moved him on to dead-end projects. Some other scientists of the time never treated Faraday as anything but a poor upstart – never as a gentleman. But Faraday continued his experiments and after Davy's death his work on electromagnetism laid the foundations for all the electrical technology around us today.

TASK

Faraday was hindered as much as helped by the scientific community of his day. What about today? Explain how scientists help each other. Then explain how and why they might try to block others' progress. Which do you think is most common?

3 Domain exploration: applying synoptic skills

Charles Darwin (1809–1882) In the 19th century in Christian societies like Britain, many believed that the world was created as described in the Bible: in six days. The huge diversity of life and the amazing adaptation of life forms to their environment – the way in which all life fitted together perfectly – was seen as proof of the greatness of God and the perfection of his creation. These beliefs are still held today by many millions of people around the world.

Charles Darwin was a naturalist and geologist who developed the theory that organisms changed over time rather than remaining just as God had created them. The process by which this occurred – natural selection – ensured that only those that were best suited to their environment survived. In this way, over millions of years, even tiny differences between individual creatures could be reinforced and enhanced until entirely different species developed from common ancestors. The Bible describes how God created humans in his own image. Darwin described how humans evolved from apes. The resulting clash between religion and science has not yet been resolved.

Darwin first planned to be a doctor like his father but couldn't bear the butchery of surgery. Then he trained to be a clergyman, but spent most of his time collecting beetles instead of studying. But the experience that changed his life was his voyage as a naturalist on board the *Beagle*, which took him all over the world and showed him the huge variety of life on Earth. It took him many years to write up his theories. He was motivated into publishing his work because other scientists had started to put forward views similar to his. However, few other scientists had the weight of evidence and the answers to as many problems and counter-arguments as Darwin, and it is his work that remains the most influential today.

Marie Curie (1867–1934) The first woman to be awarded a Nobel Prize (for physics, shared with her husband) and still the only woman to have been awarded two Nobel Prizes in different areas (physics and chemistry), Marie Curie was a Polish–French scientist who first explored radioactivity: a term she coined. She and her husband, Pierre, discovered the two elements polonium and radium and identified many of the properties of radioactive elements.

Marie Curie is still one of the relatively few famous female scientists and she has been a very important role model for all scientists but especially for women. Her daughter Irene also won a Nobel Prize for her work on radioactivity.

Despite her fame and the prestige of her Nobel Prizes, the French public were often critical of her Polish birth and upbringing and it was not until some years after her death that she became a heroine of France as well as of Poland. Interestingly, like Darwin, she lost much of her religious faith after family tragedies. Her work with radioactive materials almost certainly contributed to her death: at the time the dangers of radioactivity were not known.

TASK

How do social beliefs affect the way science works and scientific progress? Darwin was deeply troubled by the impact of his theory on religious belief – but published anyway. Why do you think he did publish eventually?

Stephen Hawking (1942–) Stephen Hawking is undoubtedly the most famous scientist alive today, which is perhaps surprising because his field of study, astrophysics, is not easily accessible to the general public. However, there are two factors that have made him stand out from other scientists writing about black holes and the formation of the universe: he is disabled and speaks through a computer, and he has written a bestselling book about his work.

Diagnosed with a type of motor neurone disease in the early 1960s, Stephen Hawking was given only a few years to live. However, following his marriage in 1965 to Jane Hawking, his condition stabilised and he proceeded to develop outstanding scientific theoretical explanations for some of the most mysterious phenomena in the universe, and about the nature of the universe itself. In 1988 he wrote and published *A Brief History of Time*, which explained his theories to the non-scientific reader and which quickly became an international bestseller.

Although his distinctive voice synthesiser is no longer manufactured, he has kept it rather than upgrade to a newer model, as he says he identifies with it and has not found a voice he likes better.

TASK

What do the biographies of Marie Curie and Stephen Hawking show about the influences society and technology have on scientific progress?

EXAMINATION TALK

This topic block is partly about science's impact on and relationship with society. Scientists think and work using a completely different set of criteria from those used in everyday life. Objectivity discounts feelings: scientific truths, however uncomfortable, have to be faced. The topic block seeks to highlight the differences between objective and subjective thinking.

Questions set in this area of the specification will reflect this dichotomy and invite you to explore it. For this reason, it is even more important than usual to read them carefully. You may be asked, for example, questions about the social consequences of a scientific discovery, or the effect of scientific scepticism and rationality on religious belief. The temptation is to write about your feelings and opinions on the topic, but if you do this you will have missed the point. Your thinking and writing will need to reflect the subject matter and exhibit the same degree of objectivity.

WHAT NEXT?

To find information on current scientific topics, and also reflective thinking on social attitudes to science, searches on these websites could be useful.

www.bbc.co.uk/science/horizon
www.bbc.co.uk/sn
will lead you to compendia of current and past broadcasts on a variety of topics. Add a topic to speed and focus your search.

www.nature.com
is the website of the weekly science journal *Nature*.

www.bbc.co.uk/radio4/science
www.bbc.co.uk/worldservice/sci_tech
www.thenakedscientists.com
are all BBC radio websites where programme summaries, information and podcasts can be found.

www.stanleymilgram.com
gives a full account of Milgram's disturbing experiments, which make a fascinating case study.

EXAMINATION PRACTICE

These questions are designed to focus your thinking on the issues dealt with in this topic block, which is why some of them are based on sources quoted above. Source material is often used in examination questions.

1 'Scientific progress makes moral progress a necessity; for if man's power is increased, the checks that restrain him from abusing it must be strengthened.' (Madame de Stael, 1766–1817). Discuss two examples of how the truth of this remark may be demonstrated.
2 Should scientists respond to social change or create conditions in which it may become possible?
3 Re-read the quotation from the website Life After the Oil Crash on page 191. What scientific and social responses would be appropriate in your view?
4 Look again at the question-and-answer sequence from the Sky News website on page 192. Evaluate both the question and the answers.
5 In what way did 'Darwin's bulldog' initiate the rift between scientists and the general public?

3.9 Social, ethical and environmental implications and consequences of scientific discoveries and technological developments

OVERVIEW

In this block of work we will look at

- the impact of ICT on those who use it
- the development of telecommunications and its influence

- agricultural practices including organic farming
- food supply and distribution
- waste disposal and recycling
- weapons and peacekeeping
- prospective inventions.

THE WILLIAMS TYPEWRITER

FOOLSCAP SIZE, Model 2.

Takes Paper 8½ inches wide.   Writes a 7½ inch line.
Dimensions : 14½ inches long, 11 inches wide, 7½ inches high.   Weight, 17½ lbs.

We recommend **Model 2** especially for Army and Navy Officers, for Clergymen, Physicians, Authors, Playwrights, Travelling Correspondents, &c.

The **Model 2 Williams** is compact, easily carried, convenient to use on steamer or railway train, and always ready for use. The **Model 2** is particularly desirable for the Blind, because of its compact keyboard and the simplicity of its mechanism.

SPECIAL PRICES.

WILLIAMS TYPEWRITER (Academy Model).
No. 2 FOOLSCAP MACHINE, with Metal Case - £15 4 0
No. 3 BRIEF MACHINE, with Metal Case - - £17 8 6
£2 2 0 DISCOUNT FOR CASH WITH ORDER.
DEFERRED PAYMENTS. 25/- on Delivery of Machine, followed by Monthly Payments of 12/6.

HEADQUARTERS FOR EASTERN HEMISPHERE ;

WILLIAMS TYPEWRITER Co. FOR EUROPE,
57, HOLBORN VIADUCT, LONDON.
BRANCHES AND SELLING AGENTS EVERYWHERE.

Figure 1

The latest technology available to authors 100 years ago might have been the typewriter illustrated here. The only resemblance it bears to a modern word-processor is the qwerty keyboard layout designed for Remington in 1874.

Let's look at how the process of publishing an article in a magazine has changed. In 1907 this involved a handwritten draft, a typewritten copy, proof reading and typesetting, as well as the commissioning of illustrations. Modern authors can proof their own work, import their own photos, add footnotes, graphs, charts and, using simple layout tools, produce copy almost ready for printing.

A process that once involved five individuals, each contributing a different skill, now involves only one or two at most. What, though, is the cost? Thanks to modern technology there is no (or less) need for copy-typists, printers, proofreaders, photographers or illustrators. One person's efficiency saving is another person's redundancy.

QUESTIONS

1. In Marshall McLuhan's 'global village', ICT has become an extension of our senses, especially those of sight and hearing. What have been the benefits and drawbacks of this?
2. The death of the newspaper and the book may be long-term consequences of the dominance of ICT. Would this be a loss or a gain?
3. 'People who buy organic food are not getting value for money, in my opinion and in the opinion of the Food Standards Agency, if they think they are buying extra nutritional quality or extra nutritional safety, because we don't have the evidence.' (Sir John Krebs, head of the FSA, August 2000) *The Times* reported this comment as being dismissive of organic food as an 'image-led fad'. What is the significance of Krebs's statement and the reporting of it?
4. Suggested solutions to the UK's traffic problems include better roads and traffic management, more bus lanes in cities, investment in rail travel and road pricing. What difficulties would be caused by these solutions?

QUESTIONS (*continued*)

5 'Our waste problem is not the fault only of producers. It is the fault of an economy that is wasteful from top to bottom – a symbiosis of an unlimited greed at the top and a lazy, passive, and self-indulgent consumptiveness at the bottom – and all of us are involved in it.' (Wendell Berry, American poet, novelist and farmer) How would you evaluate this statement?

6 Can the Nuremberg defence – that those who staffed German concentration camps were following orders they could not disobey – be used by scientists to mitigate the consequences of their inventions?

7 'A little knowledge is a dangerous thing: so is a lot. Only two things are certain: the universe and human stupidity, and I'm not certain about the universe.' (Albert Einstein) Will human stupidity always get in the way of the right use of knowledge?

8 Does it matter that hardly anyone understands the principles on which their personal technology – computers, DVD and CD players, iPods – works?

9 What scientific invention would you disinvent if you could? What would be the practical and social consequences of this?

10 The year 2057 will see the centenary of the launching of *Sputnik I*, the first artificial satellite of the Earth. By then, many readers of this book will be in their late 60s. What kind of world, for better and worse, will they be living in?

3.9.1 The impact of ICT

The work of a modern writer is only one example of how **information and communications technology** has revolutionised daily life for most people in the developed world. The speed at which the technology has developed has meant that someone born in the UK at the end of the Second World War has not only seen many new technologies develop from exotic novelties into everyday items, but has also seen many others become obsolete.

KEY TERMS

Information and communications technology is concerned with the storage, retrieval, communication and management of information.

TASK

Conduct a survey among your class of the use of ICT in our daily lives. This should include all current ICT media – television, radio, DVD, CD, iPods, e-mail, the internet and mobile telephones. Design the survey to differentiate between work and leisure use, school/college-based and home use, types of ICT used and time spent using them. Discuss the results of your survey, paying particular attention to anything which surprised you.

Many people who are now in their 60s first saw television in 1953 because their parents had bought a TV set to watch, on 2 June, the coronation of Queen Elizabeth II. The typical television set was the size of a modern washing machine, received a black-and-white 405-line picture on a screen measuring 30cm by 20cm – a sheet of A4 paper in landscape format – with only a single BBC channel to watch.

When not watching TV, that 1953 family might well have listened to their radio – in mono, AM only, choosing from the BBC *Light Programme*, *Home Service* or *Third Programme*, with Radio Luxembourg for variety on evenings when reception was good. If there was nothing on the radio, they could have listened to a gramophone record – played at 78 rpm, made of shellac, the size of a dinner plate and weighing about the same, lasting four minutes at most.

In 50 years, music reproduction has developed from those cumbersome gramophone records to the iPod, which can store hundreds of hours' worth of music in stereo. Three other formats have been developed and discarded in the process. The vinyl long-playing record (initially mono, then stereo), the reel-to-reel tape and the cassette tape are now obsolete, along with other ICT blind alleys such as the videodisc and the Betamax videotape.

The key to the ICT revolution has been the way in which information is now stored, transmitted and reproduced. The systems described above used analogue technology – where sounds are transformed into electrical frequencies and stored on media which were capable of being read by apparatus that converted electrical frequencies back into sound.

The digitisation of information – where it is generated, stored and processed in terms of binary codes – is what has led to the development of the latest music technology. Whether this will, in time, become obsolete will depend on new directions in scientific research.

3.9.2 The development of telecommunications

When, in August 1883, the volcanic island of Krakatoa erupted with an explosion heard 4,000 miles away, it generated four gigantic tsunami which rolled round the whole world, one even registering as a small tidal surge in the English channel. This catastrophe was the first event to take place in what the American sociologist Marshall McLuhan called the global village (in this case created by undersea telegraph cables, the first phase of modern telecommunications).

Land telegraph lines criss-crossed Europe and continental America by the 1850s, and the first successful undersea cable was laid in 1850 between Dover and Cap Gris Nez in France. By 1866, the first successful trans-Atlantic cable – 1,852 miles (nearly 3,000 km) of it – connected Ireland and Newfoundland.

The telegraph was capable of transmitting **Morse code** messages at 20 words per minute, and the telephone, which carried an electrical replica of the human voice rather than the on-off signal of the Morse code key, developed from it. Initially, fierce competition from the telegraph companies hindered the development of telephone networks, but by 1879 the British Telephone Company had set up the first exchanges in London, three of which connected 200 subscribers.

Owners and users of a telephone in Victorian England belonged to an exclusive group. A British Telephone Company subscription in 1880 cost £20 annually – roughly the equivalent of £3,000 today.

The technical developments of the telephone – automatic exchanges, direct dialling, long-distance telephony, as well as the provision of public telephone kiosks – refined analogue technology to a sophisticated level but were tied to the physical network of landlines. The first cell phones, appearing in 1985, freed the telephone from this limitation, and the telephone radio mast began to feature in the urban landscape. Miniaturisation and digital technology put the mobile phone in reach of younger and less well-off consumers. The take-off year for mobile phones in the UK was 1999, when a new phone was sold every four seconds.

Today, three billion telephones are in daily use – roughly one for every two people on the planet – and, of these, nearly two billion are mobiles.

The development of telephone networks also facilitated the growth of the internet as a means of communication. In 1990, fewer than 30 countries had access to the internet. Now, almost every country in the world is online, and the number of internet users exceeds one billion.

If we define the term 'e-mail' to mean information transmitted electronically, then the news of Krakatoa which reached Europe the day after the eruption was an early example of it. The direct descendants of these communications were the first e-mail messages sent between groups of US Department of Defense computers in 1971.

However, what distinguishes modern telecommunications from earlier versions is their accessibility, cheapness and versatility. A mobile phone is more than a means of talking and listening. Cameras, video-recorders, radios, music, internet access, games and a wide range of useful gadgetry are standard equipment on most of even the cheapest mobiles – a shelf-load of ICT in your pocket.

3.9.3 Agricultural practices, pesticides, herbicides and organic production

In its simplest form, agriculture consists of subsistence farming, where an individual produces food for his or her own needs with no surplus for marketing. In practice this is very difficult if a balanced diet is required. Diversifying agriculture into dairy farming (eggs, milk, butter, cheese), livestock farming (beef, pork, lamb, venison, poultry) and arable faming (grain, fruit, vegetables) was a logical development, especially when allied to a marketing and exchange system.

In practice, agriculture in the UK has tended to rely either on mixed farms, which combine elements of all three divisions, or on regional specialisms – for example, sheep in the Lake District and Scotland, grain in the southern counties of England.

In the past agriculture was labour intensive, but since 1945 the growth of intensive system farming (factory farming) has transformed the process of food production. Poultry, cows and pigs in particular lend themselves to indoor, high-density cultivation which treats these animals as elements in a production line. In recent years, salmon and other fish have also been farmed successfully.

Biotechnology is useful in ensuring the health of livestock. Synthetic growth hormones increase yield, and vitamin supplements replace elements missing from the animals' diet due to their being deprived of natural grazing. Vaccines against contagious animal diseases, and pesticides to prevent microbial and parasitical infestations are also standard.

Factory farming applies economies of scale to food production, lowering costs and standardising quality. It also causes sharp controversy among those who see it as cruel, inhumane and degrading to animals. Some aspects of a factory-farmed animal's life are unpleasant, such as the practice of de-beaking poultry in order to prevent the birds fighting, killing and eating one another.

The use of biotechnology in factory farms, as well as the use of herbicides and artificial fertilisers in arable crop production, means that the chemicals used in them, accumulated in meat and grain, can enter the food chain. Thus, the use of antibiotics may help to create antibiotic-resistant pathogens, and in the longer term, growth hormones may affect those whose diet consists of factory-farmed products.

These considerations, along with concerns about the longer-term dietary effects of genetically modified grains, fruit and vegetables, have led to a growth in the organic farming movement. Organic farmers produce food grown without artificial fertilisers, herbicides or pesticides. Traditional crop rotation and natural fertilisers ensure that the life of the soil is maintained. Animals feed as naturally as possible with minimal medical intervention.

Organic farming also aims to work with the environment, encouraging wild animal and plant life to co-exist, as far as possible. The drawbacks – loss of crops due to natural infestation, smaller yields – lead to organic food being more expensive.

KEY TERMS

Biotechnology is the use of applied biology in agriculture, brewing and baking. The term has recently come to include the manufacture of products using genetic modification.

TASK

Organise debates on the following topics, and write a brief report of the conclusions reached.

- Factory farming – efficient food production or systematic cruelty to animals?
- Biotechnology in farming – do the benefits outweight the drawbacks?
- Organic food – media-led fad or healthy eating?

This part of the specification needs a more secure knowledge base than some others. However, since much of its content is subject to argument, even controversy, your knowledge needs to be processed and balanced. As consumers – both of ICT and food – you will have views, possibly strong ones, on your rights, needs and wishes in this area. However, the objective viewpoint needed for this topic block will require you to take account of those of others too, which is why the tasks have been designed to make you aware of them.

When writing a discursive essay in this area, you will rarely be able to draw a firm conclusion, for the simple reason that so many of the issues involved are still open and developing. Acknowledging this fact is not a weakness. Indeed, anyone who was sure enough of themselves to draw firm conclusions about (say) the use of pesticides probably does not know enough to know that this is not yet possible.

WHAT NEXT?

Much useful information on the issues of this topic block can be found on these websites:

The Economic and Social Research Council – **www.esrc.ac.uk** – follow the links for Global Media and Communication.

The Department for Environment, Food and Rural Affairs – **www.defra.gov.uk** – deals comprehensively with topics concerning farming and food production.

It will save time if you make a detailed plan in note form of answers to these questions. These notes can also serve as useful revision.

1 What differences do the media use to report a news story – television, radio, newsprint – have on the story itself? Are these differences positive or negative in their effect on the consumer?
2 If e-mail and the telephone were abolished tomorrow, what would be the social impacts of these changes? Would the overall effect be beneficial?
3 'Opposition to factory farming by those happy to eat organically farmed meat is mere sentimentality, since both kinds of food production involve dead animals.' Evaluate this statement.

3.9.4 Food supply and distribution

Four British supermarket chains – Tesco, Asda, Morrisons and Sainsbury's – control 80 per cent of our food supply. More than half the food we eat in this country is imported, but because we buy most of it from our local supermarkets, and because food is not always labelled with its country of origin, it is easy to forget this.

A typical day's menu could start with eggs, bacon, toast and butter, washed down with coffee or tea. Add a light lunch – say a brie and olive sandwich with salad – and a traditional English roast beef dinner with a glass of wine, and in the course of a single day you may well have consumed the produce of up to 22 different countries.

It has been estimated that if food were to be marketed within 30 miles of where it was produced, a huge saving would be made not only in transport costs – road, rail, sea and air – but also in terms of environmental damage and pollution.

Several issues arise from this, the most important being that of **food miles**. A trailer for a debate 'Food miles: should we be buying food from abroad?' promoted by the Economic and Social Research Council summarises the issues as follows.

KEY TERMS

Food miles are the distances travelled by food from farm to plate – from producer to consumer. High food mileage indicates a substantial environmental impact.

'Do you know where every item of food on your dinner plate comes from? Does it matter? With food available from around the world in our supermarkets, should we have a conscience about buying locally? Transporting food has an increasing effect on greenhouse gas emissions, local employment, and consumer choice. Is there a conflict between the increased choice of foods that we have today and a sustainable agricultural system world-wide? Alternatively, do we have a responsibility towards poor consumers and developing country farmers to open up our food markets much more to imported food? What attitude should we take towards food imported from other countries including developing countries?

A report commissioned by Defra last year showed that food transport has a significant and growing impact on road congestion, road accidents, climate change, noise and air pollution. The report estimated that the social and environmental costs of food transport in the UK are around £9 billion every year, with more than half the costs due to road congestion.'

As well as the logistical issues surrounding food supply, there is also concern about the mark-up of prices between wholesale and retail. The Fair Trade Foundation has done much to ensure that food growers in the developing world receive a fair price for their produce. Closer to home, dairy farmers' organisations claim that their milk is being sold to supermarkets at a loss of four pence a litre. If there is any economic sense in such transactions, it is far from obvious.

TASK

Keep a supermarket bill from a weekly family shop and list the products. Using the food labels and internet research, list the countries of origin of the food your household consumes in a week. What impact, in terms of transport costs, environmental detriment and the economy of the countries of origin, does your shopping basket have? Share and discuss your findings with your group.

3.9.5 The management of transport systems

'Doublethink' has been defined as believing two contradictory ideas at the same time. Some would say that the public's thinking about transport in this country seems to be characterised by it.

In a 2007 survey jointly conducted by the Departments of Transport and the Environment, 56 per cent of those interviewed claimed that they used public transport wherever possible. In fact, the number of bus journeys made in the UK (excluding London) has fallen by 4 per cent since 2006.

Similarly, 75 per cent claimed that they avoided unnecessary car journeys, and drove only 'worthwhile' distances. In fact, 63 per cent of all journeys are made by car and, in 2005, British motorists travelled 12.5 billion miles further by car than they did in 2001. Moreover, the average length of all car journeys in the UK is only nine miles.

Despite widespread public agreement that cycling and walking are better modes of transport from both personal and environmental points of view, both habits are in decline. The average individual distance walked per year fell between 2004 and 2008 from 237 miles to 191, a decline paralleled in the number of cycle journeys. Cyclists do not receive much encouragement: compared with many European cities, English towns make little provision for cycle tracks, and cyclists often share their lanes, hazardously, with taxis and buses.

Motorists also tend to think of themselves as being victims of government policies which aim to price them out of their cars. In fact, the cost of private motoring has increased less, and at a slower rate, than the cost of using public transport.

Faced with these contradictory attitudes and beliefs, the management of public transport systems becomes more and more difficult. Many people say that they will support park-and-ride schemes to relieve congestion in city centres – but many cities lack sites where the vast car parks needed could be built. They also say that they would not drive their children two miles to school if local authorities ran school bus services – but complain vociferously when local taxes go up to pay for them.

Efforts to integrate transport systems seem to be overtaken by continuing increases in car usage, which often result in more roads being built. A government plan, unveiled in 1998, promised a cut in traffic congestion of 6 per cent by 2010: the latest forecast is for an increase of 20 per cent by then.

The successful management of transport could, unfortunately, require the kind of political courage which could guarantee the loss of a general election. A package of measures aimed at reducing traffic on urban roads and motorways could include, say, petrol rationing, greatly increased petrol duty, more toll roads and congestion charges, and prohibitive road tax increases for second

> **INTEGRATING KNOWLEDGE**
>
> Look back at AS 1.2.7 on transport issues. What are the key transport issues where technology makes on impact?

cars. Compulsory car-sharing schemes for commuters could be implemented, as could a ban, on workdays, on all single-occupancy vehicles in city centres.

Such a policy package might have the desired effect on congestion as well as providing revenue for much-needed investment in improved public transport. The crucial question is: would any government advocating such policies stay in office long enough to implement them?

KEY TERMS

Carbon footprint is a measure of the total amount of carbon dioxide (CO_2), or other greenhouse gases, omitted by a product or process over its lifecycle or the amount of CO_2 produced by an individual's activities over one year.

KEY TERMS

Biodegradable substances decompose naturally in normal conditions.

Landfill sites are large outdoor sites for waste disposal. They have been associated with pollution and contamination and strict controls now operate on landfill sites in the UK. This has made it much harder to find new sites to use for the every increasing amounts of waste needing disposal.

INTEGRATING KNOWLEDGE

You studied pollution and its management at AS in topic 2.1.8. To what extent is waste a pollution problem we can fix?

TASK

Log the use of transport your family makes in a typical week, recording the length of journeys, their purposes, the transport used and the cost involved. Is your family's transport **carbon footprint** larger or smaller than you imagined? What steps could be taken to reduce it? By discussing your transport log with your group, try to determine how typical it is.

3.9.6 Waste disposal and recycling

Half a billion tonnes of waste is generated in the UK each year, 30 million of it by households, which is approximately half a tonne per person. Half of this – kitchen and garden waste – is organic, and thus potentially pollutant. A quarter of it – glass, plastic, metal – is not **biodegradable**.

Waste is dealt with according to a waste hierarchy which ranges from the most desirable outcome to the least. These are prevention and minimisation, re-use and recycling, and finally – the least-favoured options – energy recovery and **landfill**.

It is better to prevent the generation of waste than to have to deal with its recycling or disposal, but this part of the hierarchy is hard to regulate. Composting garden waste on site is the ideal solution for organic waste, but it takes time, trouble and space. Cardboard boxes, plastic packaging, carrier bags, newspapers, disposable nappies, household appliances – all of these items, which we think of as indispensable, generate waste that could be prevented or minimised.

Putting out empty bottles for the milkman is the simplest example of waste re-use, but is becoming rarer as daily milk deliveries decline. It is common sense to re-use plastic carrier bags as bin-liners, or to repair broken domestic equipment rather than replace it. However, how many people ask about the availability of spare parts for a new washing machine, or how easy it is to repair? Also, it is often cheaper to buy a new product than to repair the old one. People buy products purely because they are disposable. How many wet-wipes, nappies, razors, plastic cups, kitchen towels, disposable cameras, computer toner cartridges and batteries do we use each year?

Finding different uses for waste products, or passing them on to other users, is one form of recycling. There are 300 furniture recycling projects currently in the UK, and such organisations as CREATE (Community Recycling Enterprise And Training for Employment) combine repair and resale of white goods with skills training.

Wastes such as paper, cardboard, glass, food tins, aluminium drink cans and foil can all be re-manufactured with little loss in quality. Six billion aluminium drink cans are used annually in the UK – and many of them return, as new, to supermarket shelves every six weeks or so.

One million computers are discarded each year. At the moment, only 20 per cent of them are recycled for use by charities, schools or low-income households, or sent to developing countries. Recycled clothes, shoes and spectacles can also be useful in the developing world.

Despite all these efforts, most non-biodegradable and currently non-recyclable waste – mainly plastics – ends up in landfill sites, or in incinerators from which only a limited amount of energy can be recovered.

In some ways the problem of waste disposal resembles that of transport management. In general, people are aware of what action could be and should be taken in the interest of the environment and future generations. However, as long as this will take effort, time and money, encouragement to take such action may not be sufficient.

TASK

List a week's waste in your household, classifying it into biodegradable, recyclable and neither. Combine your findings with those of the rest of your group. Apply the waste hierarchy to these findings and work out ways of making your generation and disposal of waste more environmentally friendly.

EXAMINATION TALK

The knowledge base you need for this topic block is quite a specialised one, and to that extent rather easier to manage than in some others. For that reason it will be useful for you to have as many facts at your fingertips as possible. Fortunately, issues involving farming, transport and waste are often newsworthy, so regular attention to news media can pay off.

The case study approach can pay dividends too. The tasks above would all provide you with sufficient material to underpin a sophisticated and knowledgeable response to questions involving the ecological, environmental and social implications of the issues involved in this topic block.

WHAT NEXT?

The website UK Agriculture **www.ukagriculture.com** contains information, policy documents and discussions on all aspects of food supply, and the ESRC website mentioned on page 203 can also be profitably searched.

The UK Commission for Integrated Transport **www.cfit.gov.uk** website is particularly valuable. It publishes reports, surveys and fact sheets as well as compiling compendia of press coverage on transport issues. There is a motorists' forum which is useful for making informal surveys of the attitudes and reactions of car-drivers.

The Recycling Consortium, **www.recyclingconsortium.org.uk**, based in Bristol, has a website which covers all aspects of waste and recycling in considerable detail.

It will save time if you make a detailed plan in note form of answers to these questions. These notes can also serve as useful revision.

1 What impacts are made by increased food miles on food producers, retailers, customers and the environment? What steps might be taken to mitigate these impacts, and what difficulties might be encountered in doing so?
2 What obstacles, social, logistical and personal, prevent the general public from making greater use of public transport in this country? What could be done to encourage this?
3 You have been asked to draft legislation to reduce the roles of incineration and landfill in waste management. What incentives and penalties would you include in such legislation?

3.9.7 Weapons and peacekeeping

Einstein's Gift, a play by Vern Thiessen

In the autumn of 2005, the New York Academy of Sciences staged a dramatic reading of two scenes from this play, which dramatises the life and work of the German–Jewish chemist Fritz Haber, and his younger contemporary Albert Einstein.

Haber's research into the fixing of nitrogen in the form of ammonia led to the development of nitrogen fertilisers. This work led to the award of his Nobel Prize in 1918. This research also contributed to the development of poison gases in 1914, a project which Haber oversaw. The project was responsible for mustard gas attacks such as those horrifically described in Wilfred Owen's famous poem *Anthem for Doomed Youth*.

Haber also led the research institute that developed an insecticide, Zyklon B, used in Nazi concentration camp gas chambers, albeit ten years after his death.

Like Haber, Einstein was also German and Jewish, but had little else in common with him. Haber valued prestige and status, was fiercely patriotic, and believed that scientific research should always have a practical aim. Einstein believed in science for science's sake, and cared little even for his personal appearance, let alone public acclaim.

The play portrays arguments between Haber and Einstein. Haber justifies his development of chemical weapons by saying that their use would save German lives. His patriotism survives even the fact that to progress his career he was obliged to deny his Jewishness, and be baptised as a Christian. Einstein, an amateur musician who would not play German music, replies that 'you cannot simultaneously prevent and prepare for war'. Haber dismisses this as cowardice and naivety.

Even the protests of Clara Haber, Fritz's wife, leave him unmoved. She feels betrayed by his applying the nitrogen-fixing technique to chemical weapons. Haber's reply, 'If I don't do it, someone else will', shows the shallowness of his thinking.

Underlying his dispute with Haber is the tragic irony of Einstein's position – he believed that his role was to practise science and leave goodness to the gods, and his pacifism was absolute: 'My reality does not include spilling blood, no matter what the cause.'

Haber's contribution to war was knowingly made; the pacifist Einstein's was not. But his letters to President Roosevelt in 1939 led to the creation of the Manhattan project, and ultimately to the atom bomb.

The themes of the play are not confined to the relationship between scientists and warfare. Ron Russell, the director of *Einstein's Gift*, said 'In 1905 science offered great promise for changing the world. In 2005, reflecting on a century of war and genocide, it seems the promise failed.'

It is in the area of war and peace that the social accountability of science and scientists is most sharply dramatised, and *Einstein's Gift* offers food for thought going far beyond the argument between a patriot and a pacifist.

TASK

Divide into small groups, allocate one extract to each, and discuss the questions which accompany them.

Report your findings to the rest of the class

a A news story from the BBC Online network, 15 July 1999

> Nuclear weapons differ in how much heat, blast, light, pressure and radiation they produce. By altering the physical structure of the device and the proportion of its explosive components, different effects can be achieved.
>
> Whereas a standard thermonuclear device will destroy buildings in a vast shockwave of heat and pressure, the neutron bomb would detonate above a battlefield with, theoretically, little risk of destroying the surrounding area. The blast would be confined to a radius of no more than a couple of hundred metres but a massive wave of radiation would knock out tank crews, infantry and other personnel. Even if the buildings did remain, survivors would soon find their bodies filled with elements such as strontium, ensuring that they eventually die of radiation poisoning.'

What ethical problems for those concerned might arise from the design, manufacture, possession and use of such weaponry?

b The doctrine of Mutually Assured Destruction (MAD)

To what extent is this statement true? What other military uses of science can you think of which had different effects, even (ultimately) beneficial ones?

> The concept of Mutually Assured Destruction was an approach to nuclear deterrence focused on the ability of a nuclear power to launch an attack after having been the victim of a first strike from another. Since both powers would be destroyed in the process, MAD had a deterrent effect against a surprise first strike. In effect, the invention and stockpiling of nuclear weaponry guaranteed world peace. The military application of science saved all our lives.

3.9.8 Prospective inventions

Scientific history is littered with predictions which time has proved spectacularly wrong. Consider this memorandum written between two officials of the Western Union telegraph company in 1876 about a new technology:

> 'This [device] has too many shortcomings to be seriously considered as a means of communication. The device has inherently no value to us.'

The device in question was the telephone.

More accurate predictions have been made by extrapolating current progress in science and technology and assessing this against social trends. Thus the Japanese Science and Technology Agency in 1960 listed 135 advanced technologies which would be developed by 2010, more than 50 of which have happened. These included mobile phones, microwave ovens, artificial insemination and the cryogenic preservation of sperm, the large-scale desalination of sea-water and voice-activated word-processing.

The problem in forecasting future inventions is that no one can foresee what new tools science will evolve as a result of pure research which then finds an application. For example, **artificial intelligence** has become a daily part of our lives, working for us in e-mail servers, satellite navigation systems and computer games. The world's most powerful computers can operate at a speed approaching that of the human brain, and on an increasingly wide range of complex tasks. Computers in the past excelled mainly at calculation, but modern versions display qualities resembling thought, enabling them to play complex games like chess, or write music and poetry.

Artificial intelligence, linked to sophisticated mechanical technology, has produced robots seemingly capable of independent action. If true artificial intelligence were created, then the Earth would be populated by two intelligent species, the artificial one possibly capable of evolving more rapidly than the natural one – a fraught prospect.

The possibilities of **nanotechnology**, which works by manipulating matter on a molecular scale, are endless, but not all of them are benign. Nanotechnology could revolutionise medicine by developing drugs targeted at individual DNA, as well as engineering replacement organs for transplant. It would be possible to use nanotechnology to provide clean water, abundant and nutritionally enhanced foods and cheap and unlimited energy. Allied to the much greater communication and information storage facilities it could develop, nanotechnology could alter irrevocably the economic and social structure of our world.

KEY TERMS

Artificial intelligence is the branch of computer science which designs programs which are able to simulate human intelligence in the machines they control.

KEY TERMS

Nanotechnology involves designs and structures on a very small scale, typically either molecular or atomic.

3 Domain exploration: applying synoptic skills

Equally, it could be used as an instrument of social tyranny, using brain implants, medical conditioning or genetic predestination. Those who possessed it would be in a position to dominate and control those who did not. Nor can there be any guarantee that such speculative technology would avoid long-term effects impossible to calculate or reverse. Some scientists scorn the notion that nanotechnology could produce self-replicating molecular machines – so-called 'grey goo' – which could overwhelm those supposedly in charge of it. Such sceptics should recall Arthur Eddington's words, which combine both a promise and a warning for all scientists '*Not only is the universe stranger than we imagine, it is stranger than we can imagine.*'

TASK

Here are four of the predictions made by the writer Arthur C Clarke of science-related developments and events during the 21st century. What do you think would be the positive and negative social, ethical and practical implications of these predictions coming true?

2009: A city in a developing country is devastated by the accidental explosion of an A-bomb in its armoury.

2024: Infra-red signals are detected coming from the centre of the galaxy. They are the product of a technologically advanced civilisation but attempts to decipher them fail.

2040: The 'Universal Replicator', based on nanotechnology, is perfected: any object, however complex, can be created – given the raw material and the appropriate information matrix. Diamonds or gourmet meals can be made from dirt. As a result, agriculture and industry are phased out, ending that recent invention in human history – work.

2045: The totally self-contained, recycling mobile home (envisaged almost a century earlier by Buckminster Fuller) is perfected. Any additional carbon needed for food synthesis is obtained by extracting carbon dioxide from the atmosphere – which will also slow down global warming.

EXAMINATION TALK

The work in this topic block shows very clearly the synoptic nature of this unit. It is almost impossible to discuss its scientific basis intelligently without considering its broader implications – social, ethical, sometimes political.

The questions which will be set, and your answers to them, must reflect those implications. In particular, the political and military implications of science need some appreciation of history if you are to deal with them fully. It would be easy to answer a question, for example, on the Manhattan project in a fairly superficial way.

A *By developing and using the atomic bomb, the United States ended the Second World War but started the Cold War. Although many fewer lives were lost in this, the waste of resources both by the US and Russia retarded public spending on health, education and infrastructure which affected their populations enormously.*

This answer suggests candidate A has made his or her mind up and is writing the answer looking for support for his or her initial opinion.

B *Supposing President Truman had decided not to use the atomic bomb, and committed the allies to an invasion of Japan instead. This would have extended the war by up to five years, in the course of which he might have lost the 1948 Presidential election to Thomas Dewey, a liberal Republican with a tolerant attitude towards communism. The Cold War thus might not have begun, or have lasted as long as it did.*

In thinking through political as well as practical outcomes of alternative courses of action, this answer is in a more scientific spirit, meshing with the synoptic nature of this unit.

Both candidates address the question but, in avoiding the obvious, B is doing so more effectively.

WHAT NEXT?

Sources for material to consider science and ethics include

www.onlineethics.org

www.i-sis.org.uk

Material on the application of science to war can be found at

www.makingthemodernworld.org.uk

Intelligent speculation about the future of science can be found at

www.sciencemuseum.org.uk

The whole Arthur C Clarke article about the 21st century can be found in the June 1999 newsletter of the Astronomy Interest Group, part of

www.dimaggio.org

On this last site you will find lots of other material which is relevant to the whole of this unit. You will need to bear in mind that this seems to be a website associated with the National Secular Society of South Africa, and that its agenda may well be reflected in some of the articles.

EXAMINATION PRACTICE

Questions requiring intelligent speculation are the hardest of all to answer. You will find it helpful to research these questions before attempting to answer them.

1 The letter on the next page was sent by Albert Einstein to the President of the United States one month before the UK and Germany went to war.
After re-reading the text on *Einstein's Gift* above, write President Roosevelt's reply. This should take account of Einstein's pacifism, nationality and birth-religion as well as the contents of his letter.
2 What major scientific developments do you expect to see during your lifetime?
In answering this question you should make clear what current scientific developments provide the starting points for your extrapolation.

Albert Einstein

Old Grove Rd.
Nassau Point
Peconic, Long Island

August 2nd 1939

F.D. Roosevelt
President of the United States
White House
Washington, D.C.

Sir:

Some recent work by E. Fermi and L. Szilard, which has been communicated to me in manuscript, leads me to expect that the element uranium may be turned into a new and important source of energy in the immediate future. Certain aspects of the situation which has arisen seem to call for watchfulness and, if necessary, quick action on the part of the Administration. I believe therefore that it is my duty to bring to your attention the following facts and recommendations.

In the course of the last four months it has been made probable – through the work of Joliot in France as well as Fermi and Szilard in America – that it may become possible to set up a nuclear chain reaction in a large mass of uranium, by which vast amounts of power and large quantities of new radium-like elements would be generated. Now it appears almost certain that this could be achieved in the immediate future. This new phenomenon would also lead to the construction of bombs, and it is conceivable – though much less certain – that extremely powerful bombs of a new type may thus be constructed. A single bomb of this type, carried by boat and exploded in a port, might very well destroy the whole port together with some of the surrounding territory. However, such bombs might very well prove to be too heavy for transportation by air.

The United States has only very poor ores of uranium in moderate quantities. There is some good ore in Canada and the former Czechoslovakia, while the most important source of uranium is Belgian Congo.

In view of the situation you may think it desirable to have more permanent contact maintained between the Administration and the group of physicists working on chain reactions in America. One possible way of achieving this might be for you to entrust with this task a person who has your confidence and who could perhaps serve in an inofficial capacity. His task might comprise the following:

a) to approach Government Departments, keep them informed of the further development, and put forward recommendations for Government action, giving particular attention to the problem of securing a supply of uranium ore for the United States;

b) to speed up the experimental work, which is at present being carried on within the limits of the budgets of University laboratories, by providing funds, if such funds be required, through his contacts with private persons who are willing to make contributions for this cause, and perhaps also by obtaining the co-operation of industrial laboratories.

I understand that Germany has actually stopped the sale of uranium from the Czechoslovakian mines which she has taken over. That she should have taken such early action might perhaps be understood on the ground that the son of the German Under-Secretary of State, von Weizsäcker, is attached to the Kaiser-Wilhelm-Institut in Berlin where some of the American work on uranium is now being repeated.

Yours very truly,

(Albert Einstein)

3.10 The moral responsibility of scientists

OVERVIEW

In this block of work we will look at

- the question of scientists' responsibility towards society
- the nature of the threats posed to society by scientific development

- the dilemmas of medical scientists and doctors
- the impact of science on the environment
- the impact of technology on the society.

Figure 1

This photograph of the nine-year-old Kim Phuc (her name means *Constant Happiness*) fleeing in terror from her Vietnamese village, napalmed by the US air force on 8 June 1972, is an iconic and terrible image of war.

Louis Fieser was a distinguished scientist who won awards for research into the chemical causes of cancer. He pioneered the synthesis of vitamin K, an agent vital to haemophiliacs, and developed anti-malarial drugs. He invented napalm in 1943, mixing powdered aluminium with petrol to produce a substance that not only burned fiercely, but also stuck itself to its target.

Dr Fieser had no reservations either about napalm or its military use, saying *'I have no right to judge the morality of napalm just because I invented it.'*

TASK

Research the lives of Kim Phuc and Louis Fieser. What might they teach us about morality and responsibility?

QUESTIONS

1 Should scientists retain control of their inventions to prevent their misuse?
2 Can science ever be morally and ethically neutral?
3 In evaluating the benefits and drawbacks of new scientific developments, who should take the final decisions? Scientists? Politicians? Civil servants? The public?
4 Science is about objective truth; political policy is about the art of the possible. Is it possible to resolve this tension?
5 'All professions are conspiracies against the laity.' (George Bernard Shaw) Has this ever been true of the medical profession? Is it true now, to any extent?
6 What are the legal and ethical issues involved in a person making a living will requesting that they should be allowed to die when their quality of life is so poor as to be a burden to them?
7 'As crude as a caveman's club, the chemical barrage has been hurled at the fabric of life.' (Rachel Carson, Green campaigner, 1907–1964) Is this a fair description of science's effect on the environment?
8 Rachel Carson's famous book, *Silent Spring*, has been described as having 'played a large role in articulating ecology as a subversive subject'. Why is ecology subversive? Does it have to be?
9 Technology provides us with tools which can also be used as weapons. Is this inevitable?
10 Is there such as thing as a completely benign technology?

3.10.1 The threats posed by scientific developments

Proponents of **genetic modification** in agriculture are positive about the benefits that it would bring if introduced on a large scale. Genetic engineering in the form of selective plant breeding has been practised for hundreds of years without damage. Why draw the line at a more scientific intervention? In any case, modification alters only a small part of the genetic profile of a plant, and rigorous testing and screening will ensure its safety.

The advantages are obvious. Genetically modified crops make more effective use of land. GM crops are bred to have a longer shelf life, so problems of shipment are solved. Because GM crops are hardier, they have greater resistance to infectious diseases, weeds and animal pests. There will be less need for herbicides and other chemical interventions. GM crops can be engineered to have better flavour, texture and greater nutritional value.

Above all, in a world where the population is increasing at an exponential rate, we need to produce as much food as we can, and genetic modification is a painless way forward. We need not sacrifice any of our quality of life in order to enhance that of others.

No one who objects to genetically modified food will be forced to eat it, so no democratic deficit is involved. GM foods will be subject to the same rigorous labelling as other products, and there is a food health and safety apparatus already in place to ensure that standards are maintained.

KEY TERMS

Genetic modification (GM) is technology used to modify the genetic material of living cells or organisms to modify their function.

INTEGRATING KNOWLEDGE

Link back to AS 2.1.6, Genetic engineering and biotechnology, as you consider these issues.

3 Domain exploration: applying synoptic skills   215

An equally strong case can be made against genetic modification. There is still a large measure of public mistrust of GM foods. Why should the public be made to accept things that they do not want? Issues such as labelling are not impossible to fudge. Nor does the 'feed the world' argument convince – world food production is already sufficient to feed everyone. The major causes of starvation are poverty, inequality and the greed of the developed world.

The experience of eating GM foods is also relatively recent, and the case for their safety is not proven. Scientific experts say that they are safe, but two generations ago scientific experts said that **thalidomide** was safe. In the 1980s experts said that beef from cattle with **bovine spongiform encephalopathy** (BSE) was safe to eat, but lacked the confidence in their own judgement to eat it themselves. Before a new drug is marketed, years of clinical trials and tests ensure its safety – and we take drugs only a few milligrams at a time. During a lifetime we ingest several tonnes of food.

Soya beans modified with a gene from Brazil nuts produced an allergic nut reaction in some who ate them. In this case the manufacturers were able to remove the gene – but can we be sure that there are not other factors about which we know nothing? How can we begin to look for something of whose existence we are unsure?

Similarly, if you breed crops with antibiotic resistance, what guarantee is there that this resistance will not be transmitted to those who eat them, with disastrous results?

Far from enabling fewer herbicides to be used, GM crops are often bred to have a heightened resistance to them. Crops can then be sprayed in quantities and concentrations which would normally kill them, and which certainly kill all of the other plants in the field, irrespective of whether they are harmful or not. This could have long-term effects on biodiversity. Agricultural land could become a desert, supporting only a single crop.

Crops are also being engineered to be poisonous to some insects which prey on them. Can anyone be certain that these poisons will not affect a broader spectrum of species than is intended?

There are other considerations too – cross-pollination between GM and non-GM crops which will mean that those who object to GM crops will end up eating them unwittingly. Cross-pollination might produce herbicide-resistant weeds. Is it natural to introduce animal or bacterial genes into plant life, interfering with the product of millions of years of evolution?

None of these arguments is, of course, conclusive, and the controversy about genetic modification will continue for many years to come. What, however, is the threat involved?

KEY TERMS

Thalidomide was a drug prescribed to prevent morning sickness in the first three months of pregnancy, and also as a sedative. In the three years before it was withdrawn, it also caused many babies – up to 10,000 world-wide – to be born with severe physical defects such as mis-shapen or rudimentary limbs. It has since been found that thalidomide can treat leprosy and some cancers effectively, but its history may prevent its widespread use again.

Bovine spongiform encephalopathy is a neurological disease of cattle, possibly transmitted through feed containing animal proteins.

There are two aspects to this. First, the misgivings about GM may be justified: indeed, they may even be understated. The whole GM movement could be a scientific experiment with the public in the role of laboratory animal. That this is unlikely does not make it less of a cause for concern. Second, and more worryingly, the average member of the public does not know enough about the scientific issues involved to be able to make an informed judgement, and has to rely on scientists for the relevant information. As demonstrated above, expert opinion can do as much to cloud an issue as it does to clarify it.

> **TASK**
>
> Using the material in this topic block as a basis, develop a case for the universal adoption of genetic modification in agriculture, and a case for its prohibition.

3.10.2 The dilemmas of scientists in the area of medicine

Constitution of British Medical Association Medical Ethics Committee

The British Medical Association Medical Ethics Committee consists of eighteen members, comprising doctors, philosophers, lawyers, theologians and lay people. It debates issues of principle in medical ethics, medical law and in ethical matters concerning the relationship between the medical profession, the public and the state.

The committee's published advice covers a wide range of issues, including consent to and refusal of treatment, confidentiality, end-of-life issues, including withholding and withdrawing treatment, cardiopulmonary resuscitation and DNAR [do not attempt resuscitation] orders, caring for children and young people, reproduction and genetics, organ donation, treating incapacitated adults, research, access to health records and the Data Protection Act, and medical reports.

From the website of the British Medical Association

'I swear by all the gods and goddesses, making them my witnesses, that I will fulfill according to my ability and judgment this oath and this covenant:

I will apply dietetic measures for the benefit of the sick according to my ability and judgment; I will keep them from harm and injustice.

I will neither give a deadly drug to anybody who asked for it, nor will I make a suggestion to this effect.

Similarly I will not give to a woman an abortive remedy. In purity and holiness I will guard my life and my art.

Whatever houses I may visit, I will come for the benefit of the sick, remaining free of all intentional injustice, of all mischief and in particular of sexual relations with both female and male persons.

What I may see or hear in the course of the treatment or even outside of the treatment in regard to the life of men, which on no account one must spread abroad, I will keep to myself, holding such things shameful to be spoken about.'

An adapted extract from the Hippocratic Oath traditionally sworn by doctors

> **TASK**
>
> Discuss the Hippocratic Oath and evaluate its relevance to modern medicine, with particular reference to euthanasia, abortion and medical confidentiality.

The BMA Medical Ethics Committee is an inclusive body. It concerns itself with questions to which there can be no clear-cut answer, where the expertise of professionals combines with the common sense of lay people to arrive at a decision aimed at the long-term best interests of patients.

Doctors can bring to discussions their medical knowledge. Philosophers may offer ideas about, say, a patient's quality of life, how aware they may be of what is happening to them, and what it means. They will find much to discuss with theologians, whose view of what is meant by the term 'life' may differ markedly from a philosopher's, especially in the case of an unborn child. Lawyers can cite precedents, and describe their legal outcomes. In the case of new problems or innovative treatments, they can advise on what current laws might apply, or need to be modified or rescinded.

All the specialist roles are supplemented by the lay persons', who are more likely to personalise what is going on: what if this disabled child was mine? Supposing I had to choose whether or not to discontinue this treatment on my own father?

The remit of the Committee is complex, the issues more so. Typical cases which the Committee might consider could include these.

- A young adult with moderate learning difficulties refuses treatment for a life-threatening illness against the advice of his GP – what issues are involved?
- A 16-year-old girl, four months pregnant, wants an abortion against the 19-year-old father's wishes – what is the best course of action?
- A woman is convinced that her husband is sexually abusing their eight-year-old son. Both deny this. What can, or should, the doctor do?
- An 87-year-old woman with an aggressive secondary brain tumour is developing pneumonia – 'the old person's friend'. Although she is now a little confused, she has indicated previously that in such a situation she would want only **palliative care**. This will make her comfortable and let nature take its course. Her son now insists that doctors attempt to cure her pneumonia. What is to be done?
- A 49-year-old man has been deeply unconscious for three years following a motor cycle accident in which he suffered catastrophic brain injuries. His family have asked for advice about what is the best way forward. What are the alternatives?
- The parents of a four-year-old girl with severe cardiac problems and brain damage sustained at birth are considering whether or not to ask for a DNAR (do not attempt resuscitation) order with respect to their child. What advice should be made available to them?

As well as dilemmas based on actual cases, ethics committees also consider more general issues, usually in areas involving cutting-edge research.

- Advances in genetic surgery and cloning technique could soon pose problems in relation to parents choosing the sex of their children. Should this be allowed?
- Developments in transplant surgery have resulted in a shortage of donated organs, and even in a black market trade in them. Organ

KEY TERMS

Palliative care is treatment given to patients with terminal illnesses. Typically it consists of the relief of pain and nausea plus emotional support from psychologists and social workers as well as spiritual sustenance. Palliative care recognises that the patient is dying, but aims to make the process as comfortable as possible for the patient without hastening it.

3 Domain exploration: applying synoptic skills

donation is currently voluntary, either with the pre-death consent of the donor or that of the relatives *post mortem*. Should it be compulsory?

- Stem-cell research offers enormous hope for sufferers from cancer, Parkinson's disease, leukaemia, spinal injuries and muscular atrophy. Stem cells can only be harvested from dead human embryos, either naturally produced or therapeutically cloned. What ethical issues are involved in such research?

TASK

In groups of five, role-play discussions of the BMA Medical Ethics Committee on the issues outlined in topic 3.10.2. The roles should be those of doctor, philosopher, lawyer and lay person. Research those aspects of your chosen discussion thoroughly before the session. The fifth member should minute the discussion and report the decision, and the grounds for it, to the rest of the class.

3.10.3 The impact of science on the environment

Biofuels: a case study

Greenhouse gases from exhaust fumes, along with inhaled particulate matter, are a major danger to air quality. Petrol and diesel engines emit large quantities of carbon monoxide, carbon dioxide, nitrous oxide and sulphur dioxide. Exhaust fumes can also cause cancer, liver or kidney damage and birth defects.

This environmental impact cannot be prevented without limiting car ownership, which is not going to happen except as a last resort. However, one of the alternatives to **fossil fuels**, biofuels, is attracting growing support. Racing drivers have used biofuels for many years: fears about peak oil (see page 136) and subsequent shortages are fuelling general interest in the idea.

The active ingredient in biofuel, ethyl alcohol, is produced initially by fermentation and then concentrated by distillation. One hectare of wheat – about 2.5 tonnes – can produce enough bioethanol to fuel a journey of 29,000 miles (almost 47,000 km).

In use, biofuels can emit 65 per cent less greenhouse gas than petrol. The fuel is relatively 'green' in use and has a smaller carbon footprint. Research has shown that the carbon dioxide emitted by biofuels in use does little more than replace what was removed from the atmosphere during the growing of the crops used to make it.

A small number of petrol stations are already selling fuel made up of 95 per cent petrol or diesel and 5 per cent bioethanol. This may become more widespread following a government pledge that, by 2010, 5 per cent of all car fuel must come from renewable sources.

Meeting this target will depend on cars being adapted to use biofuel. Bioethanol attacks rubber and degrades aluminium, so the conversion process consists mainly of replacing seals and coating vulnerable components, which is relatively simple and cheap.

KEY TERMS

Greenhouse gases **prevent solar radiation from escaping from the atmosphere. They include water vapour, ozone, chlorofluorocarbons, carbon dioxide, carbon monoxide, methane and nitrous oxide.**

Fossil fuels **are formed from decayed plants and animals and include oil, coal and natural gas.**

INTEGRATING KNOWLEDGE

AS 2.1.2 and 2.1.3 provide a good foundation of information for this case study. What political and social issues are involved with fuel use and fuel prices?

Two major car manufacturers have marketed models adapted to run on bioethanol/petrol mixtures. They will cost approximately £600 more than equivalent petrol-only models, will reduce carbon emissions by up to 70 per cent, deliver a more powerful performance and offer fuel savings of up to 15 per cent.

Although the environmental advantages seem to be clear, there are some snags. Fuel transporters with stainless steel tanks, costing £120,000 each, are needed for delivery. It has proved difficult to persuade supermarkets to allocate tanks and pumps to what is still a minority fuel. Biofuel producers have had to offer substantial incentives to get forecourt space. Britain's first full-scale biofuel plant will produce 131 million litres of bioethanol from 340,000 tonnes of wheat when it reaches full capacity. However, a production cost of 35p per litre will not make it cheap. Ten such plants will be needed to meet the government's 2010 target.

Biofuels reduce carbon emissions, although many see them as an expensive way of doing this. Doubt has also been cast on their efficiency as fuels – they may be more effective when used to generate power and heat than as motor fuel. Expense and efficiency are not the only concerns, however.

By 2020, the EU wants 20 per cent of European fuel needs to be met by biofuel. Recent studies imply that meeting this target could have a severe environmental impact in agricultural terms, with consequent effects on food production and pricing.

Internationally, nearly 10 per cent of the world's agricultural land would need to be given over to biofuel crops in order to replace 10 per cent of the world's petrol consumption by biofuels. This could result in a reduction of land available for food production in countries where food shortages and famines already occur. In some areas, large tracts of **rainforest** could be felled to clear space in which to grow biofuels. This would involve a huge energy expense as well as accelerating climate change already caused by rainforest depletion. In the UK, the Royal Society for the Protection of Birds (RSPB) has campaigned against biofuels, claiming that the 'current rush to biofuels is causing nothing short of a disaster for wildlife habitats across the world.'

Recent studies have shown that some biofuels may produce more greenhouse gas emissions than they save. Biodiesel fuels manufactured from maize and rapeseed produced an average of 60 per cent more nitrous oxide than fossil fuel oil – and as a greenhouse gas, nitrous oxide is 300 times more detrimental than carbon dioxide. The reason for this is both simple and ironic. Up to 5 per cent of the nitrogen in the fertiliser used to grow the crops is converted into the biofuel and emitted as nitrous oxide in exhausts.

The search for alternatives to fossil fuels will continue, but, barring some radical change of scientific direction, the goal of a cheap,

KEY TERMS

Rainforests are dense, warm and wet forests. They are havens for millions of plants and animals, many of which are still unknown to science.

3 Domain exploration: applying synoptic skills

renewable source of fuel with no environmental impact will remain remote. The case of biofuels re-emphasises a basic truth about the relationship of science and technology to the environment, which is that in terms of fuel and energy there is no such thing as a free lunch.

3.10.4 The impact of changing technology on society

All technology has a social impact. Humankind's ability to make fire was a crucial milestone in technological and social evolution. Later, the making of tools enhanced human capacity, enabling the killing, butchering and eating of animals, the preparation of their skins for clothing, and the beginnings of organised agriculture.

Subsequent technologies have been about making better and more focused tools, a notion caught in the famous ox-bone to space-ship dissolve – 'the longest fast-forward in film history' – from Stanley Kubrick's film *2001: A Space Odyssey*.

Figure 2

So long as humans control the technology they develop, it can enable progress and prosperity for those who own it, although its misuse and abuse can never be ruled out.

Many concerns about technology centre on issues of personal privacy and control. George Orwell's **dystopia**, *Nineteen Eighty Four*, foresaw a society in which central government spied on, supervised and regulated every action of its citizens. A generation later, we live in a society where technology records much of what we do, both publicly and privately.

In the UK, 15 million CCTV cameras watch the public in all phases of life. Every time a credit or debit card is used, a record of the transaction is made. A customer loyalty card used in a supermarket logs every item purchased. Mobile phone calls track movements when people are out of CCTV range.

In private, every computer keystroke leaves a trace, search engines record every query, and commercial companies record telephone

KEY TERMS

Biometric information is derived from measuring and analysing bodily characteristics. These include fingerprints, retinas and irises, as well as vocal and facial patterns.

calls 'for training purposes'. Personal details including health records are stored on databases. A national DNA database is a strong likelihood, as are identity cards carrying **biometric information**.

Citizens leave abundant electronic traces in many places, and technology now exists which could link all these traces together in a comprehensive and detailed electronic profile. Should this happen, then the crucial question becomes who would be able to access that profile, and why?

The potential positive use of such technology is enormous: in preventing and solving crimes, preventive medicine, effective marketing leading to economies of scale, traffic control and accident prevention.

KEY TERMS

Identity theft involves an individual impersonating someone else for criminal gain. This is often done using stolen electronic data.

However, the potential for criminal and illegal abuse is, if anything, greater: **identity theft**, social control, abuse of information in commerce and finance, blackmail and fraud. Is it fanciful to see such possibilities also as the technical equipment for a police state?

TASK

Organise debates on these motions.

a 'The innocent have nothing to fear from a national DNA database.'

b 'CCTV is the most effective weapon in the fight against crime since the invention of fingerprinting.'

c 'Identity cards will prevent identity theft, terrorist conspiracy and illegal immigration.'

EXAMINATION TALK

The scope of this topic block is relatively wide and so you will benefit from looking in depth at a small number of case studies from which general principles about the topics may be deduced.

Answers should concentrate on these general principles, using the knowledge base to illustrate and clinch your points. Giving a narrative summary of a case study will take time which would probably be better spent deciding on which aspects of it are relevant to the question.

Science students in particular need to be wary of using their specialist knowledge simply because they can. A General Studies examination does not test what you know so much as how you can use what you know.

WHAT NEXT?

It is difficult to research the moral responsibility of scientists as a topic, since it is so diverse. In looking for help in this area on the web it is better to search for websites dealing with topics where moral responsibility, scientific development, medical dilemmas and the environment are relevant issues.

So, Googling topics such as cloning, stem cell research, abortion and euthanasia should put you in touch with useful back-up material. Should you use such websites, take care to identify any social, religious or ethical agenda they might have, so that you can evaluate their information as objectively as possible.

A good example of such a site is **www.gmwatch.org**, which carries this message on its front page:

> 'We are confronted with the most powerful technology the world has ever known, and it is being rapidly deployed with almost no thought whatsoever to its consequences.'

Dr Suzanne Wuerthele, US Environmental Protection Agency toxicologist

There is no reason why such a website should not prove useful, but its claims should not be accepted without investigation and checking.

EXAMINATION PRACTICE

1 'I have no right to judge the morality of napalm just because I invented it.' Napalm has no morality, but its use does. On what grounds can its inventor claim that this has nothing to do with him?
2 The general public lacks the scientific knowledge properly to evaluate the views of experts, and thus is liable to assent to developments it does not begin to understand. What responsibility should scientists take in this situation?
3 'Thou shalt not kill, but needst not strive officiously to keep alive.' (Arthur Hugh Clough, *The New Decalogue*) Evaluate this idea as a basis on which doctors could assess end-of-life dilemmas. What might be the unintended consequences of using it?
4 'If any student comes to me and says he wants to be useful to mankind and go into research to alleviate human suffering, I advise him to go into charity instead. Research wants real egotists who seek their own pleasure and satisfaction, but find it in solving the puzzles of nature.' (Albert Szent-Gyorgi)
'Imagination is more important than knowledge.' (Albert Einstein)
Is the egotism of scientists, coupled with a lack of imagination, responsible for the impact of science on the environment? What other explanations might there be?
5 What safeguards are needed to ensure that technology can serve society rather than endanger or limit its freedom?

3.11 The relationship between technology, science, society and ideology

OVERVIEW

In this block of work we will look at

- what we mean by resource exploitation
- the concept of sustainable development
- the meaning of stewardship

- industry and ecology
- intermediate technology and its uses
- natural hazards and disasters and issues of relief and rescue.

Figure 1

Exploitation often means…

'…the improper use of an individual or country's resources for another's profit'

Exploitation should mean…

'…the extraction and sale of a country's natural resources to provide raw materials for its industry, or wealth to fund the country's development.'

A country rich in resources is entitled to exploit them, by extraction and trading, or by licensing other countries to do so. Wealth thus generated can be used to promote national development. Criminally motivated exploitation of natural resources finances organised crime, terrorism and political oppression and causes countries to regress.

1 Natural resources are allocated by chance – should their exploitation reflect this fact so far as their profits are concerned?

2 Should natural resources be political as well as economic and practical assets?

3 Is the practice of sustainable development in developing countries liable to cause impatience with the slower progress it tends to support?

4 How should the balance between sustainability and stewardship be regulated and maintained?

5 Can traditional heavy industry and ecological stewardship ever co-exist?

6 The Gaia hypothesis says that living and non-living parts of the Earth are a complex, interacting and self-regulating system that can be thought of as a single organism. If this is so, why is humankind responsible for the Earth's ecology?

7 Can intermediate technology only be applied in developing countries? Could it not be used to solve some of the problems of developed ones?

8 Is imposing intermediate technology on developing countries a form of technological colonialism?

9 Should a permanently staffed international relief and rescue organisation be created to coordinate organised responses to disaster?

10 Should rebuilding after disasters be regulated to follow the principles of sustainable development?

3.11.1 Resource exploitation

Case study 1: mining in Tibet

Tibet is resource-rich, having large deposits of iron, copper, coal, gold, silver and quartz. No Tibetan employees are involved, however, in operating the many mines in Tibetan territory currently occupied by the Chinese. They are staffed and run entirely by Chinese workers.

The Chinese government claims to be developing those mines for the benefit of Tibet. Tibetans claim that China is simply stealing their country's natural resources. No Tibetan employment is being created, and none of the economic benefit accrues to Tibet. Tibetans claim also that China's motives are political as well as economic, since the infrastructures involved in mining – machinery, roads and communications – will enable further consolidation of its control of Tibet.

It is alleged that two of the companies involved in advising and supplying equipment to the Chinese government are British.

Whatever the rights and wrongs of the issue, it is clear that technology here is being used, at least in part, to exploit resources for political as well as economic purposes.

Case study 2: blood diamonds from Africa

Diamonds represent one of the most portable forms of wealth. As well as being easily traded, they are inflation-proof and easy to smuggle. Anyone seeking to launder money would always consider the diamond trade as a *modus operandi*.

Much of the world's diamond stocks are in African mines – in Angola, Botswana, the Democratic Republic of Congo, the Republic of South Africa and Zimbabwe. Diamonds are a natural resource of enormous economic and political potential.

In some countries, revolutionary groups who have taken over the diamond mines use their proceeds to finance their operations. The trade in 'blood diamonds' has also been implicated in money-laundering by Al Qaeda, Hezbollah and, allegedly, Hamas.

As a result, few African economies have benefited directly from their own diamond mines, whilst others, Liberia, Sierra Leone, Angola and the Democratic Republic of Congo, have been laid waste in conflicts financed by the illicit diamond trade.

Estimates of how many blood diamonds are traded each year vary between 4 per cent and 15 per cent of total world output. Even at the 4 per cent rate, blood diamonds (sometimes known as conflict diamonds) would generate vast profits – several billion pounds at least – which could transform the economies of the countries owning the mines.

The legitimate diamond industry designed the Kimberley Process, ratified by the United Nations in 2003. The process requires governments to certify that shipments of rough diamonds exported from their countries are free of blood diamonds. Despite this, the trade continues and, as long as it does, the populations of African diamond-producing countries will continue to be exploited by organised crime and corrupt politicians, both local and international.

TASK

1 Prepare a short (five-minute) talk on resource exploitation in the developing world, based on one product or service. These could include timber, minerals, tourism or food production.
2 Research examples of sustainable development in those same areas, and compare the social and environmental outcomes.

KEY TERMS

Sustainable development is economic and social development that respects and preserves natural resources.

3.11.2 Sustainability and stewardship

The concept of **sustainable development** grew from the realisation that scientific and technological development which met only current social needs would probably work against the interests of future generations. Scientific research and improvements in technology led to ever more efficient resource exploitation. Many resources are finite,

3 Domain exploration: applying synoptic skills

or, if renewable, replaced only at a pace which cannot be accelerated. The result of this 'efficiency' was development that, in the end, led to the running down of industries for lack of raw material.

A change from profit-led resource exploitation to sustainable development became essential to the survival of a number of industries. Of these, perhaps the most striking example is fishing, where technological development and more efficient processing caused a partial collapse of the industry, from which it has still to recover.

Fifty years ago most British seaports had fleets of trawlers, drifters and other small boats. These have largely disappeared, replaced by large factory ships able to stay at sea for weeks at a time. At sea they can receive the catches of their accompanying hunting ships and process, freeze and can them. They return to port only when their holds are full.

In addition, net mesh-sizes were reduced to trap smaller fish in an effort to increase catches. Allied to the indiscriminate nature of net-fishing, this led to great waste. For example, for every tonne of prawns caught, three tonnes of other fish are killed and dumped. Porpoises and dolphins also die in large numbers through indiscriminate fishing.

Scientifically efficient fishing began to run fish stocks down. A smaller herring population also reduced the number of cod, which are predators of herring. The over-fishing of sand eels, a popular catch in the Shetland Islands, led to a decline in the puffin population, with colonies failing to breed for some years.

Bans on fishing for endangered species have done something to restore fish stocks, although it is likely that some areas – the Icelandic cod banks for example – will never recover. Environmental scientists have called for even more stringent measures such as bans on fishing in a third of British territorial waters and strict quotas applied to the rest.

Whether these measures are effective ultimately remains to be seen. Humankind does not own the world and its resources in any significant sense. Rather, our role may be seen as being that of **stewardship**, with the responsibility to leave the Earth as we would wish to have found it.

> ### KEY TERMS
>
> **Stewardship** is the responsible management of resources – human, physical, biological and environmental.

3.11.3 Industry and ecology

A case study: Middlesbrough, Teesside

The industrial revolution began in Britain in the early 19th century and was marked by change which was both wholesale and precipitate. In 1800 Middlesbrough consisted in its entirety of a large farm on the south bank of the River Tees, with 25 agricultural workers and their families living on it. By 1871, it was a booming industrial town with a population of 40,000. Thirty years later, it was the biggest town on Teesside, 90,000 strong.

The town's industrial development can serve as a model for what happened not only throughout the UK but also internationally.

Improved transport was necessary both to industry and to those who worked in it. The Darlington and Stockton railway, opened in 1825, initiated a railway boom connecting the town with its raw materials – coal from County Durham and iron ore from the Cleveland hills. A canal extended sea-access so that large vessels could service the export trade in coal.

Iron (and later steel) production could be completed from start to finish in the town. By 1880 the Tees was known as the Steel River. London's famous Big Ben was cast on Teesside in 1855, and 'Made in Middlesbrough' is stamped in the steelwork of Sydney Harbour Bridge.

By 1900 shipbuilders on the Tees made a major contribution to the total tonnage produced in the north east, which then accounted for over 40 per cent of the world's merchant fleet. Chemical industries began at Billingham on the north bank, and in 1926 Imperial Chemical Industries was formed from a series of amalgamations. ICI later became a leading world brand in medical and industrial chemistry.

The story of Middlesbrough's industrial revolution can be duplicated all over the world. Much of this development took place without systematic regard to its effects on the environment. These can credibly be described as catastrophic. Soil pollution, the loss of tree cover through erosion, dangerous – occasionally lethal – levels of air pollution in urban areas, toxic chemicals in coastal, estuarine and river waters – all of these have left legacies which later ecological concerns and projects have had to redress.

KEY TERMS

Regeneration involves investment into an area to 'breathe new life' into it.

A huge effort of **regeneration** has gone into Middlesbrough's now derelict industrial sites, and the remaining industry is much greener than before. Local water quality is in the top 2 per cent for urban areas, and its air quality has won awards. A seal colony and abundant bird-life feature at the Teesmouth Nature Reserve.

The industrial revolution brought material prosperity and social progress to a mass of the population. It also began the process of increasing, by 13-fold, the mass of atmospheric carbon dioxide. Whether this process will render our planet uninhabitable remains to be seen. Can modern ecological awareness and practice undo damage that has already been done?

TASK

Using local history resources, trace one of the ecological effects of the industrial revolution in your area. What has been done to repair the damage?

WHAT NEXT?

www.afrol.com is the website of Afrol News, an independent news agency dedicated to covering the African continent. The coverage is very comprehensive and covers all aspects of life in 59 African countries. Government websites can often offer useful information, though it is often sensible to cross-check facts with another source. **www.kenya.go.ke** is an example.

www.treehugger.com is a website devoted to a wide range of Green viewpoints on transport, science, technology, design, architecture, travel, food and health.

Many sources on sustainable development can be found by using a search engine. This could lead, for example, to such websites as **www.darwin.gov.uk** which details the work of this Defra-funded initiative.

EXAMINATION PRACTICE

1 Companies exploiting natural resources do so for profit, which must be maximised for the benefit of their shareholders. Can this motivation be reconciled with the concept of sustainable development?

2 'We must strive to become good ancestors.' (Ralph Nader)
'The first steps toward stewardship are awareness, appreciation, and the selfish desire to have the things around for our kids to see. Presumably the unselfish motives will follow as we wise up.' (Barbara Kingsolver)
What do you think your great-grandchildren will make of our stewardship of the world we are creating for them?

3 What environmental lessons can we learn from the industrial revolution and its ecological outcomes? Are there any lessons we have refused to learn?

3.11.4 Intermediate technology and development

Electricity supply in Africa is not accessible everywhere and is not affordable by all. Those in rural areas may rely on candles or paraffin lamps to light their homes. Whilst many possess torches and radios, batteries are expensive. Solar power is appropriate technology for Africa, but the installation of even a modest solar electricity system would cost too much for most households.

Hence the Sollatek GlowStar lamp (right). It is charged by a solar panel, delivers up to six hours of high quality light, and can also power a small radio.

Figure 2: Sollatek GlowStar lamp

3 Domain exploration: applying synoptic skills

Intermediate technology is designed with local cultural, social and environmental needs in mind.

What are the links between population dynamics and development? Link back to AS 2.1.5 as you consider this.

The solar lamp is an example of **intermediate technology**, as well as being a good example of sustainable development, in that the only energy source it needs – sunlight – is locally in plentiful free supply.

Intermediate technologies are developed from a close study of problems on the ground, and finding solutions using materials and skills already to hand.

For example, women in sub-Saharan Africa spend hours each day gathering firewood for cooking-stoves that are both inefficient and smoky. This leads to under-cooked food (and possible parasitical infections) and chronic respiratory problems. Intermediate technologists designed an efficient ceramic stove for local manufacture, and then trained potters in making the stove. These potters manufactured the stoves on their own account and also trained others to make them.

This simple project produced many benefits. Women spent far less time gathering wood, so forests began to recover. Food was properly cooked, and respiratory problems disappeared. The women had time to undertake more constructive pursuits – paid work or education – and manufacturing the ceramic stoves became a national cottage industry.

Most of the ideas developed by intermediate technology are simple. An African blacksmith who can make spades and axes can learn how to make a more efficient ploughshare, or even small turbines to drive simple machinery.

Not all intermediate technology projects deal with local manufacture, however. Providing a farmer with a bicycle and trailer, for example, enables him to take his produce to market much more easily. Customers enjoy a wider variety of choice, the farmer can sell more, and his bicycle has little environmental impact after its manufacture.

More importantly, local economies grow at a natural rate, with modest progress unlikely to cause unrest or strain. Giving that same farmer a tractor which he can neither use nor repair is to see his problem in the light of our own preferred solution, which could not be less appropriate.

TASK

Re-read the section on intermediate technology above. What other solutions to the problems outlined – electric light, better cooking facilities and the transport of produce – can you devise? Assess your solutions according to the principles of intermediate technology.

3.11.5 Natural hazards and disasters, relief and rescue

During the eight months leading up to October 2005, a series of **natural disasters** took place world-wide, beginning with the Indian Ocean earthquake, which triggered the catastrophic tsunami on 26 December 2004. Hurricane Katrina's progress through North America the following summer caused the destructive flooding of New Orleans. In October, El Salvador's highest volcano, Ilamatepec, erupted, and a week later Hurricane Stan hit the country, causing catastrophic floods and mudslides. At almost at the same time, an earthquake in Pakistan devastated large areas of Kashmir.

In natural disasters, the aftermath may cause as much loss of life as the original event. In developing countries, soil laden with water is liable to liquefy during an earthquake. This undermines fragile building and road construction, causing much additional damage and many more casualties. Poor sanitation and contaminated water supplies contribute to disease epidemics. Cholera, dengue fever, malaria, typhoid, diarrhoea and vomiting spread rapidly in such situations and medical aid is often overwhelmed.

Relief efforts need to be systematic. The rescue of trapped casualties, the triage of others, emergency medical treatment, clean water, food and shelter – these are immediate needs. The dead must be identified, listed and given decent burial.

Longer-term assessments of damage to the infrastructure and how it may be repaired require different expertise – civil engineers, architects, town planners. Later still comes the rebuilding of destroyed cities and towns to withstand future earthquakes, floods or hurricanes. This usually takes place long after the television cameras and journalists have moved on, so few people are aware of how long these processes last, or how much they cost.

Earthquakes, floods, hurricanes, volcanic eruptions and tsunami are classified as natural disasters, and, whilst they may not be preventable, it is growing increasingly possible to forecast them with a useful degree of accuracy. The practical usefulness of such forecasts is, however, questionable. Had the 2004 tsunami been forecast for 26 December, would there have been time to minimise casualties?

We should be less fatalistic about other disasters. The locust swarms that destroyed the crops in Niger in 2005 could have been prevented in a country with better pest control. However, the fact that four million people – a third of Niger's population – were still starving three years later is no longer the responsibility of the locusts. The 2005 Gleneagles G8 summit pledged its members to more sustained and focused efforts to aid sub-Saharan Africa. Turning that pledge into action would have prevented Niger's natural disaster from becoming a human-made one.

KEY TERMS

A natural disaster is a physical event such as a volcanic eruption, earthquake, flood or landslide. If subsequent disaster relief is delayed or inadequate, it may turn into a humanitarian disaster.

TASK

Natural disasters cannot be prevented, but steps can be taken to mitigate their effects. In groups, discuss possible methods of preparing for floods, earthquakes, hurricanes, tsunami and volcanic eruptions in such a way as to protect people from them. Prepare a poster on your findings.

EXAMINATION TALK

Some aspects of this topic block are historical, others are more like current affairs. Still others combine technology and social awareness. Questions asked will reflect this eclectic approach; good answers should do the same.

For example, a question may ask about ways of regenerating damaged land following industrialisation. A good answer will describe the damage and how it occurred, perhaps illustrating the points by reference to a local or recent example. Straightforward knowledge of, for example, reforestation techniques will be useful, as will awareness of how such a project could serve a social need, for example, by providing cycleways or a park serving the local community.

The knowledge base need not be extensive or detailed; but it needs to be versatile. In this book there are references to global peak oil in the sections on ideology, scientists' moral responsibility, and nature of scientific progress. This illustrates the synoptic nature of this unit, as well as the integrated thought needed when preparing for the examination.

WHAT NEXT?

Use the following websites to find information and ideas on aspects of this topic.

www.itdg.org is the website of Practical Action (founded in 1966 as the Intermediate Technology Development Group by EF Schumacher, the author of *Small is Beautiful*).

www.practicalaction.org will take you to the same website.

www.disasterrelief.org is a general site about disaster relief.

www.iiaa.iix.com/disastrs.htm is a website maintained by the Independent Insurance Agents of America to give information about natural disasters.

www.miamisci.org is the website of the Miami Science Museum and gives information on hurricanes.

quake.wr.usgs.gov is maintained by the US Geological Survey and is devoted to the study of earthquakes.

www.volcanoes.com offers general information on volcanoes and some history of eruptions.

www.oxfam.org.uk has an excellent section on disaster relief.

EXAMINATION PRACTICE

1 According to the Practical Action website, intermediate technology must
   a meet the needs of both women and men
   b enable people to generate income for themselves and their family
   c be designed, improved, managed and controlled by local people
   d be affordable
   e use local skills and materials as much as possible
   f have a limited impact on the environment.
   According to these criteria, evaluate the three examples of intermediate technology described in section 3.11.4.
2 What factors cause natural disasters to develop into human-made ones? Illustrate your answer by referring to *one* disaster in the western world, and *one* in the developing world.

4.1 Synoptic assessment: exploring stimulus material

OVERVIEW

In this block of work we will

- increase your understanding of the connections between different elements of the subject

- integrate knowledge from a range of disciplines in order to develop an understanding of the interrelationships between them
- examine questions from a broader standpoint than that of a single discipline.

At A2 you will need to think synoptically (see page 8), which means looking at connections and relationships from a wider perspective than in just one unit of work. Your last A2 exam for General Studies will test your ability to make connections between the domains. The exam is called Culture, Science and Society: Making Connections. You will be required to answer two questions which will present you with a range of source materials (perhaps two or three) on a particular theme and then ask you to write an essay using the sources and your own ideas and beliefs about the way this theme connects with culture, science and society in the world today. Each of the two questions is worth 50 marks.

Since the theme chosen for the exam could be anything, there is not a great deal a textbook can tell you about *what* you could write for your Culture, Science and Society: Making Connections exam. But your whole General Studies course will have prepared you for it, because the key skill here is to be able to make connections between the three domains and put forward your answer logically and creatively, using your thinking and analysing skills from Unit 3. As you make your connections, you need to put them into a well-structured argument, assessing each point for its strengths and weaknesses and coming up with a justifiable conclusion.

A really good starting point is the Venn diagram (see Figure 1). A Venn diagram provides an excellent way to get your synoptic thoughts together because it shows where social, scientific and cultural domains might overlap on any given theme.

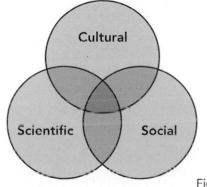

Figure 1

To show how this could work, let us consider the topic of euthanasia – a very challenging ethical dilemma that for many people provokes very strong feelings.

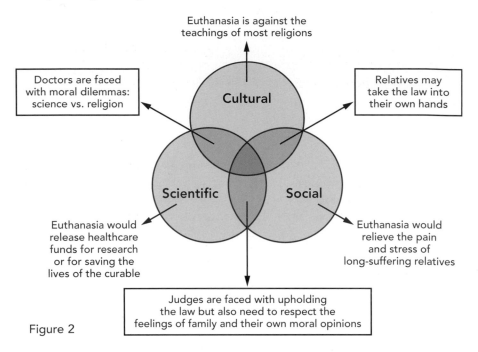

Figure 2

4.1.1 The overlap between domains

It is almost impossible to classify any individual, event or series of events as belonging solely to the social, or cultural, or scientific domain. Each domain impacts upon, or is affected by, the others in varying ways and to varying degrees.

For example, subjects such as health have been affected in many ways by both cultural and scientific issues. For example, in some parts of the world some kinds of cancer are almost non-existent because of dietary influences (e.g. the low-fat, high-fish, traditional diet of Japan). Equally, scientific advances have ensured that, in other parts of the world where these types of cancer are common, a much higher percentage of those diagnosed with the disease do now recover than was the case 50 years ago.

Synoptic assessment requires you to see and understand the interrelationship between the domains. You should develop further understanding and awareness through discussion and deliberation and form your own opinions. All issues impact upon the way we live now and will live in the future. We should all be aware of the benefits and drawbacks of these events and their effect upon us.

TASK

- How has the invention of the telephone affected society and culture?
- What cultural trends have influenced the design and features of mobile phones?
- How have changes in the culture of communication affected society now that mobiles mean we can communicate all the time, wherever we are?

---

4 Culture, science and society: making connections

The following two sections look at synoptic issues in the scientific, social and cultural domains and provide examples to help you understand how to pick up links and follow connections and relationships. Remember that the Venn diagram can help you with this.

TASK

Identify links from science to society and culture from the three topics below. Use a Venn diagram approach if it helps.

4.1.2 Synoptic issues and the scientific domain

The scientific domain offers a number of opportunities for discussion about synoptic issues. Here are some examples.

Space travel

Apart from the level of scientific and technological development required for travel in space, there are some who believe that space travel will offer opportunities to develop tourism, as well as provide solutions to population concerns in different parts of the world (see topic 2.1.5). Others think that there might be other forms of life that might integrate with our own cultures. However, some people question whether it is morally right that vast amounts of money are spent on space exploration when, in our own world, there is poverty, a lack of universal primary education, and many oppressed peoples, etc.

Stem cell research

Some people are concerned about how this new technology might be applied. Others would stress the benefits for all.
- Use of the knowledge for research into cures for illnesses
- Storage of 'cord blood' (blood taken from umbilical cords, which is otherwise thrown away immediately after birth) to assist research into stem cell technology
- The ability to 'create' new skin for burns victims from stem cells instead of using skin grafts.

However, consider the following
- The creation of 'designer babies' – whether to gain a cure for a sibling, or because parents have three boys and would like a girl, or because the father wants a sporty son?
- Cloning – if we can clone human beings, how would society treat them? What would be their identity and their parents' identity?

Energy production

What will happen when supplies of the non-renewable energy resources that we rely on are exhausted? Should we be looking for a technological solution to replace non-renewables with everlasting power, like nuclear power, solar power or tidal power? The social consequences of diminishing supplies of energy are the great challenge of modern times. Should developing nations, for example, have to limit their energy use – and their development – when it is the developed world that has drained the planet of resources? To what extent will people accept higher petrol prices and increased road tax? Culturally, are we ready to change our energy-intensive lifestyles – and morally do we have any alternative for using less energy if our children are to live happy and peaceful lives?

4.1.3 Synoptic issues and the social and cultural domains

The social and the cultural domains also offer opportunities to consider issues in a synoptic way. For example, Britain has been described as having a 'throwaway' culture. We deposit more rubbish in our landfill sites than any other country in Europe. We throw away one third of the food we buy without using it. As a result of this, there are social and scientific issues that impact upon, or affect, our lives. There are connections here to issues such as poverty and malnutrition around the world; to the way we can control or influence how people choose to live their lives; and to science and technology and the development of new kinds of foods with new properties – such as food that stays fresh for longer in the fridge.

TASK

1 Investigate the history relating to the tobacco plant and how it came to be introduced into Britain.
2 Investigate the health risks associated with tobacco, smoking and passive smoking.
3 Consider the issues of tobacco growth and production, and sales of cigarettes.
4 Assess the merit of tobacco firms promoting cigarettes to people living in developing countries.
5 Explain why the NHS goes to such great lengths to advertise the various methods of 'kicking the habit' of smoking.
6 Identify which information and knowledge you have gathered relates to each of the domains.

WHAT NEXT?

Mother dies after refusing blood transfusion

A Jehovah's Witness died shortly after giving birth to twins because her faith prevented her from having a blood transfusion. Emma Gough, 22, began haemorrhaging but because her beliefs did not allow her to receive blood she slipped into unconsciousness and died.

Read the complete article from November 2007 about the Jehovah's Witness who died rather than have a blood transfusion at **www.telegraph.co.uk**.

Jehovah's Witnesses believe that they must follow their religious principles even when the law of a country goes against them. They are a useful example to research, as their beliefs give them a very different perspective on medical technology from that of most people in the UK.

EXAMINATION PRACTICE

Examine the value of the tobacco industry and its impact upon science, society and culture. How far should the issue of 'giving up' be a matter of individual responsibility rather than a collective national one? [50 marks]

4.2 Extended writing in essay form

> **OVERVIEW**
>
> In this block of work we will
>
> - consider how to plan and write an essay for synoptic assessment.

In your examination, quality of written communication is assessed in all units within Assessment Objective 4 and credit may be restricted if communication is unclear.

You need to

- ensure that text is legible and that spelling, punctuation and grammar are accurate so that meaning is clear
- select and use a form and style of writing appropriate to the purpose and to complex subject matter
- organise information clearly and coherently, using specialist vocabulary when appropriate.

4.2.1 Key things to remember about synoptic assessment

There are rarely 'right' or 'wrong' answers – just some answers that are better constructed than others. You need to be able to demonstrate what you know, understand, are aware of and have an opinion about. Within the essay you need to be able to discuss issues, show the interrelationship between the domains and offer some individual thoughts about the subject and its impact on our lives.

You have only 45 minutes to read or look at the stimulus materials, formulate your thoughts and then write your essay.

Think of the essay as a monologue where the other person is the examiner who only listens, and cannot offer any contribution. You are therefore 'thinking aloud' about the issues.

4.2.2 Planning and writing

The key to success in essay writing is the planning, or 'thought showering', that you can do before you begin to write.

Be aware that time is tight. Once you have considered the stimulus, read the question, formulated some thoughts and opinions, and decided what you want to tell the examiner, *you only have 30 to 35 minutes of writing time*. Planning is therefore essential, not only in the examination but beforehand as well. You should put some time aside to practise planning and writing essays.

> **&& Failing to plan is planning to fail. &&**

- Do not describe what is in the stimulus at the expense of giving your knowledge and understanding of the issues which arise from it. This will gain only the minimum of marks as nothing new is brought to the discussion.
- Make sure you consider your opinion, ensure that you cover all three domains in your discussion, decide what you want to say about how the stimulus relates to the domains and then begin.

A basic essay plan would be a paragraph as an introduction and then three more paragraphs, each one discussing issues related to each of the three domains.

A better plan enables you to

- show an ability to consider individual issues within the question
- consider these in relation to each of the domains
- assess the relative impact of each of the domains upon the issue raised.

You might find that the Venn diagram approach helps you here (see page 233).

Identifying issues in a question

Let's consider the examination question given on page 236: Examine the *value of the tobacco industry* and its impact upon science, society and culture. *How far should* the issue of 'giving up' be a matter of individual responsibility rather than a *collective national* one?

It is always a good idea to pick out the *key words* and *phrases*.

- *Value of the tobacco industry*
  This suggests that two views, positive and negative, are possible. Identify the main reason for each view. There might be more than one of each, but you do not have a lot of time so one reason for a positive view and one reason for a negative view is a good place to start. You will need to talk about at least one of each and perhaps refer to others.
- *How far should…*
  This phrase suggests a continuum between total individual responsibility and total collective national responsibility. Where along this continuum will your final opinion lie? You might have an opinion before you begin the essay, but it might change by the time you reach the end after having considered a number of issues. Do not express your opinion at the start of the essay, save it for the conclusion.
- *…collective national…*
  Are you clear in your mind about what you understand this phrase to mean? 'National' is a reference to the whole country, but the use of 'collective' indicates that the whole nation should be equally responsible for the issue of giving up. What do you think?

What to include in the paragraphs

In order to offer the best possible answer, the essay might be split into eight separate paragraphs. Having identified each element of the essay you should think about what you want to include in each paragraph. For each paragraph you need to consider your knowledge and opinion in relation to each.

Your knowledge has many sources. For example, what you have been taught in GCSE or AS/A2; what you have read; or what you have experienced at first hand. Ideally, there should be a balance between knowledge, opinion, fact and analysis.

Here are some ideas about what you might include in your essay. There are more ideas here than you might find in a typical plan, because we've had more time to think about it!

· *Introduction to the essay*
Brief history of how smoking arrived in this country, some information about number of smokers, smoking related illness/death, initial identification of why this might be an issue worthy of discussion

· *Examining the value of the tobacco industry*
Economic value: income to government, growers and producers, employment, costs of production (15p per cigarette), profits, value in terms of research into flavours and varieties of cigarettes

· *Considering its impact on science*
Research into production methods, research into illnesses as a result of smoking, research into cures of these illnesses, research into products to help people give up (or become addicted to something else?)

· *Considering its impact on society*
Cost to individual when purchasing cigarettes (disposable income and also tax paid), effects of mixing with smokers – clothing, smells, passive smoking issues, government income through taxation which might mean increased taxation in other ways if smoking declined, cost to individuals who do not smoke through increased taxes to fund NHS treating people who are ill as a result of smoking and smoking-related illnesses, recent law to ban smoking in public places and workplaces (possibly comment about other EU countries having introduced the ban earlier than the UK)

· *Considering its impact on culture*
Smoking under age, smoking and health, previous images of smokers of cigarettes, cigars and pipes, does it still look cool?, does it still seem rebellious?, will the end to smoking in pubs lead to changes in the culture of who goes to pubs and clubs?

· *Giving up as an individual responsibility*
Willpower or use of other methods, benefits in relation to health and income, individual choice about giving up, longer life-span as a result

· *Giving up as a collective national responsibility*
Encouragement of others to give up can be seen as positive – NHS already produces adverts, helplines, CDs, leaflets, etc. in order to help people give up; campaigns by shops such as Sainsbury's and Boots to encourage people who are considering giving up; introduction of legislation which affects everyone can be interpreted as a collective national responsibility

· *Extent to which you feel the issue of giving up is an individual or national responsibility*
Considering the impact of the issues you have identified and discussed. Reaching a conclusion that identifies your position on the imaginary continuum.

EXAMINATION PRACTICE

1 Write a plan for the following question: Using your own knowledge and views, compare the impact of increased levels of obesity on culture, science and society in the UK. How would you advise governments to tackle the problems of an increasingly obese population?
2 Review your work and decide how you can improve your speed at planning, creating and writing an essay. It might be an idea to use key words instead of complete sentences and phrases in the planning phase, or practise writing more quickly without sacrificing legibility.

4 Culture, science and society: making connections

Index

Acknowledgements

The authors and publishers would like to thank consultant editor Justin Woolliscroft for his contribution to this project.

Photo credits

Cover Digital Vision/Getty Images; **p.2** Corbis/The Gallery Collection; **p.10** CartoonStock.com; **p.12** *t* Corbis/Hulton-Deutsch, *c* Alinari/TopFoto, *b* PA Photos/Thibault Camus/AP; **p.17** Cartoonstock.com; **p.21** Lorna Ainger; **p.24** *cl* Corbis/Hulton-Deutsch, *c* Alinari/TopFoto, *cr* PA Photos/Thibault Camus/AP, *br* Advertising Archives; **p.28** Cartoonstock.com; **p.30** *l* Alamy/Guy Croft, *tc* Alamy/Patrick Steel, *cr* Royal National Lifeboat Institution, *br* Alamy/Joe Fox; **p.36** Cartoon by Nicholson from The Australian www.nicholsoncartoons.com.au; **p.38** Airbus/exm company H Goussé; **p.42** Airbus/Andrew H Walker; **p.43** *l* Corbis/Ashley Cooper, *r* Alamy/A Room with Views; **p.46** *l & r* BFI; **p.47** PA Photos/Chris Young; **p.51** Akg-images; **p.57** *t* Rex Features/Nils Jorgensen, *b* BBC; **p.59** Getty Images/Timothy Clary/AFP Photo; **p.60** Rex Features/Andrew Murray; **p.63** *t* Alamy/Rolf Richardson, *cl* Corbis/Swim Ink, *cr* Rex Features; **p.65** Arts Council England; **p.67** Alinari/TopFoto; **p.76** CartoonStock.com; **p.79** *tl* NASA/Jet Propulsion Laboratory, *tr* NASA, *bl* NASA/Marshall Space Flight Center; **p.95** *tl* Peter Welleman; **p.101** Lake District National Park Authority; **p.102** Rex Features/The Travel Library; **p.113** Science Photo Library/Kaj R. Svensson, **122** *tl* NASA/Jet Propulsion Laboratory, *tc* Alamy/David Cook/www.blueshiftstudios.co.uk, *tr* Alamy/Digifoto; **p.124** *l* Alamy/David Levenson, *r* Alamy/Martin Shields; **p.132** Pacemaker Press International; **p.137** PA Photos/Scott Heppell/AP; **p.140** Alamy/Classic Image; **p.144** Corbis/Archivo Iconografico, S.A.; **p.145** *t* Akg-images/Ullstein Bild/Granger Collection, NY, *b* Bridgeman Art Library/Bibliotheque Nationale, Paris, France, Lauros/Giraudon; **p.156** PA Photos/Sergei Grits/AP; **p.166** *t* Getty Images/Tim Graham, *b* CartoonStock.com; **p.173** Alamy/Mary Evans Picture Library; **p.174** Rex Features/Sipa Press; **p.179** Corbis/Bettmann; **p.187** *l* Mary Evans Picture Library, *r* Science Photo Library/Colin Cuthbert; **p.189** *t* Alamy/Mary Evans Picture Library, *c* Corbis/Hulton-Deutsch, *b* Corbis/Hulton-Deutsch; **p.191** NASA; **p.198** Advertising Archives; **p.214** PA Photos/AP; **p.224** Khalil Bendib; **p.229** Sollatek.

Written sources

p.19 from Ipsos MORI poll, 28 October 2007; **p.26** *UK Census 2001*, www.nationalstatistics.gov; **p.27** *Social Trends*, No. 37 (2007); **p.32** Home Office immigration tables; **p.33** 'Must I Work Harder?', Jean Lambert, MEP, *The Guardian* (14 February 2007), by permission of the author; **p.37** 2007 Annual Survey of Hours and Earnings (ASHE); **p.41** 'Credit where credit's due', Alan Milburn, MP, *The Guardian* (23 November 2006), by permission of the author; **p.55** the Church Society table on church attendance, www.churchsociety.org, by permission; **p.61** Statistics and table on Internet use, *National Statistics Online* – all copyright © Crown, by permission; **p.64** from 'The Role of the Arts in Regeneration', Alan Kay and Glenys Watt, Blake Stevenson Ltd (October 2000); **p.77** from 'Galaxy Song', Eric Idle, from the Monty Python film, *The Meaning of Life* (1983); **p.82** United Nations, Department of Economic and Social Affairs, Population Division (1999), from Table 2: 'The World at Six Billion' (ESA/P/WP/154), by permission; **p.99** Case Study: The Lake District National Park; **p.103** from *2007 IUCN Red List of Threatened Species*, www.iucnredlist.org, downloaded on 22 February 2008, by permission; **p.110** Mapping the Spread of Viruses, created at the Centers for Disease Control & Prevention, Atlanta, Georgia, USA, downloaded from www.orgnet.com/contagion.html; **p.213** Einstein letter to F. D. Roosevelt, August 2, 1939, The Albert Einstein Archives, © The Hebrew University of Jerusalem, by permission.

Thanks to the Northumberland Rock Art website for permission to adapt one of their illustrations (p.177).

Thanks to OCR for permission to reproduce examination questions.

Every effort has been made to trace all copyright holders, but if any have been inadvertently overlooked the Publishers will be pleased to make the necessary arrangements at the first opportunity.